THE MEDALS DECORATIONS & ORDERS
OF THE GREAT WAR 1914–1918

'Pip, Squeak, and Wilfred' – The medals of the Old Contemptibles,
August–November, 1914 (The 1914 Star and Bar, British War Medal,
Victory Medal with oakleaves for mentions in despatches).

THE MEDALS
DECORATIONS & ORDERS
OF THE GREAT WAR
1914–1918
Second Revised Edition

Alec A. Purves

Fellow of the Royal Numismatic Society
President of the Orders & Medals Research Society
1956–60

J. B. HAYWARD & SON
Polstead, Suffolk
1989

First published 1975; 2nd edition 1989
© Alec A. Purves, 1989

ISBN 0 903754 38 X

By the same author
THE MEDALS, DECORATIONS & ORDERS OF WORLD WAR II, 1939–1945.
J. B. Hayward & Son, Polstead, Suffolk

COLLECTING MEDALS AND DECORATIONS
B. A. Seaby Ltd., London

ORDERS AND DECORATIONS
Hamlyn All-Colour Paperback, No. 91, London

FLAGS FOR SHIP MODELLERS AND MARINE ARTISTS
Conway Maritime Press Ltd., London

Typeset by Roger Booth Associates, Newcastle upon Tyne
Printed and Bound in Great Britain by Athenæum Press, Newcastle upon Tyne

TO
MY SON, JOHN,
*In the hope that, unlike his father
and grandfather, he will not be called upon
to serve in a world war*

Contents

The letters in brackets ( ) indicate the abbreviations used in the Index.

Photographic Illustrations

Line Drawings in the Text

Acknowledgements

The research in connection with this book has been spread over some six or seven years, and many collectors and dealers have willingly assisted by allowing me to examine medals and decorations in their collections or stocks. To them I am extremely grateful.

In particular I would like to express my sincere thanks for information supplied by the following.

Dr P. F. King, of Northwood, Middlesex, for details of some Italian awards.

Dr K. G. Klietmann, of Berlin, for information on some German decorations.

Heer C. P. Mulder, of Rotterdam, and Heer B. W. Wagenaar, of Castricum, The Netherlands, for details of Dutch medals.

Messrs G. E. Lundberg and T. H. Sharland for very kindly lending ribbons from their collections, and mounting them for photography.

Mr R. J. Scarlett, for undertaking the photography of the medals and emblems.

Mr E. C. Joslin of Spink & Son Ltd., for the loan of several medals and decorations.

Mr J. B. Hayward for the loan of medals, and considerable encouragement.

Mr W. G. C. Webb, for the loan of medals.

M. Ivo Suetens, of Borgerhout, Belgium, for notes on Belgian awards, etc.

The Public Record Office, London, for information regarding the Royal Red Cross.

Mr Hugh Murray, for information on the British Red Cross Society War Medal, etc.

M. Vaclav Měřička, of Prague, for information on Czechoslovak and Austrian awards.

Mr J. M. Sanfourche, for notes on an Estonian award.

Dr Franco Bigatti, of Savona, for details of some Italian awards.

Introduction to the Second Edition

IT IS NOW nearly seventy years since the end of the Great War – or World War I, as our American friends call it – and, apart from the first edition of this work (1975), no book has appeared dealing exclusively with the host of medals and decorations issued by the many countries, of both sides and neutral, during or in connection with the four-year struggle and its immediate aftermath.

Admittedly many of the awards have been included in various medal books, but some have never been described in English. It is impossible to pretend that the present work is complete, as, with the many political changes since 1918, verified information has sometimes been unobtainable, while many archives have been mislaid or destroyed in the 1939–45 conflict, In consequence there are bound to be some items which are either unknown to the author or about which no details can be obtained.

The items described are those which were instituted or revived in connection with the war, but, apart from listing them, we omit those already in existence unless new classes or distinctive emblems were introduced; to include full details of existing awards would require several more volumes, for the many hundreds of orders, decorations, and medals which, although awarded during the war, were not instituted for that particular purpose and are adequately dealt with elsewhere.

Among British awards, while the Military Cross and Military Medal rank for inclusion, the Distinguished Service Order would be merely listed (as it was established long before 1914) but for the fact that bars were authorised in 1916; the Prussian Iron Cross qualifies as it was not a permanent award, being discontinued after the Franco-Prussian War, 1870–71 (as it had been after Waterloo), and was re-instituted, with a variation in detail, in 1914.

In some instances descriptions or details of institution are of necessity meagre, despite many enquiries; sometimes information has been conflicting; in such cases the author would be grateful for authoritative data or supplementary details.

With many of the foreign decorations, slight differences of size and design may be encountered. Although in some instances copies may have been made, usually such variations are due to the insignia having been produced by more than one manufacturer, particularly those awarded in large quantities. There are some awards, more particularly foreign orders, where recipients have to purchase their insignia, consequently many continental jewellers and tailors carry stocks of these, of varying quality of workmanship, to suit all purses. Most of them conform to type, but minor details and sizes often vary, as also do the ribbons. Thus one might find a small item of ornamentation shown as a five-pointed star on one model, a six-pointed star on another, while a third example might have a five-petalled rosette or a spur-rowell. Unless an official sealed pattern or a definite written description shows which is correct, these minor variations are usually accepted.

In describing the insignia, particularly the shape of crosses, some conventions have been used. A cross *patée* indicates one with curved widening arms, with straight ends, like the Prussian Iron Cross – the Victoria Cross (often wrongly called a Maltese cross) would be described as a straight armed cross *patée*. A cross with narrow straight arms, also widening, is quoted as a *St. George cross*, being similar in shape to the Russian cross of that name. *Maltese cross* is used to indicate one with deep-cut V's and arms narrowing to a central point (or nearly

11

so), like that of the Order of St. John, while a *Bath cross* means one with shallower V's in the ends, like that of the military division of the Order of the Bath. A cross *patée* with slightly concave ends, like the Austrian Order of Leopold, is designated a *Leopold cross*, but apart from these, the normal heraldic terms have been used as far possible.

A crown of two arches shows three semi-arches, while a four-arched crown shows five semi-arches. However, for convenience these are described according to the number of semi-arches seen, thus the former is shown as 'a three-arched crown'.

Swords, as used on decorations *with swords*, are of the 'antique' type, with cross hilts, unless stated to the contrary.

Occasionally there is a discrepancy among sources of reference as to which is the *obv* (obverse, or front) and which the *rev* (reverse, or back) of some decorations. Hessenthal & Schreiber, in their authoritative book, *Die Tragbaren Ehrenzeichen des Deutschen Reiches*, include a number of items where the *obv* (according to text) is designated as the *rev* on the plates. And current practice of wearing does not always assist, as photographic evidence is often conflicting.

Dimensions also vary, and one must accept a certain amount of leeway. Also, in some countries semi-miniature insignia, slightly smaller than statute size but larger than the usual 'evening dress' miniatures, are permitted to be worn in certain orders of uniform – Lord Roberts used to wear orders and medals in semi–miniature, according to photographs. These semi-miniatures find a place in the collections of continental collectors, as do miniatures of all sizes, but British collectors (who must be on their guard when buying from foreign dealers or in foreign auctions) usually regard them as unofficial and of little interest, except perhaps to represent the full-sized medal until a genuine one turns up.

In order to avoid fruitless correspondence, the author would like to make it clear that he is quite unable to supply any medals or ribbons for medals, and while it is possible to obtain a few foreign medal ribbons from the leading medal dealers in Great Britain, in most instances it will be necessary to write to firms in the country concerned, usually in the capital city or the largest towns. A few names and addresses of firms who may be able to supply ribbons are given in Appendix II.

In the lists of existing awards, items where there is an addition or amendment in connection with the war, are marked with an asterisk, *.

Items for which the ribbons are shown in the Ribbon Charts are marked R, while those for which photographs are included are marked P.

Ribbon Charts

Inter-Allied Victory Medal. The standard ribbon used by Belgium, Brazil, Cuba, Czechoslovakia, France, Great Britain, Greece, Italy, Japan, Portugal, Rumania, Siam, Union of South Africa, and USA

BELGIUM Order of Leopold with gold stripes for special Services

Order of the Crown: ribbon for 6th Class.

Croix de Guerre

Yser Medal and Yser Cross

Croix du Feu

Maritime Decoration

Civic Cross, 1914-18, (1st and 2nd Class, with gold stripe)

Civic Medal

King Albert Medal

Queen Elisabeth Medal

War Medal, 1914-18

African Campaigns, 1914-17

Cross for Deportees, 1914-18

Colonial Medal, 1914-18

Combatant Volunteers' Medal

Medal for National Restoration

Liège Medal, 1914

BRAZIL Campaign Cross 1917-18 Ribbon for Auxiliary Services

EGYPT Order of Mohammed Ali

Order of the Nile

EGYPT Order of El Kemal

Medal for Meritorious Acts

Military Star of Sultan Fouad

FRANCE Legion of Honour
with Grand Cordon rosette

Croix de Guerre
with Bronze Star

Croix de Guerre
with Bronze Palm

Croix du Combattant Volontaire

Médaille de Evadés

Medal for Victims of Invasion

War Commemorative Medal

Médaille d'Orient

Médaille des Dardanelles

Croix du Combattant

Medal for Civilian Prisoners,
Deportees, and Hostages

Médaille de la Reconnaissance
Française

Decoration for
Military Wounded

Médaille de la Fidélité

GT BRITAIN Victoria Cross with
miniature on ribbon (1917)

Order of the British Empire
Civil Division (1917)   Military Division (1918)

Order of the
Companions of Honour

Military Cross

Distinguished Flying Cross
Original ribbon (1918)   Revised ribbon (1919)

GT BRITAIN Air Force Cross

Original ribbon (1918)   Revised ribbon (1919)   Distinguished Service Medal

Military Medal   Distinguished Flying Medal
Original ribbon (1918)   Revised ribbon (1919)

Air Force Medal   Revised ribbon (1919)   1914 Star, with silver rose,
Original ribbon (1918)   indicating bar

1914 Star (without bar);   British War Medal   Mercantile Marine War
1914-15 Star   Medal

Victory Medal with Oakleaf   Territorial Force War Medal   RAF Meritorious Service
Spray (Mention in Despatches)   Medal

Special Constabulary   Allied Subjects' Medal   First Aid Nursing
Long Service Medal   Yeomanry War Medal

GREECE War Cross 1916   Medal for Military Merit   **ITALY** War Cross, 1915

War Medal, 1915-18   Medal of Merit for Volunteers   Medal for Mothers and
Widows of the Fallen

ITALY Occupation of Fiume

JAPAN War Medal, 1914-15, 1914-20

LUXEMBOURG Medal for Volunteers

PANAMA Medal of Solidarity

PORTUGAL War Cross

Medal for Wounded

Medal for those Promoted for Bravery

RUMANIA Order of Michael the Brave

Commemorative Cross, 1916-18

Medal for Volunteers (Ferdinand Medal)

RUSSIA Order of St. Nicholas

SERBIA All orders and medals awarded for war service

Serbian Retreat Medal

SIAM Military Order of Rama, and Rama Medal

War Medal

USA Distinguished Service Cross

Distinguished Service Medals

Army

Navy

Navy Cross

Distinguished Flying Cross

Army of Occupation of Germany (Original ribbon)

Army of Occupation of Germany (Revised ribbon)

AUSTRIA Order of Franz Joseph
(War ribbon); Medal for Bravery;
Cross for Military Merit, &c

Karl Truppenkreuz

Medal for Invalids

Medal for Wounded
(2 wounds)

Tyrol Commemorative Medal,
1914-18

War Commemorative Medal

BULGARIA War Medal
(Combatants)

(Combatants)

GERMANY-ANHALT Friedrich Cross
(Non-Combatants)

Marie Cross

BADEN War Merit Cross

Cross for Voluntary War
Assistance

BAVARIA Order for Military Merit: ribbons for officials
(a) 'with swords'   (b) 2nd Class

Order of Military Hygiene

King Ludwig's Cross

BRUNSWICK Cross for War Merit
(Combatants)

(Non-Combatants)

Bremen War Cross

THE FREE HANSA TOWNS
Hamburg War Cross

Lübeck War Cross

LIPPE Cross for War Merit
(Combatants)   (Non-Combatants)

War Medal of Honour
(Ribbon when won in
enemy country)

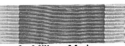

SCHAUMBURG-LIPPE Medal
for Military Merit

MECKLENBURG–SCHWERIN
Cross for Military Merit

Cross for Military Merit
(Philanthropic war work)

Franz Friedrich Cross

OLDENBURG Friedrich August Cross
(Combatants)   (Non-Combatants)

PRUSSIA Iron Cross, 2nd Class
(Combatants)   (Non-Combatants)

Cross of Merit
for War Aid

SAXE-WEIMAR Cross for Merit in
the Homeland

SAXE-ALTENBURG Medal for
Bravery

SAXE-MEININGEN Cross for War
Merit (Combatants)

WÜRTTEMBERG Order of Military
Merit (1914 ribbon)

Wilhelm's Cross

Charlotte Cross

DENMARK Slesvig Medal

Red Cross Medal for
Aid to Prisoners of War

NETHERLANDS Mobilisation
Cross

Amsterdam Burgerwacht Medal

Amsterdam Burgerwacht
Cross for ex-Mobilised Men

·CZECHOSLOVAKIA War Cross

Medal of the Revolution

Order of the White Lion

SLOVAKIA Cross for 1914-18,
'Substitute' Medal 2nd Class

ESTONIA Cross of Liberty
1st Grade

2nd Grade

Cross of Liberty, 3rd Grade

War of Liberty Medal

HUNGARY War Medal
(Combatants)

War Medal
(Non-Combatants)

FINLAND Cross of Liberty, 1918

Medal of Liberty, 2nd Class

Order of the White
Rose

War of Liberty Medal
(1919 ribbon)

LATVIA Order of Lacplesis

War Commemorative Medal

LITHUANIA Order of the
Cross of Vytis

Medal for Volunteers in
Independence Campaign,
1918-20

POLAND Order 'Virtuti Militari'

Cross of Valour

War Commemorative Medal

Independence Cross and Medal

I
The Allies and Associated Countries

Belgium

The kingdom of Belgium dates only from 1830, when she broke away from the Netherlands and became independent. The great powers had undertaken by treaty to respect her neutrality, and ostensibly it was to honour this undertaking when Germany invaded Belgium in August 1914, that Britain declared war on Germany.

EXISTING AWARDS

* Order of Leopold (1832)
* Order of the Crown (1897 in the Congo; 1908 in Belgium)
* Order of Leopold II (1900 in the Congo; 1908 in Belgium)
  Order of the African Star (1888 in the Congo; 1908 in Belgium)
  Royal Order of the Lion (1891 in the Congo; 1908 in Belgium)
  Décoration Militaire – Article 4 (awarded for bravery) (1873)
  Décoration Civique (1867)

NOTES
1 Certain decrees and amendments affected orders and decorations in general. A royal decree *(Arrête Royal)* of 15 November 1915, provided that military recipients of orders who were cited in an Army Order of the Day should wear a *palme* (palm leaf bearing the royal initial, A) on the ribbon, in silver for *chevaliers* (the lowest class), and in gold (silver-gilt) for *officiers*; commanders and grand officers were to wear, in addition to their normal insignia, an officer's cross with gold *palme*.
2 The *Commission de la Reconnaissance Nationale* (Commission of National Gratitude) was created by royal decree of 5 April 1919 to consider, *inter alia*, the means of indicating awards of the Belgian orders made to civilians for deeds of heroism, devotion to duty, and specially distinguished services rendered during the war. This was achieved by embellishing the ribbons with a gold thread centre stripe, by gold thread side stripes, or with gold (gilt) stars, under a royal decree of 24 June 1919.

Civilian recipients of awards of the national orders for outstanding war services whose names appeared in an Order of the Day had gold side stripes added to the ribbon and a five-pointed gilt star. For the grade of commander (3rd class), the neck ribbon had two stars, one on each side of the cross, while grand officers (2nd class), who normally wore only a breast star, also had an officer's cross (4th class) with gold side stripes and a star. Those who received similar awards but not appearing in an Order of the Day, had the same ribbons but without the star.

Awards for special services rendered in the course of hostilities carried a central gold stripe. If gazetted in an Order of the Day, the star was added to the ribbon.

Some of the ribbons were manufactured with the gold centre or side stripes woven into the material, but in many cases stripes of gold tape were sewn on in the appropriate position.

When an award was made for charitable or benevolent services, the ribbon bore a silver star.

3 The *Décoration Militaire* can be awarded in two distinct categories: (1) for long service, with a red ribbon having four narrow black stripes each flanked by narrow yellow stripes; (2) when given for gallantry, and described as *Décoration Militaire (dite Article 4)*, it has a red ribbon with black, yellow, and red edges. For specially meritorious cases the 1st class can be awarded, distinguished by a gilt chevron (point uppermost) on the ribbon.

4 The Belgian Military Cross *(Croix Militaire)* instituted in 1885, is purely a long service award for officers.

5 A Royal Decree of 17 March 1920 authorised mothers of Belgians killed in the war to wear their sons' decorations, military and civil, including those awarded by the allies. By a further decree of 21 April 1920, all such Belgian decorations were to be distinguished by having a black enamel bar, 36 x 3mm, with a narrow silver edge, 0.5mm wide, placed horizontally in the centre of the ribbon.

6 A Royal Decree of 14 February 1939 authorised crossed swords to be worn on the ribbons of any of the national orders awarded for war services, King Leopold III 'particularly wishing to honour those who served in the campaign of 1914–1918'. The emblem was to be in silver; Grand Officers and Commanders, in addition to the breast star or neck badge, were to wear an Officer's Cross with the crossed swords on the ribbon.

NEW AND AMENDED AWARDS

Order of the Crown   R
Originally the ribbon of the 6th Class of the order – *Palmes,* in gold or silver – and of the medals of the order, was red-brown with 3mm white stripes inset 3mm from the edge. According to the late M. Henri Quinot, the white stripes were altered in 1918 to 6mm in width, inset 1mm. There does not appear to be any decree authorising this modification, and M. Ivo Suetens, the leading modern authority on Belgian awards, feels that the alteration was made much earlier, probably before the war.

War Cross (Croix de Guerre)   RP
Six months after France had instituted her *Croix de Guerre*, Belgium followed suit, on 25 October 1915, with a very similar decoration of the same name.

The decree stated that the cross was to be conferred by the commander of the army for acts of bravery in the face of the enemy, and was to be worn on the left breast immediately after Belgian orders. It could be conferred collectively or individually, could be worn at all times, and remained the property of the family of a deceased recipient. In addition to its award for bravery, it could also be given for long service at the front.

The cross is of Bath type, bronze, with shallow angles to the ends of the arms and with bronze ball finials on the eight points; crossed swords appear between the arms. The central medallion shows the Belgian rampant lion on the *obv*, and the royal initial, A (Albert), on the *rev*. Suspension is by a riband hinged inside the crown, through the orb of which is a ring to take the ribbon, which is red with narrow green side stripes and three narrow green central stripes.

A Royal Decree of 15 November 1917 authorised the addition of a bronze lion emblem, 5mm high, to the ribbon for each mention in an Army Order of the Day, and five bronze lions were to be replaced by a silver lion. A further decree of 26 February 1919 amended this to a more complicated system according to the grade of the Order of the Day, using lions or palms in bronze, silver, or silver-gilt; for a mention in a Regimental Order, a bronze lion; for a Divisional Order, silver; for *Division d'Armée*, silver-gilt; for mention in an Army Order, a bronze palm; five bronze palms were replaced by a silver palm, while five in silver were replaced by one in silver-gilt. The same decree of 26 February 1919 also granted the *Croix de Guerre avec palme* to recipients of Belgian or foreign orders or decorations awarded as a result of an Army Order of the Day citation. Other decrees authorised the award to various other categories, such as those who died of wounds, those who escaped from German prisons and rejoined the Belgian army, volunteers over the age of forty or under sixteen, etc. As late as September 1950, the Prince Regent authorised the award of a supplementary palm leaf to the ribbon of the 1914–18 Croix de Guerre for ex–prisoners of war, honourably captured, who had escaped and rejoined.

Yser Medal, later the Yser Cross   RP

From 17 to 31 October 1914 the Belgian army fought an outstanding and most gallant action against the might of General von Falkenhayn's attack along the River Yser. The Belgians won undying glory but suffered some 60,000 casualties, over a third of their strength.

To commemorate this action, a decree of 18 October 1918 instituted the *Médaille de l'Yser*, for those who had participated with distinction (which apparently meant all present), and was awarded to allied troops as well as to Belgians if they fulfilled the conditions.

The medal, 35mm diameter, was of artificially patinated bronze, of a greenish shade (verdegris), with a small 15mm medallion incorporated at the top. The *obv* has a nude helmeted male figure standing, rt, holding a lance and symbolising barring the way to the enemy; to the right are the dates in three lines, 17—31/OCT./1914. The upper medallion has the word, YSER on a green enamelled background. The *rev* has a wounded lion sitting, left, with a sketchily delineated battlefield in the background; below, in the exergue, is again, YSER. The upper medallion has a crowned A on a green ground.

The medal, which was worn immediately after the Croix de Guerre, has a 37mm ribbon, black with a 15mm fire red centre stripe. The regulations stated that the ribbon could not be worn without the medal, but in practice this was not enforced.

A Royal Decree of 5 February 1934 changed the title to *Croix de l'Yser*, but oddly enough no change was specified in the design. However, this was dealt with by a further decree of 22 August 1934. The new cross was 42.5mm across, still in green patinated bronze, with the old 35mm medal superimposed, thus only the very short ends of the arms of the cross *patée* are apparent, and the upper medallion covers most of the top arm of the cross. The ribbon remained unchanged. Recipients of the Yser Medal could wear whichever decoration they preferred, but many preferred to wear the original medal, rather than purchase the cross (since this was not distributed by the government).

Croix du Feu   R

A decree of 14 May 1932 instituted a document called the *Carte du Feu*, indicating that the holder had served at the front, under fire, for certain minimum periods (according to circumstances). A further decree of 27 April 1933 provided a distinctive badge for these people (for which no ribbon appears to be specified), in gilt metal, and called the *Croix du Feu*, literally the Cross of Fire. This was a cross *patée*, 20mm across, with swords between the arms. The *obv* has an allegorical battlefield scene, described as a 'vision of death', with a helmet on a bayonet, a gas mask case, barbed wire, etc., all within a laurel wreath. On the *rev* the centre has the words, in four lines, SALUS/PATRIAE/SUPREME/LEX (The safety of the fatherland, the supreme law). This was worn as a lapel badge.

On 6 February 1934 a Royal Decree established a new *Croix du Feu*, for the same purpose. This was of patinated bronze, in the form of what might be described as a Greek cross quadrate; the horizontal arms are much wider than the vertical ones, and overall is a vertical rectangle, with side panels each containing a stylised laurel spray. The centre panel, which is about the same width as the vertical arms, shows an allegorical battlefield scene rather similar to the one on the earlier cross, with a steel helmet and bayonet as the central motif. The *rev* has the same inscription as before, on the panel across a laurel spray; above is a crown and below are the dates, 1914, 1918.

The ribbon, 36mm, is red with a 4mm blue centre stripe and similar side stripes near the edge. The cross is worn immediately after the Yser Cross, in which case the earlier lapel badge was not worn (although it was still worn in civilian dress).

Maritime Decoration, 1914–1918 R

This decoration, created by decree of 19 November 1918, consisted of five classes to reward distinguished services at sea, as follows: Cross, 1st class (gold, ie. silver-gilt); Cross, 2nd class (silver); Medal, 1st class (silver-gilt); Medal, 2nd class (silver); and Medal, 3rd class (bronze).

The badge of the first two classes is a Bath cross, 35mm across, enamelled white, with crossed swords in the angles. the central medallion has the royal monogram, A, on both *obv* and *rev*. The medal of the three lower classes is not enamelled, and consists of a Bath cross with the spaces between the arms filled in and showing the diagonal limbs of the Cross of Burgundy; the central circle has the royal monogram; above the medal are crossed swords.

For all classes the ribbon is sea green, 37mm wide, with two 6mm stripes each having five narrow stripes – red, yellow, black, yellow, red. On the ribbon are two crossed anchors of the same metal as the decoration, those of the first two classes being slightly larger than those of the lower grades.

Although a decree of 31 December 1924 ruled that the decoration would not be awarded after that date, a further decree of 4 June 1949 allowed retrospective awards to be made to fishermen and merchant seamen who had sailed for at least a year during the hostilities, or who had been torpedoed or taken prisoner before having served a full year.

Civic Decoration, 1914–1918 R

A Royal Decree of 18 May 1915 created the *Décoration Civique* 1914–1915, which was replaced under a further decree of 12 December 1918, by the *Décoration Civique* 1914–1918, and these must not be confused with the *Décoration Civique (Type 1867)* which was awarded in two categories – for long service and for acts of courage, devotion, and humanity. Because of the special nature of services rendered by civilians during the war, King Albert decided to institute this special version of the award.

Like the 1867 award, the new decoration was in five classes; Civic Cross, 1st class (gold or silver-gilt) and 2nd class (silver); Civic Medal, 1st class (gold or silver-gilt), 2nd class (silver), and 3rd class (bronze). Both cross and medal were similar to the earlier insignia but with minor differences. The cross is of Bath type, 35mm across, enamelled white, as for the Maritime Decoration; the medals are also the same as those of that award. The 1914–15 decoration bore the monogram of Leopold II, two interlaced Ls, but the 1914–18 insignia had the cypher A, of King Albert. We understand that the first badges were made in Paris, but are almost impossible to find.

The ribbon was 37mm wide, in a pale green with edges of the national colours in 3mm stripes of black (inner), yellow, and red (outer). A decree of 14 June 1919 provided that the ribbon for the *Croix Civique 1914–1918* should have, for the 1st and 2nd class, a centre stripe of gold thread; although the width was not specified, it was usually 4mm wide; after World War II the gold thread ribbon was no longer made, and modern ribbons have a yellow stripe in lieu.

The first crosses and medals had a bar on the ribbon, 5mm wide, in the same metal as the decoration, bearing the dates, 1914–1915. This was changed to 1914–1918 on the revised issue.

King Albert Medal R

The *Médaille du Roi Albert* was instituted by decree of 7 April 1919, as an award for both Belgians and foreigners who had rendered outstanding services in charitable and humanitarian work in assisting Belgians in distress.

The medal is 37mm in diameter, in patinated bronze. The *obv* has the head of the king, left, with the legend, ALBERT ROI DES BELGES, within a laurel wreath which gives the medal an irregular outline. The *rev* bears the engraved name of the recipient within the inscription, EN TÉMOINAGE DE RECONNAISSANCE NATIONALE À ... 1914–1918 (In witness of national gratitude to ...). The medal was also struck with the *rev* inscription in Flemish, ALS BLIJK VAN'S LANDS ERKENTELIJKHEID, AAN ...

The ribbon, 37mm, is a rich amaranth crimson, with a narrow central stripe of black, yellow and red. In cases where the award was made in connection with the re–victualling of occupied Belgium, the ribbon has two stripes of the three national colours, with black nearest the edge on each side.

Queen Elisabeth Medal RP

This decoration was instituted on 15 September 1915 for Belgians and foreigners who had given valuable services to Belgian civilians or soldiers in connection with the war and particularly with nursing and care of the sick and wounded, for a period of not less than one year prior to 30 September 1919.

The medal is 35mm in diameter, of dulled bronze, circular but with slight extensions at the four cardinal points, giving a stylised effect of a cross with convex ends to the arms, extending barely 1mm beyond the circular disc of the medal. The *obv* shows the bust of the queen, right, with the inscription, ELISABETH REINE DES BELGES. The *rev* has a female figure in nurse's dress, left, symbolising the spirit of sacrifice and devotion; the legend is PRO PATRIA, HONORE ET CARITATE (For Fatherland, honour and charity), with 1914–1916 in the exergue.

At the top of the medal is a laurel wreath with a cut-out centre, when the medal was awarded for hospital services, an enamelled red cross appears in the centre of this hole.

The ribbon is described as blue but is actually grey, with 4mm rose edges.

Medal for Combatant Volunteers, 1914–1918 R

It was not until 17 June 1930 that this decoration was created, to reward both Belgians and foreigners who had served under a voluntary engagement. There were various categories which gave entitlement to the medal, the length of combatant service required varying with age at entry.

The medal, in bronze, is of peculiar shape, described as oval, 28mm wide by 34mm tall, but this is not accurate. It is in fact a circular medal, 28mm in diameter, with a crescent shaped extension at the top, giving an additional height of some 6mm. The *obv* bears two heads, left, one representing the volunteers of 1830 and the other, those of 1914–18. The *rev* has the inscription, VOLUNTARIIS 1914–1918 PATRIA MEMOR (Some examples have VOLONTARIIS). The ribbon is plain royal blue.

Medal for War Volunteers

This medal was instituted on 7 April 1952, and could be awarded to, *inter alia*, ex–volunteers of the 1914–18 war who did not receive the Medal for Combatant Volunteers, 1914–18. In these cases a bar, 1914–18, was worn on the ribbon.

The medal, 37mm in diameter, is in bronze and shows a nude male figure standing behind a low wall, head to left, holding a sword pointing downwards; behind him are rays incorporating the letter V. The *rev* has a lion and the word, VOLUNTARIIS. The ribbon is in 17 stripes, nine dark blue and eight red.

Victory Medal   RP

Instituted by Royal Decree of 14 July 1919, the *Médaille de la Victoire* was awarded to all who had served between 1 August 1914 and 11 November 1918. Various decrees up to 17 August 1951 extended the scope of the award, to include white and coloured troops who had served in Africa, personnel of the merchant marine and fishing fleet, also civilians who had been awarded the Medal for Political Prisoners (*qv*).

The bronze medal, 36mm in diameter, follows the usual allied style, with the *obv* having a winged victory with head facing right, arms outstretched downwards, holding a sword in the right hand, and standing on a segment of a rayed globe.

The *rev* has the arms of Belgium in the centre, surrounded by a laurel wreath; outside this is a ring of nine shields of the principal allies superimposed on two oak branches; starting at the top and moving clockwise, these are: France, USA, Japan, Rumania, Brazil, Serbia, Portugal, Italy, and Great Britain. Outside these is the usual inscription, in Flemish and French; DE GROOTE OORLOG TOT DE BESCHAVING – LA GRANDE GUERRE POUR LA CIVILISATION. The ribbon is, or course, of the usual 'double rainbow' pattern.

War Medal, 1914–1918   RP

A Royal Decree of 21 July 1919 instituted the *Médaille Commémorative de la Guerre, 1914–1918*, for all who served during the war under the same conditions as for the Victory Medal.

The medal is of bronze, of unusual shape, approximately an isosceles triangle with the left and right side bent outwards, giving an outline rather like a bishop's mitre. The *obv* has the bust of a soldier, left, wearing a steel helmet on which is a spray of laurel (one writer describes him as King Albert I, but we understand that this is not correct, despite some slight resemblance). This is set in a central circular depression, above which is the Belgian lion flanked by branches of oak and laurel. In the bottom corners are the dates, 1914, 1918.

The *rev* has the dates in large figures, 1914, 1918, with the inscription above (in French) and below (in Flemish): MÉDAILLE COMMÉMORATIVE DE LA CAMPAGNE – HERINNERINGS MEDAILLE VAN DE VELDTOCHT. Above is the royal crown.

The ribbon, 37mm, has a 15mm central stripe of yellow, flanked by 1mm pin stripes of black and 10mm red edges.

Quite a number of embellishments have been authorised for wear on the ribbon. Volunteers have a 6mm gilt crown; service bars, 2mm wide, were worn (the first for twelve months' and subsequent ones for each six months' service) in silver, with a gilt one replacing five of silver; small crosses in red enamel indicated war wounds; a five-pointed silver star was worn by those who returned to active service after war wounds or sickness contracted on service. By a decree of February 1920, officers of the intelligence service who had been awarded a Belgian Order wore a silver crown, 6mm, on the ribbon of their War Medal, while in 1921 the award of the medal was extended to the merchant navy, with a 10mm bronze anchor on the ribbon.

A decree of 31st March 1933 provided that the medal could henceforth be awarded to all who had served during the war in the Belgian intelligence service or in the intelligence service of the allies; these were to have the silver crown on the ribbon, while those who had served in the Belgian intelligence wore, in addition, a silver lion rampant.

As late as November 1950, the Prince Royal authorised a gilt bar, known as the *Agrafe Russie*, 5mm wide, with the inscription, **1916–R–1918,** for members of the Belgian Expeditionary Corps who served in Russia (This decree regularised an unconfirmed royal order of 1931, authorising a similar bar, **1916–R–1917**). The decree also authorised two crossed anchors, 6mm in bronze, for Marines. Finally, a law of 24 June 1952 authorised uniform chevrons for military personnel captured by the enemy during 1914–1918; these were also to be indicated on the War Medal ribbon by plain black bars, 2mm wide, similar to the silver bars for service at the front.

Commemorative Medal for the African Campaigns, 1914–1917   R
Originally instituted by Royal Decree of 21 February 1917, to commemorate the campaigns in Africa during 1914–1916, the period was extended by a further decree of 28 September 1931, to include actions in East Africa in 1917.

The medal was in two classes, in silver for Europeans and in bronze for native soldiers, who had served in war actions in the Cameroons, Rhodesia, German East Africa, or on the eastern frontiers of the Belgian Congo. The *obv* has the frontal view of a seated lion with its front paws on a rock. The *rev* bears the dates, 1914–1916, and the names of the principal countries or areas in which the troops were engaged. In the middle of the names are two horizontal laurel branches. Above the medal is the royal crown. The ribbon is 36mm wide, of pale blue with 4mm yellow edges.

One bar was authorised in 1931, of the same metal as the medal, inscribed, MAHENGE, for those who participated in the capture of that place, in German East Africa, in 1917.

By virtue of the decree of 28 September 1931 mentioned above, the dates of the *rev* should have been amended to 1914—1917, but according to the late Henri Quinot (a noted authority on Belgian decorations), this was never put into effect as by this time all those entitled had received their medals, and the manufacturers could see no likelihood of selling the re-designed medals.

Political Prisoner's Medal, 1914–1918
A Royal Decree of 26 December 1930 established the *Médaille du Prisonier Politique*, for those Belgians who had been imprisoned by the enemy for a month or more, for acts of heroism and devotion in the support of the allies, and also for foreigners similarly imprisoned for helping Belgians.

The medal, 37mm across, is of patinated bronze, with the head of Albert I, left, on the *obv*. The surrounding laurel wreath gives an irregular edge to the medal. The inscriptions on *obv* and *rev* are in either French or Flemish, as appropriate to the recipient. In French, they are *(obv)*, ALBERT, ROI DES BELGES, and *(rev)*, EN TÉMOINAGE DE RECONNAISSANCE NATIONALE (Albert, King of the Belgians. In recognition of the country's gratitude). The Flemish equivalents are, ALBERT, KONING DER BELGEN, and ALS BLIJK VAN'S LANDS ERKENTELIJKHEID. Below, on the *rev*, are the dates, 1914–1918.

The ribbon is bright blue with a horizontal stripe, 4mm wide, of the national colours, black, yellow, and red, the last being nearest the medal.

By a decree of 17 August 1951, civilian recipients of this medal were also deemed to be entitled to the War Commemorative Medal and Victory Medal. Some 5000 awards have been gazetted.

Cross for Deportees R

This decoration was instituted on 27 November 1922, for Belgians who had been deported into enemy territory for refusing to work, or who had been conscripted into forced labour.

The cross is of maltese type, with shallow cut ends to the arms, of patinated bronze, with the dates, 1914, 1918, on the horizontal arms. The V of the top arm of the cross is filled with an ornamental pattern, to take the suspension ring. The ribbon is crimson, 38mm wide, striped with narrow chevrons (points downwards), 5mm apart, of the national colours, black, yellow, and red, with the red nearest the medal.

Deportees who died during their deportation were not only awarded a posthumous cross, but also the 5th class of the Order of Leopold II with the gold centre stripe on the ribbon.

Colonial Medal, 1914–1918 R

On 20 June 1935 the *Médaille Commémorative Coloniale* was instituted virtually as the civilian counterpart of the medal for the African campaigns. It was awarded to civilians whose official functions or other duties prevented them from serving in the fighting forces, or who, having joined the army, were recalled to the Belgian Congo to carry on their civilian professions.

The medal, which had to be purchased by entitled personnel, is of bronze gilt, with a five-pointed star and the rampant Belgian lion in the centre. Between the arms of the star is tracery. Silver-gilt examples also exist.

The ribbon, 37mm, is bright blue with 3mm edges of black, yellow, and red, with black on the outside, and it carries a narrow bar of bronze gilt, 5mm wide, with the dates, 1914–1918.

Medal of the National Committee for Assistance and Food Supply

Soon after the end of the war it was felt necessary to provide a decoration for those who had worked under the auspices of the National Committee, in distributing food and other needs to the population (presumably since almost every other category – military and civilian – had been given a medal). Thus by Royal Decree of 31 May 1919, this award was instituted in four classes, the first two in bronze gilt (the first class having a rosette on the ribbon), the third in silvered bronze, and the fourth class in bronze.

The medal is 34mm in diameter, with the *obv* showing a crowned female bust, left, representing *la Belgique*, within a wreath of oakleaves. The *rev* has the initials, C.N. *(Comité National)*, and the dates, 1914–1918. Below is the inscription in French and Flemish, EN SOUVENIR DE SA COLLABORATION – TER HERINNERING AAN ZIJN MEDEWERKING (In memory of his, or her, collaboration – it will be noted that *collaboration* had a happier meaning than during the 1939–45 war). The ribbon is 37mm wide, red with 8.5mm white edges.

During the war those distributing food had, of necessity, to hand out considerable quantities of dried beans, and consequently the medal has become known as *la Médaille du Haricot* – the Haricot Bean Medal.

Medal for National Restoration R

With the enormous work of rebuilding and restoring home life, industry, commerce, and culture, after the devastation four years of war, it is not surprising that a Royal Decree of 22 May 1928 created this award for meritorious service by administrators, commissioners, and others who had shared in this work.

The bronze gilt medal, 35mm in diameter, has a female head, left, representing

Belgium, with a low relief indication of reconstruction work in the background. The *rev* shows the ruins of Ypres, the dates, 1914–1918, and a panel inscribed, SOUVENIR DE LA RESTAURATION NATIONALE, and the Flemish equivalent, AANDENKEN VAN DE NATIONALE HERSTELLING.

The ribbon is scarlet with 5mm light blue side stripes, inset 5mm.

Liège Medal   R

Several unofficial medals were struck by local authorities in Belgian towns, but with one exception, they were not permitted to be worn, and do not come within the scope of this work.

However, the council of the city of Liège struck a medal which was first awarded in April 1920, for the gallant defenders of the city in August 1914, under the command of General Leman. The presentation was made by Prince Leopold, Duke of Brabant (later Leopold III), and although never officially sanctioned, the wearing of the medal in uniform was tolerated. It was also awarded to citizens of Liège who received the Political Prisoner's Medal, having been sentenced at Liège by German tribunals.

The medal is of bronze, edged on both sides with a laurel wreath. The *obv* shows the *Perron* of Liège — a column or statue — with a surrounding inscription, LA VILLE DE LIÈGE À SES VAILLANTS DÉFENSEURS (The town of Liège to her brave defenders). The *rev* depicts a battle scene.

The ribbon, 37mm wide, is half red, half yellow – the colours of the city of Liège.

Brazil

Brazil was one of the several countries which declared war on Germany in 1917, following the entry into the war of the United States of America, but played little if any active part in the fighting.

NEW AWARDS

Campaign Cross, 1917–18   R

Instituted by decree of 11 August 1922, this is a cross *patée* with rounded ends to the arms, 40mm wide, in bronze gilt.

The arms have a stippled field with a plain border, while the central medallion has the four stars of the Southern Cross set horizontally, surrounded by the inscription, PELA JUSTICA E PELA CIVILIZACÃO (For justice and for civilisation). The top of the upper arm has roman numerals, for the number of half-years' service.

The *rev* is similar, but the medallion bears the dates, 1917, 1918 (one above the other), with the surrounding circle lettered, GRANDE GUERRA (Great War) above, and BRASIL below.

The ribbon is 33mm wide, orange with a 3mm black centre stripe and edges, for combatants, and with similar white stripes for auxiliary services.

Victory Medal   R

By decree of 22 June 1923, Brazil instituted a Victory Medal, in bronze, 34mm in diameter, with the usual 'double rainbow' ribbon. The *obv* follows the usual style, with a winged Victory carrying a branch of laurel and palm. The *rev* has the shields of the allies, with that of Brazil in the centre, with the inscription, GRANDE GUERRA PELA CIVILIZACÃO.

China

Following the example of several other countries, China declared war on Germany on 14 May 1917, after the USA had entered the war, but did not take any significant part. However, large numbers of Chinese served with the Labour Corps and RAMC, and many British officers, particularly in those two corps, received the Order of the Striped Tiger (Wen-Hu), while a smaller number were awarded the Order of Chia-Ho.

EXISTING AWARDS

Order of Wen-Hu, or the Striped Tiger (1912).
Order of Chia-Ho, or the Excellent Crop, or Golden Grain (1912).
Decoration for Bravery (c 1912).

NEW AWARDS

War Commemorative Medal
In 1918, at the time of the armistice, on the suggestion of Marshal Toan, this silver medal was struck and awarded to all allied officials and military guards at allied legations in Pekin, as well as to a number of Chinese officers and officials.

The medal is 40mm in diameter and slightly convex. The *obv* has three Chinese flags, enamelled; the centre one is the national flag, in five horizontal stripes of red, yellow, blue, white, and black; on the left is the maritime ensign, red with a blue canton containing a white 'sun' with twelve small pointed rays; on the right is the flag of the army, red with a 9-pointed black (or blue?) 'star' with a yellow ball on each point; on the star itself are ten yellow balls. The three flag-staves are tied where they cross with a tasselled cord. The *rev* has four central Chinese characters in a stylised laurel wreath, indicating *In Commemoration of Victory*; around, outside the wreath, in ancient Chinese characters is *7th Year of the Chinese Republic, 28th of the 11th Month, Conferred by the President Hsiu Chu Chang*.

The ribbon is in five equal stripes, as the national flag but vertical, of red, yellow, blue, white, and black.

Cuba

Cuba declared war on the Central Powers, in common with several other American countries, in 1917, and appears to have issued a War Medal and a Victory Medal.

War Medal, 1917–19
From an unrecorded source we have noted details of a bronze medal, 30mm in diameter. The *obv* shows the waves and the sea shore, with a hut and flagstaff; on the right, in the background, is a rayed sun; the dates, 1917–1919, are in a panel below. The *rev* has the inscription, within a wreath of oak, CAMPAÑA POR LA HUMANIDAD, LA JUSTICIA, Y EL DERECHO. The arms of Cuba appear on a shield at the base.

The ribbon is half black, half red with a narrow white centre stripe.

Victory Medal   RP
With the usual 'double rainbow' ribbon, the bronze medal, 35mm, has the winged Victory (wings drooping somewhat) with outstretched arms, and holding a sword, point downwards, in her right hand and a flaming torch in the left. The *rev* has the

arms of Cuba surmounted by a cap of liberty, and flanked by oak and laurel sprays; around the top is LA GRAN GUERRA POR LA CIVILIZACION, while on each side of the lower half are the names of the allies – FRANCIA, INGLATERRA, ESTADOS UNIDOS, RUMANIA, BRASIL, RUSIA, GRECIA, BELGICA, ITALIA, SERVIA, MONTENEGRO, PORTUGAL, JAPON, CHINA.

Egypt

Under the sovereignty of Turkey before the war, Egypt became virtually a British protectorate when Turkey joined the Central Powers. The Khedive chose to remain in Constantinople, was deposed, and his uncle, Hussein Kamil, was elevated to the rank of Sultan. It became necessary for the allies to protect Egypt and the Suez Canal from Turkish invasion and thus the Egyptians became, somewhat reluctantly, drawn into the Allied side.

EXISTING AWARDS

Medal for Bravery (1913)

NEW AWARDS

Order of Mohammed Ali   R
In 1915 the Sultan instituted this order as the senior Egyptian award, for special merit or exceptional services to the country; it was very rarely awarded. There was a special grade of Collar, with the grand cordon insignia, awarded only to royal personages, heads of states, etc., and just two classes, grand cordon (sash) and commander (neck badge), limited to 30 and 100 members respectively.

The badge is most attractive, being a green bordered, white enamelled medallion, covered with gold stylised Arabic inscriptions indicating *Charity, Justice and Freedom from Vindictiveness are the strength of a Kingdom;* in the centre is a green disc, lettered (in Arabic), *Mohammed Ali,* in white. The medallion is set in an ornamental six-sided 'star' of joined arcs, with bud-like finials, in gold, green, and blue.

The ribbon is in the Moslem colours of dark green with white edge stripes.

The star of the order (worn on the left for grand cordon and on the right by commanders) has twelve points, with the badge superimposed.

In connection with the order are two medals, in gold and silver, awarded for bravery by personnel of the army and navy.

Order of the Nile   R
The Sultan instituted this order in 1915, for services to the country, and many British officers received it.

There were five classes, the two highest having a breast star – grand cordon (sash badge, and star on the left breast), grand officer (neck badge, and star on the right breast), commander (neck badge), officer and chevalier (badge worn on the left breast, with a rosette for officers).

The badge is a ten-pointed star of alternate gold and silver rays, the five larger points being set with two pointing upwards, two laterally, and one downwards, with the other five points somewhat shorter, giving a very unbalanced effect. Superimposed is a white enamelled 5-pointed star (with one point downwards) with a pale blue central medallion, edged gold, with an Arabic inscription declaring, *What*

31

benefits Egypt owes to the Nile, her source of prosperity and happiness! Later this was altered to a gold or silver centre with pale blue lettering. Above the badge, hinged, was a 5-arched crown.

The ribbon is a mid-blue with yellow side stripes, while stars for grand cordons and commanders are similar to the badge but larger, and the crown was set in the angle of the top rays of the white star.

Order of El Kemal R

Instituted in 1915 exclusively for ladies, this order would not really rank as one connected with the war but for the fact that (as with several other similar decorations) some awards were made for war services.

It was in three classes, the first class wearing the badge on a narrow sash and a star on the left side, while the second and third class badges were worn from a bow, the second class having a small rosette.

The badge is a dainty piece, consisting of a small white centre, with blue writing indicating *El Kemal;* from this centre radiate ten flowers, blue and white – five long ones, somewhat like *fleurs de lis,* and five shorter, like tulips. Above the badge was a crown.

The ribbon is a bluish-grey, with narrow gold thread edges. The star is gold with the badge superimposed, and on the points of the star, in high relief, are the Arabic signs for *Charity, Duty, Devotion, Nobility*, and *Pity*.

Medal for Meritorious Acts R

In 1917 the Sultan instituted this medal, in silver and in bronze, for meritorious services in all walks, including the forces, nurses, police, etc. The *obv* bears the Sultan's emblem and the date, 1335 (=1917 AD). The *rev* has an Arabic inscription indicating *Sultan of Egypt's Medal for Meritorious Acts. The most useful among you are the best.* The medal is named, and hangs from a clasp inscribed with the date of the award. The ribbon is plain violet.

Military Star of Sultan Fouad R

We have been unable to ascertain whether or not retrospective awards were made of this decoration for services during the Great War, but in view of its creation shortly after the war, on 6 December 1919, and the fact that it was for award both to Egyptian officers and to foreign officers attached to the Egyptian army, mentioned in despatches for merit or distinguished services in action, it seems probable that it should be included.

The decoration (officially termed an Order) is a five-pointed star of the shape of the Khedive's Star, 1882, enamelled white, edged gold and with a gold centre stripe to each ray; the large central medallion has a gold laurel wreath on a red circle, enclosing a blue ground with two crossed swords; at the top of the wreath is a crown. The *rev* is rather similar, with a central inscription indicating *The Military Star of Sultan Fouad.* The suspender bar is straight, and the ribbon was in five equal stripes of Nile blue, buff, black, buff, and blue.

The star was worn immediately after the Order of the Nile and before all other decorations, and bars were awarded for subsequent entitlements.

France

After her defeat by Prussia in 1870–71, France founded the Third Republic, which continued until the second German victory in 1940.

Germany declared war on France on 2 August 1914, ostensibly because of France's 1890 Alliance with Russia, on whom Germany had already declared war the previous day.

EXISTING AWARDS

* * Legion of Honour (1802/4)
  Médaille Militaire (1852)
* * Medal of Honour of the President of the Republic (*c* 1870)
* * Colonial Medal (1893)

NEW AND AMENDED AWARDS

Legion of Honour   R
In 1916, in order to distinguish between the various classes when ribbons only were worn, a system of rosettes and gold and silver braid strips were introduced. Chevaliers wear the plain red ribbon, while officers have a small red rosette (representing the large rosette worn on the ribbon with the badge itself). For commanders this rosette has a short strip of silver braid underneath, extending on each side; grand officers have gold braid on one side and silver on the other, while grand cross is indicated by gold braid on each side. A decree of 5 July 1918 authorised these distinctive emblems to be worn also in civilian dress.

Colonial Medal
Normally awarded with a bar for the relative campaign, by decrees of 27 March 1914 and 5 October 1920, the Colonial Medal could be awarded without bar for specified periods of service in overseas territories (In 1962 the name was changed to *Médaille d'Outre-Mer* – Overseas Medal).

Croix de Guerre, 1914–18   RP
With military awards for gallantry in action limited to the Legion of Honour and the Médaille Militaire, there was felt a need for a lower award, particularly for those who had received a *citation à l'ordre*, ie. a mention in despatches, so that a decoration could be awarded immediately by the commander-in-chief on the field of battle. As a result the *Croix de Guerre* (War Cross) was instituted by a law of 8 April 1915, to recognise, from the outbreak of hostilities, individual mentions in despatches of armies, army corps, divisions, brigades, and battalions or corresponding units. It could be conferred on both Frenchmen and foreigners, and also on civilians who had been the subject of a *citation*. For maritime personnel, similar regulations applied.

The cross was also awarded, automatically, to recipients of the Legion of Honour for gallantry in action or the Médaille Militaire, whose award was gazetted in the *Journal Officiel*, equivalent to a *citation à l'ordre*.

The decoration is a bronze St. George cross, 37mm across. The arms have a pitted sunken surface with plain raised edges; the *obv* central medallion has the head of *La République*, right, with RÉPUBLIQUE FRANÇAISE and conventional laurel branches in the surrounding circle. The *rev* of the medallion bears two dates, 1914 above and dates between 1915 and 1918 below, according to when it was struck. Between the arms of the cross are two crossed antique swords. Suspension is by a ring through a ball and ornamental double curl fitting.

For the ribbon, a modern weave of the St Helena Medal ribbon was used – 37mm green with five narrow red stripes and narrow red edges – but with a brighter green than that of the earlier ribbon.

On the ribbon one usually finds one or more emblems, according to the nature of the 'mention'; for a mention in an Army despatch, a bronze *palme* or laurel branch (and known as *Croix de Guerre avec palme*); for five bronze ones, a silver *palme* could be substituted according to a decree on 8 January 1917, but in practice most recipients preferred to have five small *palmes* on their ribbon; for an Army Corps mention, a gilt star was awarded; for Division, a silver star; for Brigade, Battalion, or similar unit mention, a bronze star was worn.

The cross was widely awarded, although the exact number is not known; according to an official publication, some 2,055,000 *citations* had been made up to 1 March 1920, to which must be added those accompanying awards of the Legion of Honour and the Médaille Militaire, and also posthumous awards.

A large number of towns and villages in France, and some abroad, were awarded the cross, and it was also awarded collectively to certain regiments, whose officers and men were allowed to wear the *fourragère*, or lanyard, in red and green, on the left shoulder.

There were many British recipients, in all branches of the forces, and groups of medals including a Croix de Guerre should be checked against the *London Gazette* for verification of the award. A note of these is sometimes given in regimental histories, but their data is not always complete or accurate.

Médaille de la Reconnaissance Française   RP

The French title of this award has no exact translation into English, the word *reconnaissance*, meaning approximately, gratitude, recognition, or acknowledgement or assistance (it has no connection with the way in which we now use the word in a military sense).

The medal was instituted by decree of 13 July 1917, as a token of gratitude for all kinds of individual and collective works of benevolence at home and abroad, in helping the sick and wounded, in caring for families of those killed in the war, the mutilated, blind, orphaned, and homeless families ruined by the German invasion. It was purely a civil decoration, for which military personnel were not normally eligible.

Awards were in three classes; for the first class the medal was in silver-gilt, with an 18mm rosette on the ribbon; the second class was in silver (a decree of 2 December 1917 provided for a 15mm blue enamelled star to be worn on the ribbon, but this does not appear in modern regulations), while the third class was in bronze. The original design, 30mm in diameter, in low relief, showed the figure of Charity raising up a wounded figure; the *rev* had a two-line inscription in small seriffed capitals, RECONNAISSANCE FRANÇAISE, with a palm leaf on the right. The suspension ring is fixed to the medal by an ornamental strip along the top of the medal (NOTE: in 1945 General de Gaulle revised the regulations, and established a new medal, 32mm in diameter, in a similar but altered design).

The ribbon is 37mm, white, watered, with a narrow red-white-blue edge (blue on the outside).

Quite a number of these medals were awarded to British personnel during the Great War, and are often seen in company with the British War and Victory Medals named to medical and nursing personnel; in some cases the French medal has the recipient's name on the *rev*, but this was probably done privately.

Medal of Honour of the President of the Republic

In 1831 or 1834, a wearable Medal of Honour was instituted for acts of courage and devotion, and this was replaced early in the days of the Third Republic (thus *circa* 1870) by a new decoration known equally by the names, *Médaille d'Honneur du President de la République*, and *Médaille d'Honneur des Affaires Étrangères*.

The medal, in gold (silver-gilt), silver, or bronze, was awarded for services to France by Frenchmen or foreigners living outside France or, exceptionally, by foreigners living in France. Awards to military personnel carried crossed swords above the medal.

In October 1917, the medal 'with swords' was redesigned. In place of just the pair of swords, the embellishment now became crossed swords on two sprays of oak leaves. The gold (silver-gilt) medal was now reserved for officers, the silver for under-officers (approximately equivalent to British warrant officers and sergeants), and the bronze medal for corporals and privates.

The Medal of Honour ranked after the Croix de Guerre, and quite a number were awarded to British officers and other ranks and ratings.

Croix du Combattant Volontaire   R

Although not instituted until 4 July 1935, this bronze cross was struck to reward volunteers who had served at the front in a combatant unit, including foreign volunteers who served with the French army.

Apparently there had been long discussions as to how this award should be constituted, and it was originally decided, with the institution of the *Médaille Commémorative de la Grande Guerre (qv)*, that a bar, ENGAGÉ VOLONTAIRE, should be worn on its ribbon. The authority for this, however, was not continued after the introduction of the *Croix du Combattant Volontaire*.

The cross has a diameter of 36mm, and is basically of the same shape as the *Croix de Guerre*, but without the swords and with a small projection along most of the end of each arm. The arms have conventional laurel leaves and a narrow raised edge, with an antique sword set vertically, point uppermost, showing behind the central medallion. The medallion shows a soldier's head, with steel helmet, facing left, within a surrounding inscription, REPUBLIQUE FRANÇAISE. The *rev* has plain arms to the cross, narrowly edged; the medallion has a conventional design and the dates, 1914–1918, surrounded by COMBATTANT VOLONTAIRE.

The ribbon, 36mm, is green with an 8mm red centre stripe, and 4mm yellow side stripes inset 1mm. The colours combine those of the Legion of Honour, the *Médaille Militaire* and the *Croix de Guerre*.

Médaille des Évadés   R

The medal for escaped prisoners of war was established by decree of 20 August 1926 to commemorate the achievements of both military and civil escapees, including natives of Alsace and Lorraine who escaped from the German Army, and inhabitants of occupied territory who made their way through the enemy lines or crossed frontiers to put themselves at the disposal of the French military authorities. Furthermore, the award of the medal was extended to prisoners of war in Germany, who escaped during the Franco-Prussian War of 1870–71.

The medal is of bronze, 30mm in diameter, with an *obv* of a familiar type – the female head of *La République*, left, wearing an oak chaplet, flanked by the legend, RÉPUBLIQUE FRANÇAISE. The *rev* is simple – just the words, MÉDAILLE/DES/ÉVADÉS, within an oak wreath. Suspension is by a plain ring, with a 36mm ribbon, green with three orange stripes, the centre one being 5mm wide and the outer ones 2mm wide, inset 2mm from the edges.

Médaille de la Déportation et de l'Internement

This title covers two distinct medals – one for acts of resistance and the other for political prisoners – and four separate ribbons. Although instituted after World War II and intended primarily for that period, the awards were extended to cover similar circumstances during World War I, and therefore fall within our scope.

The medal for acts of resistance was instituted by a decree of 6 August 1948, and was awarded to those deported or interned for such acts. The bronze pentagonal design, point downwards, is unusual, and is 36mm wide by 34mm high. The *obv* shows two chained hands, crossed at the wrists, with flames behind. The *rev* has the legend, RÉPUBLIQUE/FRANÇAISE/MÉDAILLE/DE LA DÉPORTATION/ET/DE L'INTERNEMENT/ POUR FAITS DE RÉSISTANCE. Below is a small cross of Lorraine.

The ribbons, 36mm, have 2mm red edges; for deportees the central portion has four pale blue and three white vertical stripes; for internees the stripes are diagonal from top right to bottom left. Recipients of the Great War period wear a bar on the ribbon, with **1914–1918**.

The medal for political prisoners is quite different. Created by decree of 9 September 1948, it is of bronze, circular, 30mm in diameter. The *obv* has as its main motif three rectangular chain links; the top and bottom ones are seen end on and project beyond the circumference of the medal, the upper link serving to hold the trapezoid suspension loop. In the chain is a small outline map of France, from which rays extend to the edge, the central and lower ones being over the central chain link, and the upper ones are below it. Along the edge is the inscription, RÉPUBLIQUE FRANÇAISE. The *rev* has the same chain motif, but with the central link broken, enclosing the dates, 1940, 1945. The surrounding inscription is, MÉDAILLE DE LA DÉPORTATION ET DE L'INTERNEMENT.

The ribbons are 36mm wide, and similar to the previous ones, but with 2mm yellow edges in each case and, similarly, recipients of the Great War period have the bar, **1914–1918**, on the ribbon.

Médaille Commémorative Française, 1914–1918   RP

On 23 June 1920 one of the first of the commemorative medals of the war was instituted. It was awarded to all members of the French armed forces who served between 2 August 1914 and 11 November 1918, also to members of the merchant navy, nurses, and orderlies, doctors, chemists, welfare workers; local government officials, police and firemen of bombed towns were eligible, also women drivers, telephonists, and secretaries serving for at least six months with military units.

The medal is in bronze, basically circular, 30mm in diameter, with a square-cut oak and laurel mount in one piece with the medal. The *obv*, in rather low relief, has a female head – presumably *La République* – facing left, wearing a steel helmet and holding a sword in her left hand, with only the hilt visible; in the background are laurel branches. The *rev* is rather plain; in the centre is, incuse, GRANDE/GUERRE/ 1914–1918, surrounded by RÉPUBLIQUE FRANÇAISE.

The ribbon is 36mm wide, in six white stripes of 3.5mm and five red stripes of 3mm. Prior to the institution of the *Croix du Combattant Volontaire*, a bar, ENGAGÉ VOLONTAIRE, was worn by those who subsequently received the cross; officially the bar was not supposed to be worn after the issue of the cross, but not unnaturally many old soldiers continued to wear it.

Médaille Interalliée or Médaille de la Victoire, 1914–1918   RP

The French version of the Victory Medal follows the general pattern, with a circular bronze medal, 36mm diameter, with the *obv* depicting a winged figure of Victory facing to the front, with arms raised. She holds an olive branch in her right hand and a laurel wreath in the left. The *rev* has, at the top, a conventional cap of liberty, flanked by the initials, R.F.; below, in five lines, is the inscription, LA/GRANDE GVERRE/POVR LA/CIVILISATION/1914–1918. The ring suspension is similar to the British one and the ribbon is, of course, identical, in the shaded colours of the spectrum, violet on the two edges and shading through blue, green and yellow, to red in the centre.

The medal was instituted by a law of 20 July 1922, and was awarded to all members of the armed forces, nurses, orderlies, prisoners of war, escapees, and others who had served for a minimum of three months. The time qualification did not apply in the case of military personnel mentioned in despatches, discharged wounded or sick, volunteers, or reservists.

The Victory Medal was worn immediately after French orders and decorations, and before colonial awards and campaign medals (including the Commemorative Medal for 1914–18).

Another design of the Victory Medal is found, which is presumably unofficial (since it is not mentioned in *Décorations Officielles Françaises*, nor in Delande's *Décorations – France et Colonies*), and probably a rejected design. The *obv* shows a frontal figure of Victory with arms outstretched, holding a sword in the right hand, below the hilt, with point downwards, and a laurel spray in the left hand. In the lower background are faint rays; near the edge, bottom right, is the signature, *C. Charles* (This design was in fact used for the *obv* of the Cuban Victory Medal. *qv*). The *rev* has the central 3-line inscription, LA GRANDE GUERRE/POUR LA CIVILISATION/ 1914–1918. Above and below are laurel sprays. Unlike the official medal, this design does not have 'R.F.' as indication of the country of origin.

Médaille Commémorative d'Orient et des Dardanelles   R

During the war it was proposed to issue a medal, similar to the *Médaille Coloniale* (which was a general service medal) for the troops who had served in expeditionary corps in the Eastern Mediterranean and at the Dardanelles. This suggestion was not adopted at the time, but was re-opened in 1925. As a result, the *Médaille d'Orient* was created by decree of 15 June 1926, to be awarded for these two theatres of war. In fact, two varieties of the medal were struck, one bearing on the *rev* the word, ORIENT, and the other, DARDANELLES, but otherwise they are identical; however, different ribbons are used.

The medals are of bronze, 30mm in diameter. The *obv* has the head of *La République*, left, wearing a helmet ensigned with an oak wreath, and the inscription at the sides, RÉPUBLIQUE FRANÇAISE. The *rev* has a collection of regimental colours, a gun, anchor, and laurel sprays, with the curved title in the upper field, ORIENT or DARDANELLES. The suspension ring is hidden by a crescent within two palm branches.

The ribbons, 36mm, are, for the *Orient*, a mid-blue with a 5mm yellow centre stripe and 2mm yellow side stripes set close to the edge; that for *Dardanelles* has six white stripes of 3.5mm, and five green ones of 3mm

Croix du Combattant   RP

In 1926 a law was passed instituting a 'Combatant's card', for all ex-servicemen who were entitled to assistance from the *Office National du Combattant*, and by a decree of 28 June 1930, the *Croix du Combattant* was created so that their fellow citizens could know and respect those who had defended the country in her hour of need.

The design is simple but effective, in bronze, 36mm wide. The cross has straight sided, widening arms, like the *Croix de Guerre*, but with slight projections as if it were superimposed on a shorter but slightly wider cross. The central medallion has the head of *La République*, left, with above and below, RÉPUBLIQUE FRANÇAISE.

Surrounding the medallion and visible between the arms of the cross, is a laurel wreath. The *rev* is similar, with a sword on the medallion, point downwards and with rays emanating from the pommel; around is the legend, CROIX•DU•COMBATTANT.

The ribbon is attractive, 35mm wide, in horizon blue with seven red stripes, 1.5mm wide.

Recipients who also qualified for a 'Combatant's card' for World War II, are entitled to wear two bars on the ribbon, **1914–1918**, and **1939–1945**.

Médaille des Victimes de l'Invasion R

In order to acknowledge the courage and spirit of those who had been rendered homeless or had endured other suffering as a result of the German invasion, the Minister for the Liberated Regions instituted this medal on 30 June 1921. There were three classes – silver-gilt, silver, and bronze – 30mm in diameter, with the *obv* in low relief showing a woman victim standing, right, with a devastated town in the far background; above, right, are the faint letters, FRANCE. The *rev* has the 6-line inscription, AUX/VICTIMES/DE/L'INVASION/LA FRANCE/RECONNAISSANTE (France is grateful to the victims of the invasion), within a wide border of stylised laurel branches with, in base, the dates, 1914–1918.

Above the medal and attached to it, holding the ribbon bar, is a mount showing on *obv* and *rev* an arrangement of chains.

The ribbon is a rich blue with a 2mm black central stripe and 5mm red side stripes inset 5mm. By decree of 10 January 1923, two bars were issued, PRISONNIERS POLITIQUES, and OTAGES DE GUERRE, for political prisoners and war hostages, respectively.

Médaille des Prisonniers Civils, Déportés et Otages de la Grande Guerre 1914–1918 R

As late as 14 March 1936, it was decided to institute a medal with this lengthy title, although it would appear that potential recipients were already catered for by various awards already in existence. Those eligible included the inhabitants of all the regions invaded by the Germans, civil prisoners, those deported as hostages or interned in concentration camps, but those who were entitled to the *Médaille des Victimes de l'Invasion* were not eligible. It is a little difficult to see the reason for the distinction, as it would seem that one medal could have covered both categories.

The bronze medal, 32mm in diameter, depicts on the *obv* a female figure standing, left, with bowed head, right arm extended and chained at the wrist, the left hand holding a flaming torch. The *rev* has the 7-line inscription, PRISONNIERS/CIVILS/ DÉPORTÉS ET/OTAGES/DE LA/GRANDE GUERRE, with a chain all round the edge.

The ribbon, 32mm, is red with a 5mm blue central stripe flanked by 2mm white stripes, and 1mm green outside edges. It is also found in the more usual French width of 36–37mm, with slightly wider green edges. It is reported that some 11,000 of those medals were issued.

Médaille de la Fidélité Française R

A medal was created by law of 3 July 1922, for inhabitants of Alsace and Lorraine who had been imprisoned or exiled by the Germans, because of their loyalty to France.

The bronze 32mm medal shows, on the *obv*, two women seated, looking out across country to (presumably) France. The *rev* has a bundle of fasces between crossed oak and laurel sprays, with a three-fold motto riband, lettered, LIBERTÉ, ÉGALITÉ, FRATERNITÉ.

The ribbon has a wide blue centre, with red (outer) and white (inner) side stripes and a narrow white edge. A bar on the ribbon is lettered, FIDÉLITÉ, and a star indicates each year of imprisonment or exile.

Decoration for the Wounded RP

In November 1916 a special ribbon was authorised for men of the French army and navy who were wounded or who were invalided through wounds or illness due to the war. The ribbon has a red centre stripe, flanked by yellow, narrow blue, and wider blue, all separated by narrow white stripes. In the centre a large red enamelled 5-pointed star was worn. (*fig.* 1a)

Many years later a medal, in the form of a red enamelled 5-pointed star on a gilt wreath (with the same ribbon) was struck by manufacturers for sale to recipients of the original ribbon.

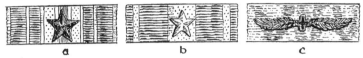

a   b   c

Fig. 1   France: a – Ribbon and emblem for military wounded; b – Ribbon and emblem for civilian wounded; c – Emblem for nurses.

Ribbon and Emblem for Civilian Wounded

Commandant Sculfort, in a series of articles in *Carnet de la Sabretache*, records and illustrates a ribbon instituted on 1 July 1918 for civilians wounded or mutilated on account of the war. The ribbon is 37mm, mid-blue with a 9mm yellow centre stripe and 2.5mm yellow side stripes, inset 2.5mm. In the centre is a 5-pointed star in white metal (*fig.* 1b)

Sculfort records that the youngest recipient was a baby, aged two months, who was wounded by a German shell fired on Paris by a long-range gun.

This award is shown (without the star) in two publications sponsored by the firm of P. Delande, but does not appear in *Décorations Officielles Françaises*, published by the Paris Mint in 1956.

Emblem for Nurses

In the same series of articles by Commandant Sculfort, he describes and illustrates *l'Insigne des Infirmières*. No date of institution is given, but as this article appeared early in 1920, it would seem likely that the badge was instituted at the same time as the previous award.

It consists of two palm leaves set almost horizontally, slightly raised as an almost flat V, and with a small red Geneva cross superimposed (*fig.* 1c). It is shown on a plain white ribbon bar, and we understand that it was worn thus, on the left side, in hospital uniform, and on the cloak, below military nursing insignia, out of doors. Sculfort states, however, that nurses who were members of nursing societies wore the badge on the ribbon of their society's medal.

The badge is in bronze, silver, or gold (gilt), according to the recipient's length of service with the wounded; for one year it was in bronze; for two years, silver; and for three years in gold. Mere length of service was not sufficient to qualify, but also a good record of devotion to duty, bravery, or distinguished service was necessary.

Like the previous award, this does not appear in *Décorations Officielles Françaises*, although it appears to have been authorised by a decree of the Under Secretary of State for Health.

Great Britain &
the British Empire

Great Britain declared war on Germany on 4 August 1914, ostensibly because Germany had failed to respect the neutrality of Belgium. Actually, it was inevitable, as all Europe had known for some years that war between the Central Powers and the Entente was coming, largely because Germany was too late in entering the race for colonial expansion, and was therefore suffering extreme frustration.

EXISTING AWARDS

* Victoria Cross (instituted 1856)
  Order of the Bath (1725)
  Order of Merit (1902)
  Order of the Star of India (1861)
  Order of St. Michael & St. George (1818)
  Order of the Indian Empire (1878)
  Indian Order of Merit (1837)
* Distinguished Service Order (1886)
* Royal Red Cross (1883)
* Distinguished Service Cross (1901, as Conspicuous Service Cross)
  Order of British India (1837)
* Distinguished Conduct Medal (1854)
* Conspicuous Gallantry Medal (1855/1874)
* West African Frontier Force D.C.M/ (1905)
* King's African Rifles D.C.M. (1905)
* Indian Distinguished Service Medal (1907)
* Meritorious Service Medal – Army (1845)

NEW AWARDS

Order of the British Empire
Order of the Companions of Honour
Military Cross
Distinguished Flying Cross
Air Force Cross
Military Medal
Distinguished Service Medal
Distinguished Flying Medal
Air Force Medal
Meritorious Service Medal (Immediate award for gallantry, &c.)
1914 Star
1914–15 Star
British War Medal
Mercantile Marine Medal
Victory Medal
Victory Medal (South Africa)
Territorial Force War Medal
Meritorious Service Medal – Royal Navy
Meritorious Service Medal – Royal Air Force
Mention in Despatches Emblem
Special Constabulary Long Service Medal
Allied Subjects Medal
Canadian Memorial Cross
British Red Cross Society War Medal, and Special Service Cross
First Aid Nursing Yeomanry War Medal (semi-official)

The Victoria Cross (Instituted 1856)   R

As the Victoria Cross was instituted in 1856, it does not fall within the normal scope of this work, but some amendments to the regulations occurring during the Great War should be noted.

Miniature VC on the ribbon. As the ribbon for army recipients was same colour as that of the Long Service & Good Conduct Medal, although 1½in wide as against 1¼in, it was felt, in 1916 (since a large number of VC's had been awarded) that some distinction should be made. Consequently the LS&GC ribbon was given narrow white edges, and plain crimson of the army VC was thus easily distinguishable.

If a bar were awarded (as in the case of Lieut. A. Martin-Leake, RAMC, 18 February 1915), this was to be indicated by a miniature of the cross worn on the centre of the ribbon strip when the cross itself was not worn (Army Order No. 290 of September 1916).

In 1917 this regulation regarding the miniature cross was revised (Army Order of April 1917). Now army recipients were to wear the miniature cross on the ribbon strip to indicate the *first* award of the VC, and a further miniature to indicate each bar (so far no second bars have been awarded).

Change of ribbon. With the formation of the Royal Air Force in 1918, it was necessary to review the then current ribbons, being crimson for the army and blue for the navy. Henceforth all arms of the services were to wear the crimson ribbon, with the appropriate miniatures to indicate first award and bar(s). These amendments were subsequently incorporated into the consolidating Royal Warrant of 22 May 1920.

During the period 1914–19, some 613 Victoria Crosses were awarded, and two bars for second awards (one each to Lieut. A. Martin–Leake and Capt. N. G. Chavasse, MC, both of the RAMC). Of the 615 awards, 415 were to the British army, 51 were to the navy and marines, 9 to the RFC and RAF, and 140 to Dominion personnel (including one Newfoundlander).

The Most Excellent Order of the British Empire   RP

After nearly three years of war it was apparent that no suitable order existed to reward the splendid services of the thousands of men and women who, by their enormous efforts at home and throughout the Empire – in factories, hospitals, voluntary services, social work, politics, and many other spheres – had materially contributed to the cause.

To meet this need King George V instituted the Order of the British Empire by Letters Patent under the Great Seal, on 4 June 1917, while on 27 December 1918 the addition of a Military Division enabled similar recognition to be made for distinguished services in H.M. Forces of a type which fell outside the category of other decorations.

The order was instituted in five classes: Knights and Dames Grand Cross (GBE); Knights and Dames Commanders (KBE and DBE); Commanders (CBE); Officers (OBE); and Members (MBE). The badge is a cross *patonce*, ie. with widening three–pointed ends. For the highest classes it is enamelled pearl (usually appearing as a bluish-grey), edged gold; the central medallion was gold (silver-gilt) with the figure of Britannia seated to right, in a red circle lettered in gold, FOR GOD AND THE EMPIRE; above the cross is the imperial crown. The badges of the two lowest classes are in the same design, but without enamel; that of an officer is wholly in silver-gilt, while that of a member is in matt silver. The *rev* of the badge has the royal and imperial cypher of George V, GRI, interlaced and with a crown above, in a cable circle.

Unlike the Order of Bath, which has a different insignia for its military and civil divisions but with the same ribbon for each, the Order of the British Empire has the same insignia for both divisions, but differenced the plain purple ribbon with a narrow red central stripe for the military division.* It is odd that the early statutes are somewhat vague about the width of the central stripe; knights grand cross wore the badge from a sash, passing over the right shoulder to the left side, 3³/₄in wide (often manufactured as 4in), the military division having a central stripe 'of about five-sixteenths of an inch'. For dames grand cross the sash was 2¹/₄in wide and the military central stripe 'about one-quarter on an inch'. They also wore an eight-pointed breast star of forty-eight rays (the vertical rays being longer than the horizontal ones) with central medallion as on the badge. Knights and dames commanders wore a similar but slightly smaller badge at the neck, from a ribbon 1³/₄in wide (with a red stripe 'of about three-sixteenths of an inch' for the military division), and a smaller breast star of forty rays with the vertical and horizontal rays equal. Commanders wore the same badge and ribbon, but without the star. Officers and members wore their badges on the left chest from a 1¹/₂in ribbon (with a one–eighth red stripe when appropriate). For all except the highest class, ladies' ribbons are made up in bow form, for wear on the left shoulder when not in uniform.

Five officials of the Order were appointed: Prelate; King–of–Arms; Registrar; Secretary; and Gentleman Usher of the Purple Rod.

Up to February 1921, which covers services in connection with the war, the approximate number of awards were: knights and dames grand cross, 102; knights and dames commanders, 561; commanders, 3,275; officers 12,196; members, 10,692.

It should be noted that recipients of the original pattern insignia could continue to wear the purple ribbon after the new insignia was introduced, or they could change to the pink and grey ribbon if they so desired.

Medal of the Order of the British Empire

In addition to the five classes described above, the *Medal of the Order of the British Empire* was instituted to reward persons whose services to the Empire warranted recognition, but for whom membership of the order was not suitable. The small medal was approximately 1.1in in diameter, of frosted silver, the *obv* design being similar to the central medallion of the badge of the order, while the *rev* had the interlaced script initials, GRI below a crown, within a cable circle. The plain purple ribbon was one and one-sixteenth of an inch wide, the military division having a red stripe of 'about one-sixteenth of an inch'. Suspension was by a ring.

Various writers have quoted misleading figures of the numbers issued up to 1922 (when a larger medal of different design, with bar suspension, was instituted), giving the impression that only some 400 were awarded. P. E. Abbot and J. M. A. Tamplin, in *British Gallantry Awards*, have recorded a total of 1,987, from entries in the *London Gazette*. The medals were issued unnamed, but one sometimes finds them privately engraved.

The Order of the Companions of Honour   RP

This is not an order of knighthood but of distinction, and was instituted by King George V on 4 June 1917, at the same time as the Order of the British Empire. It has been described as in the nature of a junior class of the Order of Merit, and similarly it carries no title or precedence. It is awarded, in one class only, to a very limited number of men and women who 'have rendered conspicuous service of national importance'.

The Order of the Companions of Honour is not a war award as such, but like the Order of the British Empire, it was created to fulfill a need which had arisen by virtue of certain exceptional services rendered during and connected with the war.

---

*The change to the present ribbon of rose-pink, narrowly edged with pearl grey, and with a narrow pearl grey central stripe for the military division, was made under the revised statutes of 30 July 1937.

The oval gold badge has a central rectangular 'medallion' depicting, on the left, a knight in armour on horseback, riding past an oak tree on which hangs a shield of the royal arms. The rectangle is surrounded by a blue band, lettered in gold: IN ACTION FAITHFUL AND IN HONOUR CLEAR. The spaces between the rectangle and the surrounding band are filled with ornamental scroll work, while above the badge is the imperial crown.

Suspension is by a ring, with a carmine ribbon, 1½in wide, with interrupted edge stripes of gold thread. The badge is worn at the neck by men and from a ribbon bow on the left shoulder by women. Members of the order place CH after their names, and in order of precedence this comes immediately after the GBE (Knight or Dame Grand Cross of the Order of the British Empire) and before the DSO (Distinguished Service Order).

There is a Secretary and Registrar appointed to the order, and he wears, according to the statutes, a similar badge 'with the addition of two silver pens saltirewise between the angles of the cross'. This is a somewhat odd description, as the badge does not appear to incorporate a cross in its design unless this refers to the four tiny members linking the scrolls to the rectangle.

The Distinguished Service Order (Instituted 1886)

Bars for second and subsequent awards were authorised by Warrant of 23 August 1916, and at the same time a silver heraldic rose indicating each bar, was authorised for wear on the ribbon strip when the decoration itself was not worn.

It is believed that the early bars were similar to the suspender bar (and upper brooch bar), ie. with conventional straight laurel sprays, but these were soon replaced by the present bar, plain with a central horizontal ridge and a crown in the centre.

The Royal Red Cross (Instituted 1883) P

When this decoration was instituted, for ladies only,* members of the Nursing Services or other ladies engaged in nursing duties, there was only a single class with a gold (later silver-gilt) and red enamel cross.

By Royal Warrant of 10 November 1915 the decoration was extended to a second class, designated as Associate (ARRC), and provision was made for recipients of the second class to be eligible for advancements to the first class.

The badge was of similar design to that of the first class (with the head of George V on the central medallion), but in silver and red enamel, and with the inscription, FAITH, HOPE, CHARITY, 1883, on the *rev* instead of on the *obv*.

A Royal Warrant of 15 December 1917 provided for the award of a bar to the first class, for subsequent awards, and this consists of a plain strip, enamelled red and edged gilt, about one inch long and about one-eighth inch wide, splayed at each end. A ring, soldered to the back of the bar, enables the badge to hang from it. We understand from the Public Record Office that no similar provision appears in regard to the second class, an it is generally believed that if an ARRC were deemed worthy of a further award, she would be promoted to the first class (RRC), thus making a bar to the second class unnecessary.

The Distinguished Service Cross (Instituted, as the Conspicuous Service Cross, 1901) P

The title of this decoration was changed from the Conspicuous Service Cross, by Order in Council of 14 October 1914, and eligibility for its award was extended from warrant officers and subordinate officers (not holding a commission in the Royal Navy) to include commissioned officers below the rank of lieutenant-commander.

---

*Since 1977 some awards have been made to male nurses.

A bar was authorised on 7 September 1916 for subsequent awards. This was a plain silver bar with arms widening at the extremities and with slightly curved ends; in the centre is a crown. By the same order the Royal Indian Marine were also eligible for the award of the DSC.

The Military Cross RP

The Military Cross was instituted by Royal Warrant of 28 December 1914, as a decoration for captains and lower commissioned officers and warrant officers in the Army, the Indian Army, or Colonial Forces, 'in recognition of distinguished and meritorious services in time of war'. In June 1917 the eligibility was extended to officers not above the substantive rank of captain who held acting or temporary rank of major, while from January 1917 onwards awards were mainly restricted to gallantry under fire.

The design is a Greek cross with the ends of the arms splayed out rather like a cross *patée*; on each arm is an imperial crown, the cross on the orb of which protrudes beyond the end of the arm; in the centre is the royal cypher. The top arm is surmounted by a lug through which passes a ring linking it to the plain suspender bar.

The *rev* is quite plain, and the ribbon, $1^3/_8$in wide, is in three equal stripes of white violet (or purple), white, although many weaves show the central stripe as $^1/_2$in wide.

The decoration was issued (in a U–shape purple case) unnamed, but many recipients or their relatives had their crosses privately engraved. Sometimes this includes quite a lot of detail, while others show just the name and perhaps the regiment and/or the date of the award (George VI and later issues have the year of award on the *rev* of the lower arm of the cross, impressed in small figures for 1938 and early 1939, engraved thereafter).

A bar was authorised for second and subsequent awards of the cross, and this consists of a plain 'slip-on' clasp with the imperial crown in the centre. This was in August 1916, and the same month saw the introduction of the silver heraldic rose for wear on the ribbon strip, indicating the bar, when the decoration itself is not worn.

Accounts of numbers issued appear to vary; one writer quotes 41,000, but this is probably an approximation including bars; we understand that *Statistics of British Military Effort during the Great War* (War Office, 1922) show 37,104 crosses (including 23 awarded at home, in connection with air raids, etc), 2,984 first bars, 169 second bars, and 4 third bars.

From the figures quoted above it will be seen that bars for the 1914–18 period are not uncommon (approximately two in every twenty-five), but an unnamed cross with a bar slipped over the ribbon does not justify any enhanced price beyond the value of the decoration plus a small amount for the bar. In a *verified* group of medals, however, whether the MC is named or not, it will have a value of twice or three times that of a similar one without bar.

Copies of the George V issue exist, and are usually appreciably thinner than normal and slightly smaller – one copy, which is quite well made, measures 1.685in across against 1.735in (although figures for the genuine cross vary slightly from one to another), with edge and centre thickness of 0.050in and 0.115in respectively, against 0.085in and 0.132in in the genuine example. Generally speaking, the copy crosses are poorly made, and it has been suggested that the well made ones were, in fact, either an economy measure or are genuine crosses made by a sub–contractor in view of the large numbers required. No definite evidence of either of these suggestions seems to have come to light, and one would require irrefutable proof before accepting them; they could be correct, either of them, and admittedly one sometimes sees such crosses in the official purple case of issue, but are they the original occupants of those cases? It might assist research if a living recipient of the

MC can testify that his original cross, as issued, was one of these smaller and thinner examples.

The award of MC can be verified from the *Army List* or from the *London Gazette* (but the latter involves a long search, unless one knows the approximate date of award), while regimental histories often list recipients of decorations, and may record the occasions on which they were won.

The Distinguished Flying Cross RP

With the formation of a new branch of the armed forces – the Royal Air Force – it was obvious that a new series of awards was necessary to recognise bravery and meritorious service in that branch.

Very approximately, one can say that the Distinguished Flying Cross is the RAF counterpart of the Military Cross and the Distinguished Service Cross. It was instituted by Royal Warrant of 3 June 1918, for award to officers and warrant officers for 'an act or acts of valour, courage, or devotion to duty performed whilst flying in active operations against the enemy'.

The Royal Warrant describes the decoration, which is of silver, as 'a Cross *flory*', but this is not heraldically correct since this term means a cross with the limbs ending in fleurs-de-lis; it is perhaps nearer to a cross *botonny* or *treflée*, ie. having each limb ending in three knobs. However, the warrant goes on to describe the cross as 'terminated in the horizontal and base bars with bombs, the upper bar terminating in a rose, surrounded by another cross composed of aeroplane propellers charged in the centre with a roundel within a wreath of laurels, a rose winged, ensigned by an Imperial Crown thereon the letters R.A.F.'. There *rev* is plain, except for a circle with the royal cypher, in script capitals, interlaced, above the date, 1918.

A lug at the top enables the flat oval ring to connect with the straight bar suspender, ornamented on its lower portion with sprigs of laurel.

The cross was issued unnamed, but examples are found privately engraved.

The ribbon, 1¼in wide, is of violet and white stripes one-eighth inch wide; originally they were horizontal, but the weave proved unsatisfactory in making up ribbon bars (when the cross itself was not being worn), and from 24 July 1919 the design was changed to diagonal stripes, at 45°, from top left to bottom right. When ribbons only are worn there should be a triangle of violet at bottom left and top right corners. Recipients were apparently permitted to continue to wear the horizontally striped ribbon until it wore out. Since medal dealers continued to stock the original design for many years, there is no doubt that many recipients continued to use it for as long as supplies were available (the author remembers an air raid warden wearing the horizontally striped ribbon during the 1939–45 war).

Bars for second and subsequent awards were authorised at the institution; they are of the slip-on type, plain silver with a horizontal ridge along the centre, and bearing the RAF eagle.

Exact numbers issued are difficult to obtain, but in the period, 1918–19, some 1,079 crosses, 69 first bars, and 3 second bars were awarded. Also it is possible that some of those awarded in 1920 and later may have been retrospective awards for actions which took place during the war.

As with the Military Cross, copies exist. Several types have been noted, but most are so apparent that nobody except the veriest beginner would imagine them to be genuine. Some, however, are well made and in one in particular is well produced by a reputable firm in the Midlands, for replacement purposes through military tailors and jewellers, and *not* to deceive collectors; in recent years this firm has marked their products COPY, but earlier ones were not so marked and are rather dangerous unless one can compare them with a genuine original. There are many differences in the

45

details, but the easiest feature to note is the apex of the central 'A' (in the monogram RAF); in the original the apex just touches the edge of the uppermost petal of the rose (*fig.* 2a), whereas in the copy it slightly overlaps it (*fig.* 2b). Also the original usually has the initials of the designer, EC^RP, in tiny letters on the outer rim on the central circle, while the copy (correctly) omits these. Unfortunately several genuine examples exist on which it is difficult or impossible to distinguish the initials, since they are not very strong at the best, and can easily have worn or disappeared from the die as later strikings were made.*

Another copy exists in which the apex of the 'A' has a short horizontal member, like serifs extending on each side (*fig.* 2c).

Fig. 2   Great Britain: Distinguished Flying Cross
a – Point of A in genuine Cross; b and c – points of A in two
types of copy Cross; d – Shape of G on *rev* of genuine Cross;
e – Shape of G on *rev* of copy Cross.

The *rev* of the DFC is plain, except for a central raised circle containing the royal cypher, script GRI interlaced, and the date of institution, 1918. In the genuine crosses the right-hand down stroke of the 'G' is almost vertical, whereas on the 'overlapping A' copy, it is very sloping, almost at 45° (*figs.* 2d and 2e).

Copies of the bar also exist, certainly made for replacement purposes rather than to defraud collectors. One type has a rather larger and cruder eagle, while the back strip is narrower than the original.

The Air Force Cross   RP

The Air Force Cross was instituted on 3 June 1918, for officers and warrant officers 'for an act or acts of valour, courage, or devotion to duty whilst flying though not in active operations against the enemy'.

The Royal Warrant describes the silver decoration as 'a thunderbolt in the form of a cross, the arms conjoined by wings, the base bar terminating with a bomb surmounted by another cross composed of aeroplane propellers, the four ends inscribed with the letters, G. V. R. I. In the centre a roundel thereon a representation of Hermes mounted on a hawk in flight bestowing a wreath ... The whole ensigned by an Imperial Crown'. The reverse, the suspender, and the bars for subsequent awards are the same as for the DFC.

The cross was issued unnamed, but examples are found privately engraved.

The original ribbon, 1¼in wide, was similar to that of the DFC, but with deep red and white horizontal stripes, and was likewise changed to diagonal stripes by Warrant of 24 July 1919. Other details regarding ribbon and naming are as for the DFC.

As with the DFC, copies exist but are much easier to detect, as, although some differences in minor details of design exist, the designer's initials are much more prominent on the originals than they are on the DFC, being clearly shown in the 'south-west' rim of the central medallion. As they are absent from the copy, this can be quickly checked. I have not heard of an apparently genuine AFC without the initials (as sometimes happens with the DFC).

---

*See *Hayward's Gazette*, No. 4 (April 1975), for enlarged photographs of these differences.

As regards the *rev*, all that has been said about the DFC applies to the AFC, but again the copies made by the makers of the 'overlapping A' type of DFC, have one peculiar feature – the original *obv* die, with the letters, G, V, R, I, on the four arms of the cross, has been used for each subsequent reign, so that in these copies (other than those of George V issues) the *obv* and *rev* do not tally. Recent issues from this firm also include the word, COPY, impressed on the edge.

A Royal Warrant of 27 August 1919 amended the eligibility so that the cross could be awarded to 'individuals not belonging to Our Air Force (whether Naval, Military, or Civil) who render distinguished service to Aviation in actual flying'.

During 1918–19 some 679 Air Force Crosses were issued, and two first bars (no second bars were awarded).

The Distinguished Conduct Medal (Instituted 1854)   P

By Royal Warrant of 7 February 1881, a bar was authorised for recipients who were again recommended for a DCM, and these bore the date of the award in raised letters (ie. they were die-struck bars), similar to the battle bars of campaign medals, with lugs for the suspender pin to go through.

These date bars continued to be awarded during the early part of the Great War, and some eighty-six were issued (one of which was a second bar) up to late 1916 when the pattern changed. From 1917 onwards a bar, made to slip on the ribbon was used, with a conventional laurel 'branch' to right and left, exactly the same as that used for the newly established Military medal and similar awards.

By Army Order No. 290, of August 1916, the silver rosette was authorised, as for other awards, for wear on the ribbon strip when the medal is not worn. Further, Army Order No. 13, of January 1918, allowed recipients to use the letters, DCM, after their names, although it would appear that this had been done unofficially for some considerable time.

The above amendments as regards the laurel-spray bar, the silver rosette, and the post-nominal letters also apply to the West African Frontier Force DCM and the King's African Rifles DCM.

The Conspicuous Gallantry Medal (Instituted 1855; re-instituted 1874)

By Order of 27 June 1916, a bar was authorised for second and subsequent awards of the medal; also seamen or marines promoted to commissioned rank (other than Quartermaster, Royal Marines) who were in possession of a CGM annuity were allowed to retain it.

It should be noted that throughout the period of the Great War the ribbon, 1¼in wide, was in the original design of three equal stripes of dark blue, white, dark blue. The change to the present white ribbon with narrow dark blue edges did not come until June 1921.

During the period, 1914–19, only 108 medals were awarded and one bar.

The Distinguished Service Medal   RP

The DSM was instituted on 14 October 1914, and was the first British award of its kind to be founded during the Great War. Ranking below the Conspicuous Gallantry Medal (originally instituted in 1855, for the Crimean War, and re–instituted in 1874), the DSM is available for petty officers and ratings of the Royal Navy, the Royal Naval Reserve, and the Royal Naval Volunteer Reserve, and non–commissioned officers and men of the Royal Marines.

The *obv* shows George V in admiral's uniform, with the usual titles, while the *rev* has FOR DISTINGUISHED SERVICE, with a crown above, within two branches of laurel tied at the base. The suspender is a straight bar.

Naming is impressed, in square seriffed capitals; usually the name of the ship is given, the location, and frequently the date of the action. Some medals omit the ship's name but have instead, FOR SPECIAL SERVICES; these are believed to be for Q–ship actions but it is possible that not all such awards are so indicated. Some awards of the DSM were made for service on land with the army, ie. awards to the Naval Brigade, but the DCM and MM were also given.

Bars, of the conventional laurel spray type (authorised on 27 June 1916) for subsequent awards, are known with the date impressed on the *rev*, in the same style as on the medal, but others have no date. Some 5,513 medals were awarded, with 67 first bars and two second bars. When ribbons only are worn, the usual silver heraldic rose indicates the award of each bar, as authorised in August 1916.

The ribbon, 1¼in wide, is dark blue with two white centre stripes.

The Military Medal   RP

Instituted by Royal Warrant of 25 March 1916, as approximately the equivalent for 'other ranks' of the Military Cross, the Military Medal was awarded to warrant officers, non-commissioned officers, and men of the army for individual or collective acts of bravery in the field. In June 1916 women were made eligible, but strangely the wording was 'for bravery and devotion under fire'.*

The medal shows the effigy of George V in field-marshal's uniform, with the usual titles, while the *rev* has the legend, FOR BRAVERY IN THE FIELD, surmounted by the royal cypher and crown, and surrounded by a laurel wreath.

The scroll suspender has a swivel mount, but occasionally a non-swivelling type may be found. These were introduced after the end of the war, and apart from a very belated original issue, are either duplicates, ie. replacements (although not at that time marked as such) or post-war issues won in India or the Middle East; these post-war awards are rare and any non-swivelling MM should be checked against the *London Gazette* in case it proves to be one of these.

The ribbon, 1¼in wide, has dark blue edges, and five equal stripes in the centre – three white and two red. Bars for second or subsequent awards are of the usual conventional laurel branch type, and are slid over the ribbon.

Naming is impressed, in narrow *sans serif* capitals, and usually the battalion, or equivalent, is shown, with Territorial units indicated by T. F. Awards to women are very much sought after, as are those to the Royal Navy (including RNR, RNVR and RM) serving in the Naval Brigade, and to the Royal Flying Corps.

The MM was widely awarded, over 115,000 being recorded, while (according to *Gallantry*, by Sir Arnold Wilson and Capt. J. H. F. McEwen) 5,796 first bars, 180 second bars, and one third bar were awarded. As with other similar awards, a silver heraldic rose was authorised for each bar, when the ribbon only was worn; this dates from August 1916.

According to the original statutes, the eligible personnel were 'non-commissioned officers and men of *Our Army in the Field*' (although the Royal Warrant of 21 June 1916 extended it to women, whether British subjects or foreign). In August 1918, eligibility was extended to Warrant Officers, 1st and 2nd Class, while in March 1919 the award of a bar for further awards to women was approved. In October 1920 the MM became available to other ranks of 'any of Our Military Forces' and equivalent personnel of Allied armies.

---

*Two awards were made to civilian ladies for services, under fire, to wounded British soldiers during the Easter Rising in Ireland, in 1916

Indian Distinguished Service Medal

By Royal Warrant of 13 June 1917 a bar was authorised, with a conventional laurel spray (as for the Military Medal), for the second and subsequent awards. At the same time eligibility for the medal was extended to non-combatants attached to forces in the field.

Meritorious Service Medal

Instituted in 1845 for award to specially selected warrant officers and sergeants (who had to be in possession of the Long Service & Good Conduct medal) for long and meritorious service, the award was extended in January 1917 to 'Warrant Officers, NCO's, and men who are duly recommended for the grant in respect of gallant conduct in the performance of military duty otherwise than in action against the enemy, or in saving, or attempting to save the life of an officer or soldier, or for devotion to duty in a theatre of war'. Such awards did not carry the annuity which normally accompanies the MSM, and are often referred to as 'immediate awards', ie. the recipient did not have to wait for many years (as is usually the case) for a vacancy to occur in the allocation of MSM to his regiment, which normally only happens when an existing recipient dies. Many of the medals which are included in 1914–18 groups can thus be eventually traced as gallantry awards.

In October 1916 the plain crimson ribbon was given narrow white edges, while in January 1917 the white centre stripe was added.

The Distinguished Flying Medal   RP

The same Royal Warrant of 3 June 1918 which announced the institution of the DFC also notified the institution of the Distinguished Flying Medal for non-commissioned officers and other ranks, and awarded for the same type of services whilst flying in active operations against the enemy.

The medal is of silver, oval in shape, with the coinage head of George V and the usual legend, GEORGIVS V BRITT: OMN: REX ET IND: IMP. The *rev* has 'within a wreath of laurel a representation of Athene Nike seated on an aeroplane, a hawk rising from her right arm above the words, FOR COVRAGE'. Around the outer edge is a wreath and 'the whole is ensigned by a bomb attached to the clasp and ribbon by two wings'.

Unlike the two crosses, the DFM was named on issue, impressed in large seriffed capitals (World War II issues were engraved, rather crudely). Bars for subsequent awards were authorised, of the same type as for the DFC.

The original ribbon, 1¼in wide, was of violet and white horizontal stripes, one–sixteenth inch wide, but, like the other RAF awards, it was changed from 24 July 1919 to diagonal stripes of the same width, at 45° from top left to bottom right.

During 1918–19 only 104 medals were awarded, and two first bars.

The Air Force Medal   RP

Instituted by the Royal Warrant of 3 June 1918, the Air Force Medal is the equivalent for non-commissioned officers and men of the officers' Air Force Cross. Like the DFM, it is oval in shape, with the same *obv*; the *rev* depicts Hermes, the messenger of the gods, standing to right on a flying hawk, and holding a wreath in his outstretched left hand. The outer edge is a conventional laurel wreath, while the mount and suspender are the same as for the DFM.

Like the other RAF awards, the ribbon, 1¼in wide, had at first horizontal stripes, red and white, one-sixteenth inch wide, but was changed to similar diagonal stripes in July 1919.

Naming is by impressed seriffed capitals, and bars for further awards are of the same type as those of the other RAF decorations.

Like the DFM, the medal is rather rare; during 1918–19 only 102 were awarded, and two first bars.

The 1914 Star   RP

In April, 1917, King George V authorised the award of this bronze star, popularly (but incorrectly) known as the Mons Star, to those who had served *in France or Belgium* on the establishment of a unit, between 5 August and midnight on 22–23 November 1914. This included all officers and men of the British and Indian Expeditionary Forces, civilian doctors, nursing sisters, and nurses, also others employed in military hospitals. Personnel of the Royal Navy, Royal Marines, Royal Naval Reserve, and Royal Naval Volunteer Reserve, who served ashore with the Royal Naval Division in France and Belgium were also eligible – which means mainly those who served in the Antwerp or Ostend areas – but those whose service during this period was only at sea did not qualify; later they received the 1914–15 Star (*qv*).

The star is basically a four-pointed one, although the top point is not visible, being obscured by a crown above which a ring is integrated, the whole design being stamped out in one piece. Across the star are two crossed swords *in saltire*, with the hilts and points protruding between the angles. An oak wreath encircles three scrolls, one above the other; the central scroll is dated, 1914, while the upper and lower are lettered, respectively, AUG and NOV. The *rev* is quite plain, apart from the naming, which is by impressed capitals. These are usually *sans serif*, square or thin narrow letters, quoting the number, rank, name, and regiment (but not the ship) of the recipient. Medals to the Royal Naval Division, which are much sought after, are named in large seriffed capitals.

The ribbon, 1¼in wide, is of watered silk, red merging into white merging into blue.

A narrow bronze bar, stitched onto the ribbon (for which a tiny hole is provided at each corner), bearing the dates, 5th AUG. – 22nd NOV. 1914, was authorised on 19 October 1919, for recipients of the star who had actually served under the fire of the enemy during that period. Unfortunately when a star has lost its ribbon, it may be very difficult to establish if the recipient was entitled to the bar unless it is known that he was wounded or killed in action, taken prisoner, or decorated for gallantry on or before 22 November 1914, or unless his personal record or service can be traced. Considerably more stars were issued without bars than with, approximately in the proportion of five with bar to seven without.

Many copy bars exist, similar to but very slightly different from the originals; the style of lettering is just not quite correct (but as the genuine bars are quite common, the collector should have no difficulty in recognising the genuine style of lettering). Often the copy is slightly thicker and more 'brassy' looking than the original. Any bar with a back strip, so that it can be slid over the ribbon can automatically be classed as a copy.

Recipients of the bar are entitled to wear a silver heraldic rose on the ribbon strip when the star itself is not being worn, to indicate possession of the bar, but unfortunately since the ribbon for the 1914–15 Star (*qv*) is the identical to that of the 1914 Star without the bar, many 'Old Contemptibles' who had the 1914 Star without bar wore (and still wear) the rosette on the ribbon under the mistaken impression that it indicates the earlier star irrespective of whether they hold the bar or not.

In recent years, not surprisingly, as serious collectors have been devoting more time to the study of 'the story behind the medal', they have come to appreciate Great War groups containing a 1914 Star to a much greater degree than in the past. They now recognise that these are the medals to the men who, for a few months, assisted the French in holding back the mighty German hordes while the new army was being equipped and trained for overseas service. The stories of the various regiments concerned, their individual parts in the actions of those first sixteen weeks – the battle of Mons, the retreat to the Seine, the battles of Le Cateau, the Marne, and the Aisne, and the first battle of the Ypres – all show how the 1914 Star (with its accompanying medals) fully justifies an honoured place in any collection.

It should be noted that the 1914 Star cannot be worn alone. It must of necessity be accompanied by the British War Medal and the Victory Medal.

The 1914–15 Star   RP

The 1914–15 Star, authorised in 1918, is very similar in design to the 1914 Star, but its eligibility covers a much wider field of service. Very broadly, it was awarded to all who served in (but not those who merely passed through) any theatre of war against Germany and her allies, between 5 August 1914 and 31 December 1915, except those who were eligible for the 1914 Star.

As far as the Royal Navy was concerned, including the Royal Marines, the Royal Naval Reserve, the Royal Naval Volunteer Reserve, the Royal Naval Air Service, and the Indian and Dominion naval forces, it was awarded to those who served at sea, or on shore in theatres of war, also to personnel of the merchant navy serving under special naval engagements (Form T124, etc), and to canteen staffs who served in a naval ship at sea. Trained pilots, observers, and men of the RNAS who were employed in flying from naval air stations on overseas patrols, were eligible. Certain services did not qualify, such as in depot ships (except those which go to sea), boom defence vessels, examination vessels, and other craft employed on harbour service; service at shore bases outside the theatres of military operations, nor services of a temporary nature in ships of war or theatres of operations, such as casual inspections, purchase of material, etc.

Service in East, West, and South-West Africa against German forces qualified, but not services in actions for which the Africa General Service medal or the Sudan 1910 medal were awarded. Also service in certain parts of India – Tochi Valley, Derajat, Mohmand, Hafiz Kor, etc. – during specified periods between 28 November 1914 and 27 October 1915 qualified for the star.

The design is identical to that of the 1914 Star apart from the centre, which bears only one scroll, with the dates, 1914–15. The ribbon is the same, but no bars were awarded. Thus there is no way of telling, from the ribbon strip when medals are not worn, whether a man holds the 1914 Star without bar or the 1914–15 Star.

Naming is on the plain *rev*, as for the 1914 Star, in thin or square *sans serif* capitals. On both stars, army officers' regiments are shown. Normally on medals to naval personnel, the ship is not shown, but medals to New Zealand personnel apparently include the ship in the naming on the *rev* or edge. I have a 1914–15 Star, British War Medal and Victory Medal to a man who served in HMS *Philomel* (handed over to New Zealand in 1913) and, contrary to UK custom, all three medals include H.M.S. PHILOMEL in the official naming.

Like the 1914 Star, the 1914–15 Star cannot be awarded alone. A recipient must also have received the BWM and Victory Medal. It is reported that some 2,366,000 of these stars were issued.

The British War Medal, 1914–18   RP

This rather uninspiring looking medal, with no bars to indicate, perhaps, service in some of the bloodiest battles ever fought, was authorised in 1919.

It was awarded, in silver, to army personnel who either 'entered a theatre of war on duty, or who left places of residence and rendered approved service overseas other then the waters dividing the different parts of the United Kingdom', between 5 August 1914 and 11 November 1918 inclusive. This was eventually extended to cover certain specified services in North and South Russia, Siberia, and some other areas during 1919 and 1920. For the navy, those who performed 28 days mobilised service or lost their lives in action before completing that period were eligible; certain extensions beyond 11 November 1918 also applied to the navy, including mine clearance at sea or service in the Eastern Baltic, the Black Sea, and the Caspian Sea to various dates up to 1920. Eligibility for the RAF was basically as for the army.

About 6½ million silver medals were issued, but in addition some 110,000 were issued in bronze, mainly to Chinese, Maltese, and Indian Labour Corps personnel, and a few other native units of a non-combatant and subsidiary nature.

The *obv* of the medal has the Mackennal coinage head of George V, with the usual short titles, GEORGIVS V BRITT: OMN: REX ET IND: IMP. The *rev* has a nude man on horseback (alleged to be St. George), trampling on a shield bearing the German eagle, beside a skull and crossbones; above is the rising sun of victory; to left and right are the dates, 1914, 1918.

The suspender is a straight bar with a non-swivelling mount. No bars were issued , although a committee investigated the matter and approved a considerable number of bars. The scheme was eventually dropped, although the naval bars were published as authorised by George V and quoted in an Admiralty Order of August 1920. Consequently one sees a number of miniature medals (for mess or evening dress wear) with a selection of the sixty-eight bars approved. A few privately made, full–sized bars have also been seen, worn (quite erroneously) by ex-service men on Armistice Day parades.

The ribbon is of watered silk, 1¼in wide, with a broad orange centre, flanked by white/narrow black/blue edges. It had been stated that these colours have no special significance.

Naming is always by impressed *sans serif* capitals, but the style varies. There are thin, narrow letters, square letters, and something in between. Army officers' medals do not show their regiment, but indication is given of R.N., R.N.R., R.N.V.R., R.M., and R.A.F. (although some medals to R.N.R. officers have been noted with only the recipient's rank and name, thus a medal to 'LIEUT. J. Q. BROWN', which cannot be traced in the *Monthly Army List*, could well prove to be an officer in the R.N.R.). For 'other ranks' in the army, the man's number, rank, and the regiment are given, while for the navy his number and rating are shown but not his ship (except in the case of New Zealanders, as mentioned under the 1914–15 Star). Medals with the designation, SERVICE WITH THE ROYAL NAVY, are believed to relate to personnel serving in ships' canteens afloat, or certain technicians and workmen whose service at sea in warships qualified them for the medal, but enquiries from official sources have failed to bring confirmation of this point. Medals which have merely a name and no other details are usually to ratings of the Mercantile Marine (with the recipient's first name), press correspondents and civilian nursing personnel who were not embodied in official organisations such as the Order of St. John or the British Red Cross (whose medals show these bodies in the naming). Furthermore, some British War Medals were apparently awarded to foreigners who had rendered services to the British Forces. Dr. F. K. Mitchell, of Cape Town (a well-known and experienced collector) has a group of awards to a Belgian citizen which includes a British War Medal named simply 'L. KEYSER', who had repeatedly assisted British and other allied soldier prisoners to escape to Holland (although one would have expected him to have been given the Allied Subjects' Medal, (*qv*).

Another variation in naming has been found on medals bought in Cairo in recent years; the following have been noted, all impressed in the usual style: 7274

ARTILLERY E.A., 1114 TRANSPORT C.E.A., 6326 6–BN.E.A. None of these has the recipient's name, but another example has been seen with no number but an Egyptian name, followed by M.W.D.E.A. These are all to personnel of the Egyptian Army, presumably officially attached to British forces. The last medal would appear to be to the Military Works Department.

With some medals to army personnel a duplicated note was enclosed, headed 'PLEASE DO NOT NEGLECT TO SIGN AND RETURN THE ENCLOSED RECEIPT'. Then follows: 'To avoid unnecessary correspondence, kindly note that the Regtl. particulars inscribed on the British War & Victory Medals are those held on first disembarkation in a theatre of war. The rank is the highest attained, PROVIDED IT WAS HELD IN A THEATRE OF WAR OR OVERSEAS PRIOR TO 11.11.18. Appointments such as L/Sgts., L/Cpl., etc., are not inscribed on medals. SPECIAL NOTE TO THOSE WHO SERVED IN RIFLE REGTS., 'Rifleman' is not inscribed on War Medals, 'Pte' being the correct designation of this rank'. While this information may be correct in many cases (and will perhaps explain some details which may have been thought to be incorrect), it certainly is not always the case, either as regards regimental particulars or 'appointments'.

Officially the size of the medal is quoted as 1.42in in diameter, but some variations occur. A considerable number were struck at the Calcutta Mint, from standard dies, and we have noted that they appear to be appreciably larger. The average diameter of some thirty British issues was 1.428in, while the Calcutta ones were approximately 0.011–0.014in (ie. eleven to fourteen-thousandths) larger. There is also a slight difference in the naming, some of the Calcutta issues being impressed in letters which are very slightly wider spaced and a little irregular in alignment.

The Mercantile Marine War Medal, 1914–1918 RP

This bronze medal, instituted in July 1919, was issued by the Board of Trade to officers and ratings of the Mercantile Marine who qualified for the British War Medal, and who served at sea on at least one voyage in a danger zone. Included were licensed pilots, crews of pilotage and lighthouse authorities or of Post Office cable ships, also fishermen, and some others.

The *obv* shows Sir Bertram Mackennal's coinage of King George V, as on the BWM and with the same legend. The *rev*, by Harold Stabler, shows a starboard bow view of a drifter steaming at speed past the bows of a sinking submarine; in the right background is a sailing ship. The exergue is lettered: FOR WAR SERVICE/MERCANTILE MARINE/1914–1918. The whole is surrounded by a conventional laurel wreath border.

Suspension is non-swivelling, by a straight bar, with a watered ribbon, 1¼in wide, half green, half red, with a one-eighth inch white central stripe; it is worn with the green furthest from the shoulder, and thus the colours appear to typify the ship's lights – starboard, green; port, red; and the central white masthead light.

The medal is worn *between* the BWM and the Victory Medal by those entitled to all three (those who served only in the Mercantile Marine received only the BWM and the Mercantile Marine War Medal, but members of the Royal Navy who served part of their time with the Mercantile Marine, or members of the MM who joined the Royal Navy, could be eligible for all three medals and also for the 1914 or 1914–15 Star). Some 113.000 were awarded.

Naming is by impressed *sans serif* capitals, and usually the recipient's first name is shown – a feature not usually seen on other medals of the period.

Medals to Australian personnel have the recipient's *initial(s)* and surname, followed by AUSTRALIA (which is located in the centre of the edge) and the man's Mercantile Marine number. Some medals have been falsified, to make them appear as the somewhat scarcer Australian awards, by adding AUSTRALIA and a number to an ordinary UK medal; in these cases, however, AUSTRALIA is not in the centre of the edge and the medal will usually show the recipient's first name.

The Allied Victory Medal   RP

In order to avoid the wholesale exchange of medals between all the allies, commemorating the victory, it was agreed that each should issue its own bronze medal, in its own design and language, but all of the same general type, bearing on the *obv* a figure of Victory, with the equivalent wording or the arms of the country on the *rev*, and all with the same 'double rainbow' ribbon of 1½in watered silk, red in the centre and the colour merging outwards through orange, yellow, green, and blue, to violet at the outer edges.

The British medal, designed by W. McMillan (who also designed the *rev* of the British War Medal) has quite a handsome figure of Victory, winged, in the classical style, but here the beauty ends. The *rev* is unimaginative, lettered, THE GREAT WAR FOR CIVILISATION,.1914–1919, within a wreath. The production is poor, with a thin brass ring for suspension, soldered on the top of the medal, like some of the cheap coronation medals handed out to schoolchildren.

Naming is as for the British War Medal, but strangely the eligibility qualifications are not identical, and consequently some recipients of the BWM did not qualify for the Victory Medal. About 5,725,000 Victory Medals were issued, some 775,000 fewer than the BWM. On the other hand, as far as we have been able to trace, all recipients of the Victory Medal also received the BWM, and all recipients of the 1914 Star and 1914–15 Star automatically received both the BWM and the Victory Medal.

Quite a number of naval reservists who were re-called, and who qualified for the BWM did not receive the Victory Medal, and it is not unusual to find groups of medals to such men consisting of, say, the East & West Africa Medal, the BWM, and the Naval LS&GC Medal (Victorian or Edwardian); on the other hand, collectors should not overlook the possibility, in a case like this, that the recipient had sold or pawned his medals and only the silver ones were accepted since the others had no intrinsic value.

Although the period of service qualifying for this medal ended, in the main, in November 1918, in at least two instances service up to midnight, 13–14 January 1919, was eligible – namely in Hedjaz and in operations conducted by the Aden Field Force. Thus the dates on the medal, though often criticised, are justified. The conditions of award have been fully covered in the various editions of Taprell Dorling's *Ribbons and Medals* (particularly in the smaller format editions appearing between 1920 and 1946).

One sometimes finds this medal in a dull, somewhat brownish brass, with rather a 'dusty' finish. Various explanations have been given, including the story that they are early issues to officers. It seems more likely that they may be the result of an experimental finish (perhaps an early one), or that a batch was made from a slightly different mixture or metals, which has reacted differently to atmospheric conditions, but it is generally agreed that for the collector they have no special significance.

Union of South Africa Allied Victory Medal   RP

All members of H.M. Forces throughout the British Empire, who were eligible, received the British medal as described above except for South Africa, whose government issued their own variety (although their troops received the normal British War Medal and, if eligible, 1914–15 Star). It has precisely the same *obv* design, but the *rev*, although very similar to the home issue, has the inscription English and Afrikaans: THE GREAT WAR FOR CIVILISATION – DE GROTE OORLOG VOOR DE BESCHAVING – 1914–1919 (At this time the Afrikaans spelling was the same as Dutch, but has since been simplified). Naming is similar to that on the UK medal, but is often slightly irregular in spacing or alignment. The ribbon is, of course, identical.

The Territorial Force War Medal   RP

The TFWM was instituted on 26 April 1920, for members of the Territorial Force and the TF Nursing Service who had volunteered for overseas service not later than 30 September 1914, and who had so served between 4 August 1914 and 11 November 1918, subject to certain conditions.

They had to be serving in the Territorial Force on 4 August 1914, or must have had not less than four years' TF service before 4 August 1914 and rejoined not later than 30 September 1914. Also they must not have been eligible for the 1914 Star or the 1914–15 Star.

Despite the last condition, a number of cases are known where the recipient received both the TFWM and one of the stars. This was, of course, and error, but since some of these double awards are supported by documents, they cannot be disputed, and the recipients continued to wear both medals on Armistice Day parades and similar occasions.

The medal is struck in bronze, with the coinage head of George V and the same titles as on the British War Medal (ie. omitting D.G. and FID. DEF.). The *rev* is unimaginative, with a laurel wreath enclosing the legend, FOR/VOLUNTARY/SERVICE/OVERSEAS/1914–19. Outside the wreath and around the top half of the medal is, TERRITORIAL WAR MEDAL.

The mount and non-swivelling suspender are the same design as those of the British War Medal, and the watered ribbon, $1\frac{1}{4}$in wide, is yellow with green side stripes. It is worn immediately after the Victory Medal.

Naming is impressed, in small thin *sans serif* capitals. Unlike the BWM and Victory Medal, officers' regiments are usually shown.

The TFWM cannot be worn alone. The recipient must also have received the BWM and, in the majority of cases, the Victory Medal; it is possible for a recipient not to have qualified for the Victory Medal yet to be eligible for BWM and TFWM, by virtue of service overseas, in parts of India and the Commonwealth which were not regarded as Theatres of War for the purposes of award of the Victory Medal, but so far we do not appear to have encountered any such authenticated groups.

It is not known why the dates on the medal are shown as 1914–19, since the final qualifying date is 11 November 1918. The fact that the Victory Medal bears the same dates is not relevant, since, in certain circumstances, services up to 13 January 1919 were eligible for that award.

Apparently some 34,000 medals were issued, and for some regiments the TFWM is quite scarce, as practically the whole of the "territorials" who might have been eligible did in fact qualify for one or other of the stars. Occasionally NCO's were (probably unwillingly) kept at home as instructors; in one regiment, where the medal is so scarce that until recently there was not even one in the regimental museum, one of the few issued proved to be to a man who was a chef in civilian life, and who was retained at depot, when the whole of the territorial battalion went overseas early in the war, for the benefit of the officers' mess.

Meritorious Service Medal (Royal Navy and Royal Marines)

Although the Army MSM had existed since 1845 (and extended to the Royal Marines in 1849), there was no equivalent medal for the Royal Navy until 25 June 1919, when King George V rectified the omission.

In view of the fact that the Naval MSM, which now included the Royal Marines in its eligibility, showed the portrait of the King in naval uniform (as opposed to the army uniform depicted on the Army MSM), this must rank as a separate award.

The *rev* is the same as for the army, with three-line inscription, FOR/MERITORIOUS/ SERVICE, below a crown and in a laurel wreath. The ribbon is also the same, crimson, with a narrow white centre stripe and edges. Like the army medal, it could be awarded for an act of gallantry on duty when not in the presence of the enemy, as well as for meritorious service afloat or ashore.

Royal Air Force Meritorious Service Medal R

With the formation of the RAF in 1918, it was necessary to include a distinctive MSM with the other special RAF awards. It was different from that of the other services in that the *obv* depicted the coinage head of George V, but the *rev* is similar to that of the Naval MSM described above.

The ribbon is half dark blue (left), half crimson (right), with a narrow white centre stripe and edges. Unlike the MSM of the other services at that time, the RAF medal was worn *before* the RAF Long Service & Good Conduct Medal.

NOTE:

We have not included the RAF LS&GC Medal in this survey, although it was instituted at the same time as the MSM, as it is purely a long service award.

Mentions in Despatches P

Although it had been the practice to record outstanding or specially meritorious service in action by mentioning names in despatches from naval or military commanders to the appropriate higher authority – sometimes with considerable detail, but often by lists of names with a general citation – and such mentions had frequently been followed either by an award or promotion, it was not until 1920 that an emblem was authorised to record this fact on a medal ribbon.

Undoubtedly the French and Belgian practice of embellishing the ribbons of their Croix de Guerre with palm leaves, stars, etc., to record various types of 'mentions', influenced the British decision to institute something similar. At first, in 1919, a special certificate was issued to all mentioned in despatches, but this was not fully satisfactory, and in January 1920, a bronze oakleaf spray was authorised to be worn on the ribbon of the Victory Medal. Unlike French and Belgian practice, only one emblem could be worn, irrespective of the number of 'mentions'. It would appear that if one did not hold the Victory Medal, no indication of a mention in despatches could be worn, but in the years after the war it was not unusual to see ex-service men, such as recalled naval personnel who were awarded the BWM but who did not qualify for the Victory Medal, with an oak leaf on the BWM ribbon.

It is not possible to quote the number entitled to wear the bronze oakleaf, but official statistics indicate that 141,082 military 'mentions' were published in the *London Gazette* between 1914 and 1920.

The emblems, which were issued loose with the Victory Medal and ribbon, were in two sizes. The larger, 1³⁄₈in long, was for wear with the medal itself, affixed to the ribbon at a shallow angle, from lower left to upper right, by two sprigs pushed through the ribbon and bent over. The smaller, about 1in long, was for wear when the ribbon alone was worn. Some examples have small holes pierced for sewing instead of the pairs of sprigs.

Silver War Badge for Services Rendered P

Strictly speaking, this item does not fall within the scope of this work, as it is a badge, not a medal or decoration. However, since it is often found accompanying groups of medals, and is the British equivalent of the medals awarded in similar cases by several countries, it has been included.

Authorised on 12 September 1916, for officers and men of HM Forces who had been retired or discharged on account of wounds or sickness caused by war service, at home or abroad, from 4 August 1914, the regulations were extended on several later dates to include wider categories, including women.

The badge is of silver, 1⅓in diameter, slightly convex, with a brooch fitting, and is a narrow circle lettered, FOR KING AND COUNTRY* SERVICES RENDERED*. The centre is openwork, consisting of the royal cypher in script, GRI, with crown above. The *rev* is plain, with a serial number impressed (agreeing with the number shown on the small box of issue), but this is not the recipient's service number; there is apparently no way of positively identifying the badge with its recipient, although some recipients had their name privately engraved on the *rev*. However, RAF personnel were given a Certificate of Award (FS Form 228) bearing the same number as that on the badge.

Imperial Service Badge

Like the previous item, this badge does not strictly fall within our scope, but as many collectors have asked for information on it, it was decided to include it.

The badge was worn on the right breast by trained soldiers of a Territorial Force unit where all members had, before the outbreak of the Great War, undertaken to serve abroad if required – at the time the normal commitments of members of the TF were for home service only. The distinction, *Imperial Service*, when awarded to a TF unit, was shown in the *Monthly Army List* by an X in a circle (a very few units also had "Imperial Service" immediately below the title of the unit. This still appeared in the September 1918 *Monthly Army List*, but the ringed X's were no longer shown).

The badge is a white metal brooch, 43 x 10mm, with a narrow plain border and raised letters, IMPERIAL SERVICE, on a grained ground; above is the Imperial crown, pierced under the arches (*Fig. 3*).

Fig. 3   Great Britain: Imperial Service Badge

Special Constabulary Long Service Medal   RP

It may, perhaps, seem a little strange to include a long service medal as a war award, but although a number of provincial police forces had instituted medals for their regular and/or special constabularies, no national medal existed – and as far as regular policemen are concerned, none was instituted until 1951. However, King George V established the Special Constabulary Long Service Medal on 30 August 1919 'in consideration of the faithful and devoted service rendered by members of the Special Constabulary during the war'. The medal was also intended for subsequent long service after the war.

Of standard size, 1.42in in diameter, in bronze, the *obv* shows the crowned bust of the King by Sir Bertram Mackennal, with the usual titles. The *rev* has the inscription, FOR FAITHFUL SERVICE IN THE SPECIAL CONSTABULARY, with laurel sprays. The straight suspender is of the usual type, to take a ribbon 1¼in wide, but the ribbon is actually 1³⁄₈in wide – a peculiarity which has never been explained – with a half-inch red centre and white–black–white edges equally divided. Naming is impressed in narrow *sans serif* capitals.

For those who qualified for the medal by service during the war a bar was authorised (with a tiny hole at each corner, for sewing into the ribbon) lettered , THE GREAT WAR 1914–1918. As with the 1914 Star, copy bars are found, often with a back strip for sliding over the ribbon. Subsequent bars were authorised for normal service, lettered, LONG SERVICE, followed by the year of the award.

Greenock (Renfrewshire) Special Constabulary War Medal (Unofficial)

In 1920 a hall-marked silver medal was awarded to the members of the Greenock Special Constabulary to commemorate their war service. The *obv* has the burgh arms with the surrounding inscription, BURGH OF GREENOCK, while the *rev* has a laurel wreath and the words, GREENOCK SPECIAL CONSTABLE, and on a scroll, the name (and sometimes the number) of the recipient.

The ribbon is plain blue, seven-eighths of an inch wide, and suspension is from a bar bearing the number of years' service, 2 YEARS, 3 YEARS, etc.

NOTE:

A number of other medals or badges were struck for war service by special constables, all unofficial or semi-official, but most of these were not intended for wearing in uniform, but more as watch-chain pendants, without ribbon.

Canadian Memorial Cross

In March 1919 the Canadian Government proposed to commemorate members of the Canadian forces who had lost their lives in action, died while on active service, or died after discharge from causes due to the war, by the issue of a cross, the Cross of Sacrifice, to be worn by mothers and widows. The authority for its institution is the Order in Council PC 2374 of 1 December 1919 and amended by PC 822 of 15 April 1922. If both mother and widow were alive, each received a cross.

The cross, in dull silver, 32mm across, is rather similar in shape to the Military Cross, being a Greek cross with slightly widened ends (a type of cross *patée*) and with shallow concave ends to the arms. The ends of the three lower arms bear a maple leaf while the top one has a crown. Superimposed is another plain cross, bevelled or ridged along its centre lines; in the centre is the Royal cypher, GRI, intertwined. The cross is superimposed on a laurel wreath, the tips of which just overlap the top arm of the cross.

Suspension is by two small rings, with a 10mm violet ribbon, and the badge is worn as a pendant round the neck.

On the plain *rev* is engraved the number, rank and name, usually in two lines; those to officers have only rank and name. Approximately 58,350 crosses were issued, in small black cases lined with white satin, with a gilt crown on the lid.

British Red Cross Society War Service Medal   P

In 1921 the BRCS issued a 31mm bronze-gilt medal for its members who had performed one year or 1000 hours voluntary service, including Voluntary Aid Detachments, during the period 4 August 1914 and 31 December 1919, and who did not receive any British War Medal for services rendered in respect of Red Cross war work. The medal, which was worn from a plain white ribbon, 1¼in wide, with a gilt bar brooch, is without enamel, and bears the Geneva Cross in a wreath of laurel. The outer circle is inscribed, BRITISH RED CROSS SOCIETY: FOR WAR SERVICE: 1914–1918.

The *rev* has the 3-line legend, INTER/ARMA/CARITAS (Amidst the arms, love), in a laurel wreath.

The medal was issued unnamed, and could only be worn on BRCS or similar uniforms.

Despite the restrictions regarding its award only to those who had not received military medals, one sometimes finds groups of 1914–18 medals with which is included the BRCS War Medal (often in its original box of issue, with a small red cross on the lid), purporting to belong to the same person; although the medal is unnamed, the name written on the box agrees with the name on the official war medals. There are three possible explanations: first, the recipient could have been entitled if his (or her) service for which the BWM was given was not the same as that for which the BRCS medal was awarded; secondly, the BRCS medal could have been awarded in error; thirdly, somebody could have written their name on the BRCS box (which does not always bear a name), to make it appear that the medal belonged to the BWM recipient.

British Red Cross Society Special Service Cross

In 1917 the BRCS instituted this cross for award to foreigners who had given distinguished service to the society, and also to persons whose names were inscribed on the society's Roll of Honourable Service for exceptionally meritorious service.

The badge is a Greek or Geneva Cross, with a 6-line inscription, mainly across the centre and the horizontal arms, FOR/SPECIAL SERVICES/TO BRITISH RED CROSS SOCIETY/1917. This appears to be the *obv*, although one writer gives it as the *rev*. The other side has the 3-line inscription, INTER/ARMA/CARITAS.

There is no ribbon, and the badge is suspended by a ring to a straight bar brooch.

The Allied Subjects' Medal   RP

During the period of the war many civilians in allied countries, particularly Belgium and France, rendered considerable assistance to British soldiers – usually escaped prisoners of war – behind the enemy lines. Such help was only given at the risk, at the best, of imprisonment and, more likely, of death.

In 1922 King George V instituted a medal to recognise such assistance, whether given by men or women. The medal, in silver or in bronze, is in the standard size of 1.42in, and has the coinage head and inscription as for the BWM. The *rev* shows the standing figure of Humanity, to left, offering a cup of water to a recumbent, steel-helmeted, British soldier; in the background are the ruins of a town. There is strangely no inscription.

Suspension is by a ring through a lug at the top of the medal, with a multi-striped ribbon incorporating allied colours; the central blue stripe is flanked by wide yellow, which is separated from the red edges by black (inner) and white (outer) stripes.

It is stated that 133 silver and 573 bronze medals were awarded, unnamed, but we have been unable to verify these figures. However, the medal is very rare, and is seldom seen on the market.

First Aid Nursing Yeomanry War Medal (semi-official)   R

This medal, although not official, was apparently to be worn in uniform, and was awarded to all members of the F.A.N.Y.

It is in bronze, 32mm in diameter, with the *obv* showing the head of a woman, right, wearing a crested helmet. One writer designates her as Bellona, the Roman goddess of war, while another calls her Minerva, who was the goddess of wisdom, war, and all liberal arts. Since the latter is almost always represented in a helmet while Bellona is usually shown with dishevelled hair, it would seem that the head is that of Minerva. Around the edge are sprays of laurel, with the dates, 1914, 1918, at the top and bottom respectively.

The *rev* has shield with a cross *moline*, ie. with the ends of the arms splayed and split into two. The shield is superimposed on 'two bandages in saltire', being strip bandages (representing nursing) set diagonally, each with a curl at the lower end. Around are the words, at left, top, right, and bottom, FIRST–AID–NURSING–YEOMANRY. The medal was not issued named, but privately named examples are known.

Suspension is by a ring from a 32mm ribbon, pale blue with 4mm light red edges. 'Fannies' who had joined before the outbreak of war had a small bronze five-pointed star, 8mm in diameter, on the ribbon.

Cadet Norfolk Artillery Medal (semi-official)

The Cadet Norfolk Artillery, founded in 1911, was one of the few such units to award a medal for wartime services. Although not official, this bronze medal could be worn in cadet uniform. The *obv* shows a field gun with the words, CADET NORFOLK, above, and ARTILLERY below, the last word on a scroll. On the *rev* is a wreath within which is, FOR SERVICES RENDERED DURING THE GREAT WAR, with the dates, 1918–19. The medal is named in engraved capitals on the rim.

Suspension is by a straight bar, with a ribbon 1¼in wide, with a red centre flanked by khaki stripes; the edges are dark blue with a narrow yellow stripe between blue and khaki.

Greece

Greece revolted against the long period of Turkish domination in 1821, and achieved independence in 1822. The First Constitution, of 1822, made provision for the institution of decorations of honour, but this could not be implemented until 1829, when the Order of the Redeemer was founded. Greece had hoped to remain neutral in the Great War, but events forced her into the war on the side of the Allies on 1 January 1916.

EXISTING AWARDS

Royal Order of the Redeemer (1829)
Royal Order of George I (1915)
Medal of the Order of George I (1915)

NEW AWARDS

War Cross, 1916 R

This decoration was instituted as the highest award for services in the field, by M. Venizelos under a decree of 28 February 1917. This was confirmed by Royal Decrees of 30 June and 31 October 1917.

The award is in three classes, according, not to rank (as in the case of the Medal for Military Merit), but to merit. They are indicated by emblems on the ribbons, but two versions are given by various authoritative writers. According to one authority, the first class has a gilt laurel wreath on the ribbon, while the second class has a silver wreath. Another states that the first class has a bronze laurel wreath, while a bronze star denotes the second class. Both agree that the third class has a plain ribbon. It would seem that the second version is probably the correct one.

The badge consists of an unusual form of cross, in dulled silver, consisting of a vertical antique short-sword, broad bladed, with point uppermost, across a tablet or strip with shallow V ends, inscribed H TAN/H EΠI/T/AΣ (Conquer or die). The cross is encircled by a laurel wreath over the horizontal strip and under the sword. The *rev* is lettered, ΕΛΛΑΣ/1916–1917. (Greece).

The ribbon is 37mm wide, black with 5mm blue edges. Five-pointed silver stars are worn on the ribbon to indicate subsequent mentions in despatches.

Medal for Military Merit R

Like the War Cross, this medal was instituted by M. Venizelos by decree of 28 October 1916, with the title of Military Medal, but confirmed by Royal Decrees of 30 June and 31 October 1917, as the Medal for Military Merit. It was liberally awarded to officers of the armed forces, the Red Cross, and other organisations, for war services of all kinds. There were four classes, indicated by emblems on the ribbon.

The decoration is of bronze, a Greek cross with slightly widened ends (not unlike the British Military Cross), having an eagle with wings raised in the centre. The arms are lettered (horizontal), ΑΜΥΝ/ΕΣΘΑΙ, (vertical), ΛΕΡΙ/ΠΑΤΡΗΣ (Fighting for the Fatherland). Surrounding the cross, but within the ends of the arms, is a superimposed laurel wreath, while between the arms of the cross are crossed swords, whose hilts and points end in balls resting on the laurel wreath. The eight intervening spaces are filled in, ie. the whole design is a solid medal with no piercing, unlike the War Cross which has four piercings. The *rev* is as the previous item.

The ribbon is 37mm, yellow (deep) with black side stripes. The first class, awarded to general officers, has a gilt laurel wreath, 15mm in diameter and 2.5mm wide, on the ribbon; the second class, for colonels, has a silver wreath; the third class, for lieut. colonels and majors, has a bronze wreath, while the fourth class, awarded to captains and junior officers, has a plain ribbon. When ribbons only were worn, they carried a laurel branch instead of the wreath, in the appropriate metal.

Victory Medal RP

The medal, following the general pattern, was confirmed by Royal Decrees of 6 October 1920 and 24 November 1922, and was awarded to all who had served in the army or navy for at least three months' active service.

The *obv* has a frontal figure of the winged Victory, holding an olive branch and a garland of laurel wreaths. The *rev* has a statue of a boy (Hercules?) coping with snakes; on a large rectangular plinth are inscribed the names of the allied countries; around is the inscription, Ο ΜΕΓΑΣ ΥΓΕΡ ΤΟΥ ΠΟΛΙΤΙΣΜΟΥ ΓΟΛΕΜΟΣ (The Great War for Civilisation); in the exergue are the dates, 1914–1918.

Suspension is by an unusual lug and link, above which is an ornamental ring through which the usual 'rainbow' ribbon passes.

There appears to be two varieties of the medal, the original, struck in France, bearing the name of the designer, Henri Nocq, on the edge of the *obv* (at 7 o'clock), and with the *rev* circumscription starting with O (The). The second, struck later (possibly by M. Delande of Paris, since it is shown in his 1934 catalogue), omits the designer's name; also on the *rev*, the first letter of the Greek word for Portugal is shown as the Greek *ro* (P = our R), thus making the word appear as RORTOGALIA, whereas Nocq's version correctly has *pi* (Π = our P). As an example of this first medal was not available, it is the later striking which is illustrated at Nos. 44, 45.

No commemorative was medal was ever struck, although the decrees instituting the War Cross and Medal of Military Merit quoted the order of precedence in which such a medal was to be worn. However, internal political differences prevented the issue of the medal.

Italy

After a period of neutrality and flirting with both sides, Italy finally decided to throw in her lot with the Allies, and declared war on Austria on 23 May 1915.

EXISTING AWARDS

Order of St. Maurice & St. Lazarus (1434/1816)
Military Order of the Savoy (1815)
Order of the Crown of Italy (1868)
* Medal for Military Valour (1833)
Medal for Maritime Valour (1836)

NEW AND AMENDED AWARDS

War Cross – Croce di Guerra   RP

King Victor Emanuel III instituted the *Croce di Guerra* on 19 January 1918, for war merit in land, sea, or air operations, after at least a year's service in the trenches or elsewhere in contact with the enemy; those who were wounded in action and who had earned the award of the Medal for Wounded, those who had performed acts of bravery but not warranting the award of the *Al Valore Militare* (Medal for Military Valour) and for those who had received promotion for a mention for war merit.

The decoration is a bronze Greek cross, 37mm across. The *obv* bears the inscription, MERITO DI GUERRA, above which is the crowned royal cypher, VE (entwined) III; below is a sword on a spray of oak.

The *rev* has a five-pointed star in the centre, on a background of rays. The ribbon is a rich blue, 37mm wide, with 5mm white side stripes inset 8mm.

For a subsequent award of the cross,a 6mm bronze crown was worn on the ribbon.

Several varieties of the cross exist, but those struck at the Rome Mint have a small R on the *rev* of the lower arm.

Medal for Military Valour – Al Valore Militare

While there was virtually no amendment to this award, it should be noted that medals issued during the Great War were engraved on the *rev* (above the recipient's name), GUERRA DI 1915–1918, whereas those issued for colonial wars were engraved with the place and date of action.

War Medal, 1915–1918   RP

Instituted on 29 July 1920, this medal, 32mm in diameter, was struck in both dark and light bronze. The *obv* has the bust of Victor Emanuel III in a steel helmet, left, with the surrounding inscription between three oak sprays, GVERRA –

PER L'VNITA – D'ITALIA (War for the unity of Italy). The *rev* has a winged Victory standing on a shield supported by two soldiers. On each side is the legend, CONIATA NEL BRONZE NEMICO (Made of enemy bronze – which may well be true as regards the official issues, but since many varieties exist, it is improbable that this applies to all examples found).

Nine bars were issued – four of the old laureated type with the years 1915, 1916, 1917, or 1918, and five of the same design, but lettered ALBANIA, followed by the year 1916, 1917, 1918, 1919, or 1920. The ribbon is 37mm wide, in 18 stripes – six lots of green, white, and red. This ribbon was first used for the medal for the wars of independence, 1848–70, and was re-introduced on 21 May 1916 purely as a ribbon (on a bar) for those who had served in a theatre of war for at least a year, with each year's service marked by a 5mm silver star (In French reference books this ribbon is described as the *ruban des Fatigues de Guerre*, but presumably this is not to be translated as 'for those who were tired of the war'). Eventually it was allotted to the War Medal when this was instituted.

Medal of Merit for Volunteers   R
Instituted on 24 May 1923 as a bronze medal, 32mm in diameter, the *obv* has the female head of Italia, right, and the legend, PER L'ITALIA. The *rev* has a veiled figure standing behind a nude warrior who has his arms extended, holding a circular shield on his arm and an ancient sword in his right hand. The inscription is VOLONTARI DI GVERRA, MCMXV–MCMXVIII (War Volunteers, 1915–1918).

The ribbon is described as plain crimson, but is actually nearer deep clover coloured.

Medal for Mothers and Widows of the Fallen   R
This medal of national gratitude was instituted by Royal Decree of 24 May 1919, and was struck in bronze, 32mm in diameter.

The *obv* has an allegorical design, with a female figure presenting a wreath to a fallen warrior, while another stands beside in an attitude of mourning. The *rev* has a verse by the poet–statesman, Gabriele d'Annunzio: IL FIGLIO/CHE TI NACQVE/DAL DOLORE/TI RINASCE, 'O BEATA'/NELLA GLORIA/ E IL VIVO EROE/'PIENA DI GRAZIA'/E TECO. (The son which thou borest, is re-born to thee, oh blessed one, in glory. He lived and died a hero. In gratitude).

The ribbon is grey, with a 6mm central tricolor stripe (green, white, and red).

Medal for Army Chaplains
This bronze medal, 38mm in diameter, has on the *obv* a standing figure of an army chaplain ministering to a kneeling soldier; to the left is a cross; the surrounding inscription is PER ASPERA AD ASTRA – PER CRVCE AD LVCEM (By hardships to the stars – by the Cross to the light). The *rev* has a cross and anchor, with the legend, FIDES, SPES, CHARITAS (Faith, hope, charity); to the left is AL/CAPPELLANO/MILITARE/D'ITALIA (To the military chaplain of Italy); above is GVERRA ITALO-AVSTRIACA 1915–18 (Italian–Austrian War).

The ribbon is yellow with three 2.5mm stripes at each edge, green (outer), white and red.

We understand that there is some doubt as to whether this medal was official.

Medal for Wounded, 1915–18
In February 1917 a wound stripe, consisting of a 50mm silver braid stripe, 5mm wide, was instituted, to be worn on the right sleeve, 15cm from the shoulder and above badges of rank and merit.

We have a note of a ribbon with ten crimson and nine yellow stripes, described as that of the Medal for Wounded, 1915–18, but cannot trace any details of the medal itself. It is probably unofficial, and from the colours of the ribbon may have been issued by the city of Rome.

Victory Medal RP

The Italian version of the Allied Victory Medal, instituted on 6 April 1922, follows the general pattern, with the *obv* having a winged Victory standing in a triumphal chariot drawn by four lions. The *rev* shows two doves with sprays in their beaks, flying out from the top of a tower. At each side are the dates, MCMXIV and MCMXVIII, while around the top is GRANDE GVERRA PER LA CIVILITA (Great War for Civilisation). In the exergue is AI COMBATIENTI DELLE NAZIONI ALLEATE ED ASSOCIATE (To the combatants of the allied and associated nations). Suspension is by the usual Italian fixed lug, and the ribbon is, of course, of the usual 'double rainbow' pattern.

United Italy Medal

The medal originally struck in 1883, with the head of Humbert I, to commemorate the unification of Italy, 1848–70, was reissued by decree of 19 January 1922, in bronze, with the head of Victor Emanuel III, left, and with the *rev* reading, UNITA/D'ITALIA/1848–1918, in a laurel wreath.

The ribbon remained the same as before, 35mm wide, with a green centre and two 6mm edge stripes of red (outer) and white (inner).

Varieties of the medal are found, some with the head to the right. F. Scandaluzzi, in his authoritative work, *Ordini Equestri, Medaglie, e Decorazioni Italiane* (1962), records a special striking with a *rev* inscription below the dates, ASS. NAZ. MADRI/ E VEDOVE DEI/CADUTI, for the National Association of Mothers and Widows of the Fallen.

Another issue of the medal occurred with the dates, 1848–1922. For this one, Scandaluzzi records a special striking with a somewhat similar *rev* inscription below the dates, ASS. NAZ. FAMIGLIE/CADUTI IN GUERRA, for the National Association of Families of Those who Fell in the War.

Medal for the Occupation of Fiume R

This medal, classified as unofficial, was instituted in September 1919 by d'Annunzio. It is of bronze, 40mm in diameter, with the *obv* showing an ancient Roman eagle standard; at the base, on each side, are three hands holding daggers, points downwards. The legend is, HIC BIMUS MANE OPTIME (or possibly, HIC MANE BIMUS OPTIME). The *rev* has a spray of laurel leaves with AI/LIBERATRI/XII SETTEMBRE/MCMXIX (To the liberators of 12 September 1919) above, and on a scroll below, FIVME – D'ITALIA. Varieties of the medal exist.

The ribbon is 40mm wide, in equal thirds of crimson–purple, yellow, and blue.

The Order of Vittorio Veneto

This award was instituted by a law of 18 March 1968, No. 262, and published in the *Gazzetta Ufficiale*, No. 36, in one class only, *Cavaliere* (knight), to commemorate the 50th anniversary of the battle of Vittorio Veneto on 30 October 1918. It was awarded to those who had been decorated with the War Cross during the Great War, and also for the war in Libya, 1911–12.

It is a bronze cross with slightly pointed ends, 41 x 41mm, with ball ring suspension. The *obv* has, in the centre, an Italian steel helmet of Great War pattern, with branches of laurel on the arms of the cross. The *rev* has a 5-pointed star, surrounded by the inscription, ORDINE DI VITTORIO VENETO, and the arms of the cross have branches of oak.

The ribbon is 37mm wide, with a centre section of white, blue, white, each 4.5mm, and with edges of six narrow stripes of green, white, red, green, white, red on each side (green being on the left in each case).

Attached to the order is a gold medal, 20mm in diameter, with a 24mm ribbon comprising four sets of narrow stripes of green, white, and red. It was awarded to those who had given at least six months service in the armed forces during the Great War or in previous wars.

The *obv* has a steel helmet surmounting crossed branches of oak and laurel; above is a small 5-pointed star; at the base is the engraver's name, L. Mancinelli. The *rev* has the legend, 50°/ANNIVERSARIO/DELLA VITTORIA/1918/1968; below are branches of oak and laurel.

Cross for the Balkans, 1914–1919

This medal, *La Croce Oriente Balcanico*, relates first to the presence of Italian troops in Albania in December 1914, five months before Italy had entered the Great War. They occupied the port of Valona after Albania had been invaded by Serbian, Greek and Montenegrin troops. The award was extended to all those participating in military operations in Albania and Macedonia until 1919.

It consists of a brass (?) Greek cross, enamelled grey, 38mm across, with angular black and white scroll ornaments in the angles. The central medallion shows a mosque and an orange sky. The *rev* is plain but for the 3-line inscription, ORIENTE BALCANICO/1914–1919/ALBANIA – MACEDONIA. At the base of the lower arm, in small letters, is the maker's name, L. FASSINO/TORINO DEPOSITATO/DIS. A. CALY.

The ribbon has a black central third, with edges of red, orange-yellow, pale blue, orange-yellow, red.

Japan

Allegedly the oldest empire in the world, founded in 660 B.C., Japan entered the war on 23 August 1814, solely to occupy the German possessions in the Pacific. When this was accomplished, hostilities ceased on 7 November 1914. However, she later contributed a token fleet to the Mediterranean, and from 1918 until 1922 Japanese troops were in Siberia, etc., aiding the allied troops, in the hope of obtaining territory there.

EXISTING AWARDS

Supreme Order of the Chrysanthemum (1876?)
Order of the Rising Sun with Paulownia Leaves (1888)
Order of the Golden Kite (1890)
Order of the Rising Sun (1875)
Order of the Sacred Treasure (1888)
Military Wound Badges (1913)

NEW AWARDS

War Medal, 1914–15   R

Imperial Edict No. 203, instituted the War Medal in November 1915, for military and naval forces who participated or assisted in the actions to capture the German colony of Kia–chow and others in the area.

It is 30mm in diameter, of darkened bronze, with the imperial chrysanthemum at the top, above crossed army and naval flags within two branches of paulownia flowers. The *rev* has seven characters placed vertically; one leading authority gives these as meaning 'Taisho (reign) 3rd–4th years war', while another gives it as 'Campaign of 1914–1915'. It would seem that the first is more likely to be the correct one. The medal is a bronze bar, rectangular with chamfered corners, with four Japanese characters indicating 'Commemorative Medal'.

The ribbon, 35–37mm, is in three equal stripes of rich dark blue, white, and dark blue.

War Medal, 1914–20   R
In view of Japan's further contribution to the allied cause, a new medal was instituted by Imperial Edict No. 41, of February 1920, but nobody could receive both medals. The new medal is similar to the previous one, but in somewhat lower relief, and the *rev* has an amended inscription in ten characters indicating 'Taisho, 3rd year to 9th year war', in three vertical lines, two above and one below. It carried the same bar and used the same ribbon.

Victory Medal   RP
When the Paris Peace Conference recommended that the Victory Medal of each of the allies should have a standing figure of Victory, in the classical style, but with individual interpretation, this posed a problem for Japan. Such a figure would have no meaning for the Japanese people, so they substituted a legendary male warrior figure, *Take-Mikazuchi-No-Kami*, from Japanese mythology, carrying a spear. The *rev* is unusual, too, with a terrestrial globe in the centre of a stylised 5-petalled cherry blossom, each petal bearing a flag with an ideograph (or Japanese word symbol) representing one of the allies – Japan, USA, Britain, Italy, and France – and, below, symbols indicating 'and the other allied nations'. Surrounding this design are characters meaning 'The Great War for Protection of Civilisation, Taisho 3rd year, Taisho 9th year'.

The ribbon is, of course, of the usual 'double rainbow' type, but those of Japanese manufacture have a rather paler yellow than those of most countries.

Copies of this medal have been made in France, for collectors, one type of which (shown in our photographic illustrations) has MADE IN FRANCE, in small impressed capitals on the rim). This copy has a gilt finish and a pierced ball for the suspension ring, instead of the 'tunnel' fitting on the genuine medal; also the *rev* has a smaller globe.

NOTE:
There do not appear to be any Japanese medals for bravery or distinguished conduct in the field, and apparently the lower classes of the Order of the Golden Kite were awarded in such cases.

All Japanese medals have a hook-and-eye arrangement on the back of the ribbon, and are worn from a metal brooch with pendant tags to which the medals are hooked and fixed by bending up the bottom of the tag.

Luxembourg

The Grand Duchy of Luxembourg was overrun by the Germans early in the war, and many of her men were unwillingly forced into service in the German army. However, quite a number deserted and managed to join the allied forces as volunteers. Although the two orders noted below were already in existence, we have not been able to trace that any awards were made for service during the war, nevertheless they must be included, in case any awards were in fact granted.

EXISTING AWARDS

Civil & Military Order of Merit of Adolph of Nassau (1858)
Order of the Oak Crown (1841)

NEW AWARDS

Medals for Luxembourg Volunteers, 1914–18   R
A Grand-Ducal decree of 10 May 1923 instituted this medal to reward the
services of those Luxemburgers who joined the allied forces as volunteers, and
was given not only to survivors but also to the next-of-kin of those killed or who
died of wounds, etc.

The medal is in the form of a cross with narrow arms, widening outwards,
with convex ends (as if inscribed in a circle), and with swords in the angles.
Superimposed is a large medallion of the seal of John of Luxembourg, the blind
King of Bohemia (1310–1346), on horseback, with the legend, LUCEMBURGUM
VIRTUTI (For Luxembourg merit). The top and bottom arms of the cross are
inscribed, CRÉCY, 1346 (at which battle King John was killed, and his badge of
three ostrich feathers, with his motto, *Ich dien*, were adopted by Edward, the
Black Prince, of England), while the horizontal arms have sprays of oak and
laurel. The *rev* has, on the medallion, a steel helmet above the dates, 1914–1918,
with branches of oak and laurel, the arms are lettered, respectively, MARNE-MEUSE
(top), YSER-VARDAL (bottom), AISNE (left), and SOMME (right), being some of the
actions in which the recipients participated.

The ribbon is striped horizontally (and slightly wavy) blue and white, with
narrow red edges.

Emblem for the Wounded
By decree of 24 May 1951, an emblem was authorised for those wounded in
action. Although applying mainly to participants in World War II, it was also
retrospective for holders of the Medal for Luxembourg Volunteers, 1914–18, who
were wounded in that war.

The emblem consists of a 5-pointed star, 6mm in diameter, worn on the ribbon
of the medal.

Montenegro

Under Turkish rule since the 16th century, Montenegro eventually obtained
independence, as a principality, in 1878, after more than twenty-five years of
fighting against the Turks. Montenegro became a kingdom in 1910, but since
1919 has been a part of Jugoslavia; many of its inhabitants are still Moslems.

EXISTING AWARDS

Order of Danilo I (1853)
Milosh Obilitch Medal (1847)
Medal for Military Valour (1841)
Order of the Red Cross (1912)

NEW AWARDS

Order for the Freedom of Montenegro
This Order (which has appeared in several continental auction catalogues as

67

Order of Victory) was instituted in January 1919 by King Nicholas I while in exile in France. In a single class, it was awarded for services aimed at restoring Montenegrin independence and the monarchy, in connection with the plebiscite and unsuccessful insurrection of 1918–19.

The badge, in gilt and enamels, 45 x 40mm, is a laurel wreath, tied at intervals with bands of the national colours, red, blue, and white, enclosing the double–headed eagle, crowned, and holding a sword and orb. On its breast is a red shield with a gold lion *passant*. Behind the wreath are crossed swords, while above is a scroll with an inscription meaning 'For the Right, Honour and Freedom of Montenegro'. The *rev* is similar, except that the top scroll is coloured red, blue, and white.

The ribbon, made up in a triangle, is a plain, slightly bluish green, which was the colour associated with those who opposed unification with the Kingdom of the Serbs, Croats and Slovenes.

Panama

It would not appear that the Republic of Panama participated actively in the war, but she issued a medal to commemorate her solidarity with the aims of the allies in the defence of right and liberty.

Medal of Solidarity   R
The Republic of Panama instituted this medal in 1918, 36mm in diameter, in three classes – in gold (silver-gilt?) for the commanders-in-chief of the allied armies, and in bronze for officers and other ranks; generals and senior officers received the second class, distinguished by a rosette on the ribbon.

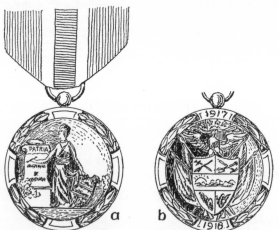

Fig. 4   Panama: Medal of Solidarity, a – *obv.*; b – *rev.*

The *obv* shows a female figure representing the republic, standing, left, holding in her left hand a shield with the arms of the state; beside her is an altar marked, PATRIA, and bearing the inscription, LA GUERRA DI DERECHO* (The war of right).

---

*This is the version given by Commandant Sculfort; L. F. Guille, in his pamphlet, *Central American Decorations*, gives it as A LA FUERZA DEL DERECHO.

The outer rim has a laurel wreath, with the arms of a cross showing at the cardinal points. (N.B. The cross does not extend outside the circle of the medal). The *rev* has the arms of Panama flanked by four flags, with an eagle above, its wings expanded. The border is as the *obv*, but with the dates, 1917 (top) and 1918 (bottom) (*figs.* 4a and b).

Suspension is from a 36mm ribbon, red with a 6mm blue central stripe flanked by 4mm white stripes. It is reported that only a hundred medals were given to each of the allied countries, so the medal is quite scarce.

Philippine Islands

The Philippine Islands were ceded to the USA in December 1898, after the Spanish–American War, and remained under US sovereignty until July 1946, when the country became an independent republic. The Philippine Constabulary was composed mainly of American army officers and American and Filipino other ranks. It was organised as an armed police force – virtually a military force – concerned largely in quelling rebellious tribes and brigands.

Philippine Constabulary World War Victory Medal
The police force regulations of 1930, para 388a, described their Victory Medal as 'a bronze World War Victory Medal of same size and weight as the United States Victory Medal... authorized for award to officers and enlisted men of the Philippine Constabulary who actively served during the World War between April 6, 1917 and November 11, 1918, inclusive'.

The *obv* has a frontal figure of a winged Victory, holding a sword in her right hand, point downwards, and a laurel branch in her left hand. On the left is the rising sun, while on the right is a smoking volcano. Above is FOR SERVICE, and below, THE WORLD WAR 1917–18. The *rev* has the arms of the state, with PHILIPPINE ISLANDS on a scroll below.

The ribbon is 1½in wide, striped in the colours of the rainbow, but not merged as in the normal ribbon for the Interallied Victory Medal.

Portugal

Traditionally Britain's oldest ally, Portugal certainly sent some troops, but they did not play a very significant part in the fighting.

EXISTING AWARDS

Military Order of the Tower and Sword (1459/1808)
Military Order of Aviz (1162/1769)
Order (or Medal) for Military Valour
Medal for Assiduous Service Overseas (1913)
Medal for Distinguished Service (1913)

NEW AWARDS

War Cross   R
A bronze cross *patée*, 42mm in diameter, but with curved ends to the arms (so that a circumscribed circle would coincide with them), the arms have plain flat

edges, with recessed centres, grained or pitted. The small central medallion has a laureated female head, right, within a circular border inscribed, REPUBLICA PORTUGUESA – 1917.

Originally instituted by Law 373 of 2 September 1915, and revised in March and November 1916, it was finally established by a decree of 28 July 1917, consequently this is the year which appears on the cross.

The *rev* is similar, but with the shield of Portugal on an armillary sphere.

Suspension is by a rather poor flattened wire loop and the ribbon is red with five equally spaced green stripes, 1.5mm wide.

The cross was awarded in a somewhat similar manner to the French Croix de Guerre, with miniature crosses, 12mm in diameter, on the ribbon to indicate the type of 'Mention', For mention in an Army or Fleet Order a silver-gilt cross was set in a laurel wreath (*fig. 5a*); for an Army Corps Mention, a plain silver-gilt cross was worn; a silver cross indicated a Divisional Mention, and a bronze one, a mention in Brigade or Regimental Orders.

Campaign Medal, 1914–18

This medal was instituted on 30 March 1916, and was in gold (gilt) for senior officers, in silver for other officers, and in bronze for other ranks; it was approximately 32mm in diameter.

 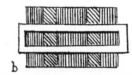 

Fig. 5   Portugal: a – War Cross emblem for Mention in Despatches;
b – Ribbon of Medal for the Wounded;
c – Emblem for Medal for Those Promoted for Bravery.

The *obv* has a laureated female head and shoulders, facing slightly to the right, with the surrounding inscription to left and right, REPUBLICA PORTUGUESA. The *rev* has, on its left side, a flying winged figure blowing a long trumpet held in the right hand at arms length; the right side has the 5-lined legend, CAMPANHAS/ DO/EXERCITO/PORTUGUES/1916 (Campaigns of the Portuguese Army). Bars were issued, including the following: SUL DE ANGOLA 1914–1915; MOÇAMBIQUE 1914–1918; FRANCA 1917–1918; CUANHAMA 1915; QUANZA SUL 1917–1918; CONGO 1914–1915; C.E.L. DEFESA MARITIMA 1916–1918 (Campo Entrincheirado de Lisboa); DEFESA MARITIMA 1914–1918; NO MAR 1916–1917–1918; FUNCHAL DEFESA MARITIMA 1916–1918; PONTA DELGARDA DEFESA MARITIMA 1916–1918; BATALHA DE LA LYS 9.IV.1918.

The ribbon for combatants is green with 5mm red edges; for non-combatants it is white with similar red edges.

Victory Medal   RP

The bronze medal, 35mm, is very similar to the French one, except that the frontal figure of Victory has the feathers of the extended wings pointing downwards instead of upwards; she holds an olive branch in the right hand and a laurel wreath in the left. The *rev* has a three-line inscription which differs from the usual one, and reads, MEDALHA DA VITORIA (Victory Medal); there is a band across the centre with five small crosses, similar to the War Cross, three in the centre and one at each end; between the first and second crosses are the arms of Portugal, the shield being superimposed on an armillary sphere, while between the fourth and fifth crosses is the DA of the inscription.

The ribbon is in the usual 'double rainbow' colours.

Medal for the Wounded   R
A medal was instituted for those wounded during the war, but no details have been traced. The ribbon is red with 4mm green side stripes inset 5mm, with an open rectangular slide bar (*fig. 5b*).

Medal for Those Promoted for Bravery   R
No details of the design of this medal have been traced, but the ribbon is red with a 6mm black centre stripe. On the ribbon is a five-pointed silver star set in an open rectangular frame (*fig. 5c*).

Rumania

The kingdom of Rumania dates from December 1861, when the Danubian principalities of Wallachia and Moldavia united. Rumania declared war on Austria on 27 August 1916.

EXISTING AWARDS

* Order of the Crown (1881)
* Order of the Star (1877)
  Cross for Military Merit (1880)
  Medal for Military Merit (1872)
* Medal for Bravery & Loyalty (Barbatie si Credinta) (1903)
* Cross for Medical Merit (1913)

NEW AND AMENDED AWARDS

Order of the Crown: Order of the Star
By a modification of the statutes in 1916, when these orders were enabled to be conferred 'with swords' for war services, they were to be worn in such cases with the ribbon of the Cross for Military Merit – red with narrow sky blue edges – instead of with their respective statute ribbons.

Medal for Bravery and Loyalty   P
From 1916, when awarded for war services, crossed swords were added above the oval medal and below the laurel wreath suspender.

Cross for Medical Merit
This decoration was originally instituted in 1913 for meritorious services in the campaign against cholera. From 1917 it was extended as an award for general merit in the military medical services. Dr. Klietmann records that from 21 July 1917 a *Kriegsdekoration* (war decoration) could be awarded, as an emblem on the ribbon, but no description is given of this.

71

Order of Michael The Brave R

This order was instituted by King Ferdinand on 13/26 September 1916 (according to Commandant Sculfort; 21 December 1916 according to Dr. Klietmann), as a reward for officers' services in the face of the enemy, in three classes – grand cross, commander, and knight. It virtually replaced the Cross and Medal for Military Merit as an award for officers, which were then reserved for other ranks.

The badge is a cross *fleurée* (rather like that of the Order of the British Empire, but without the central medallion) in blue enamel, edged in gold or silver. In the centre is the Royal cypher – two F's, back to back and joined at the foot – with a crown above. The *rev* has the year of foundation, 1916. Above the cross is a 5-arched crown.

The ribbon is claret-crimson with gold thread side stripes near the edge.

Commemorative Cross RP

This decoration, instituted on 8 July 1918 for all who served during the war, including foreign members of military missions, is in two styles – for other ranks it is in green bronze while for officers the edges and raised part of the central medallion are gilt (but this embellishment is probably unofficial). The ends of the arms of the cross widen at an angle, with three points (heraldically, a cross *urdy*). The edges are plain and flat, while the field is *quadrillée*, ie. pitted with small squares. The central medallion has only the Royal cypher, as in the previous item. The *rev* has the dates, 1916, 1918, in the medallion, and the whole *rev* field is *quadrillée* like the *obv*. At the top is a ball, pierced to take the suspension ring.

The ribbon is 37mm wide, in seven stripes, four of 5.5mm blue, and three of 5mm green, and carries bars of battles in which the recipient participated; we have noted the following: 1916; 1917; 1916–1918; 1918–1919; SIBERIA; OITUZ: DUNAREA: TARGUL–OCMA; TURTUCAIA; MARASESTI; DOBROGEA; MARASTI; BUCURESTI; JIU; CERNA; CARPATI; ARDEAL; ITALIA; OLT; PORUMBACU; TABLA BUTII; ROBANESTI; NAMOLASA; SIRET; CIRESOAIA. There was also a bar, TRADITIE, for the eldest son of a deceased recipient of the cross, if the son was an active officer.

Queen Marie Cross

Commandant Sculfort gives the date of institution as September 1916, but Dr. Klietmann quotes 17 March 1917. The cross was awarded in three classes, to medical personnel, members of the health service, ladies of the Red Cross, and those who had given distinguished services in helping the wounded or prisoners of war.

The design is an odd type of swastika, with the turned ends cut off at an angle and pointing anti-clockwise. The first class, worn at the neck, was in silver-gilt, about 49mm across (but larger and smaller examples exist), enamelled white on both sides, with a crowned M in gold, in the centre of the *obv*, while the *rev* had a Red Cross. Variations exist, including one with the red cross on the *obv*. The 2nd and 3rd Class badges are approximately 40mm across, in gilt and bronze respectively, with the crowned Royal cypher on the *obv*, and the date, 1917, on the *rev*. The ribbon is plain orange.

Badge for the Wounded

This consisted of a piece of the ribbon of the Cross for Military Merit – red, with narrow sky blue edges – with a gilt laurel wreath superimposed.

Victory Medal RP

The Rumanian version of the Victory Medal has a less pleasing frontal figure of Victory than is usually found. She holds a sword, point downwards, in her right hand and a palm branch in her left. Some minor varieties exist in the *obv* design. The *rev* has the inscription, MARELE RAZBOI/PENTRU/CIVILIZATIE (which we assume to mean 'The Great War for Civilisation'); behind this is a double-headed axe, with a spray of laurel (left) and oak (right); all this within a circle of twenty chain links. The usual 'double rainbow' ribbon is used.

Medal for Volunteers (Ferdinand Medal) 1916–18 R

We have a note of the ribbon of this medal – blue with a narrow red centre stripe – but no details have been traced of the medal itself. There was, however, the Medal of Ferdinand I, instituted in 1929 (attached to the Order of Ferdinand I, instituted for merit in the Unification of all Rumanians) with the same ribbon, and thus there appears to be some confusion here.

Russia

The thousand-year turbulent history of Russia, with its wars, assassinations, insurrections, espionage, double-dealing, and treachery, to say nothing of autocratic despotism, came to a breaking point in 1917, with the utter defeat of the Imperial Russian army by the Germans, followed by the fall of the monarchy – the Romanov dynasty – and the Red Revolution. Germany had declared war on Russia on 1 August 1914; on 17 December 1917 an armistice was arranged between the Central Powers and Russia, followed by the Peace Treaty of Brest Litovsk, on 3 March 1918.

EXISTING AWARDS
(all abolished following the Revolution of 1917)

Order of St. Andrew (1698)
Order of St. Alexander Nevsky (1725)
Order of the White Eagle (1705 in Poland, 1831 in Russia)
Order of St. George (1769)
Order of St. Vladimir (1782)
Order of St. Anne (1735 in Schleswig-Holstein, 1797 in Russia)
Order of St. Stanislas (1765 in Poland, 1831 in Russia)
Cross of St. George (1807)
* St. George Medal (1913)
Medal for Zeal (1826)
Medal for Bravery (1826/1878)

NEW AND AMENDED AWARDS

St. George Medal

Werlich, in the 2nd edition (1974) of *Orders and Decorations of all Nations*, records this as the revised name of the Medal for Bravery, from 1913, and continuing with numbering the medal and stating the class (the Medal for Bravery, not entitled 'St. George', now having the *rev* inscription in a semi-wreath, and no number or class). He also lists a variety of the St. George Medal,

73

issued by the Provincial Government (presumably the first revolutionary government, or perhaps the Kerensky regime?), with the *obv* showing the mounted figure of St. George, left, killing the dragon. No dates are given, and we have been unable to locate any further information.

NOTE:
Shortly after the overthrow of the monarchy in 1917, it was ordered that medals of the Russian orders, bearing the Czar's portrait were to be worn back to front, treating the *rev* as the *obv*, so that the Royal effigy was hidden.

Mobilisation Medal, 1914

This medal was instituted either in December 1914 or 13 February 1915, for meritorious services in connection with the mobilisation. It is 29mm in diameter, in bronze, with the *obv* showing the head of Nicholas II, left, without any surrounding inscription. The *rev* has a 5-line inscription (in cyrillic), ZA TRUDY/PO OTLICHNOMU/VYPOLNENPO VSEOBSHCHEI/MOBILIZATSII/1914 GODA (For work of distinction performed in the general mobilisation, 1914). Examples also exist in silver-gilt, with the Czar's titles on the *obv*.

The medal was worn with a dark blue ribbon – the colour of the ribbon of the Order of the White Eagle.

Order of St. Nicholas the Miracle Worker   R

We have a note of an order of this name, established in 1929 by the Grand Duke Cyril in exile, to commemorate the Great War. The badge is a 36mm cross *patée*, enamelled white and gilt, with the central medallion depicting St. Nicholas. Griffins appear between the arms, also crossed swords. It could be purchased by any Russian veteran of World War I.

The ribbon is in three equal stripes of black, yellow, and white, the Romanov colours.

This order must, of course, be ranked as unofficial, but examples of the insignia appear to come into continental auction sales fairly frequently.

Serbia

The long history of the Serbs is one of successive domination by Austria and Turkey, but Serbia was declared independent by the Treaty of Berlin, in 1878.

Following the assassination of the Austrian Prince Franz Ferdinand at Sarajevo, Austria declared war on Serbia at the end of July 1914, so sparking off the Great War. Shortly after the end of the war, Serbia was the main partner in the Union of the Southern Slavs – Jugoslavia – incorporating Slovenia, Croatia, Bosnia & Hercegovina, Montenegro, and Macedonia.

EXISTING AWARDS

* Order of the White Eagle (1883)
* Order of St. Sava (1883)
* Order of the Karageorge Star (1904)
* Cross of Mercy
* Gold and Silver Medals for Bravery (Obilitch Medals)
* Gold and Silver Medals for Zeal or Devoted Service in War
* Medal for Military Virtues

NEW AND AMENDED AWARDS

All Orders and Medals – Ribbon for Wartime Awards R

On 22 November 1914, regulations were signed by Prince (later King) Alexander for King Peter I, affecting wartime awards of all Serbian orders and medals. These regulations largely specified which classes of orders and medals could be awarded to various ranks and for which type of services. The important item, as far as we are concerned, is para 19, which states that all orders and medals which can be awarded in peacetime must – if received for war services – be worn with the ribbon of the Order of Karageorge Star 'With Swords', ie. a plain red ribbon, watered. There is nothing in the regulation to say whether or not this applies to awards made to foreigners, and one sometimes sees groups of 1914–18 war medals to British recipients which include a Serbian order or medal with its statute (or peacetime) ribbon, while others appear to have followed the Serbian regulations and used the red ribbon.

Order of the Karageorge Star P

According to Commandant Sculfort (but not recorded by other writers), the four classes of this order (reserved exclusively for officers) were increased by two further classes, date not specified, for acts of bravery by under-officers, corporals, and privates; the badge for under-officers was in gilt, with silvered rays between the arms of the cross, while that for other ranks was silvered, with gilt rays. He also reports that crosses of the order awarded during the war bore, on the *rev*, one of the pairs of dates, 1914–16, 1914–17, or 1914–18.

NOTE:

The illustrations of the badge of this order in all editions of Taprell Dorling's *Ribbons and Medals* before the 1974 edition, show the *rev* with the meaningless inscription on the central medallion, ДЕТАРІ: this is an error for ПЕТАР I, being the cyrillic letters for PETAR I, the founder of the order.

War Commemorative Medal P

On 1 December 1920, the Crown Prince Alexander, in the name of King Peter I, instituted the 'Commemorative Medal of the War of Liberation and Unity', to be awarded to all those who served in the war, including ministers and members of parliament, all members of the Montenegrin forces, volunteers, hospital personnel, and members of foreign military missions.

The medal is in bronze, 39mm across, circular with U cut-outs at the NE, NW, SE, and SW positions, thus giving the appearance of a cross with a very large central medallion. At the top and bottom are, respectively, the dates, 1914, 1918, and the hilts and points of antique swords appear in the U gaps, ie. between the arms of the cross. The medallion bears the head of King Peter I, right, with the surrounding title (in cyrillic letters), PETAR I KRAL. SRBIJE (Peter I, King of Serbia), all encircled by a wreath of laurel and oak. At the four cardinal points are small balls, with the one at the top somewhat larger and pierced to take the suspension ring.

The *rev* has the double-headed Serbian eagle with a crown above; on its breast is the shield of the Royal arms – a cross between four fire-steels. At the bottom, left, and right, are the respective dates, 1915, 1916, 1917.

The ribbon is in equal stripes of red, blue, and white – the Serbian national colours – made up into the usual triangular form.

Commemorative Medal for Albania (Serbian Retreat Medal)   R

This attractive but sad medal was instituted by decree of 5 April 1920, to commemorate the retreat from Albania in 1915, and was awarded to all who took part, including members of foreign military missions. Thus a number of British personnel received it, mainly men and women engaged in medical or hospital work.

The bronze patinated medal, 28mm high by 32mm wide, consists of a double–headed eagle, bearing the Royal arms and surmounted by a crown. Superimposed on the eagle is a circular wreath containing the portrait of Crown Prince Alexander, with a surrounding inscription in old cyrillic letters indicating *To his comrades in arms – Alexander*. The *rev* inscription means *For loyalty to the Fatherland* – 1915.

The ribbon, 36mm is bright green (for hope), with 5mm black side stripes (for sadness in this heroic effort), inset 2mm.

NOTE:

Strictly speaking, the last two items should be listed under Jugoslavia, as the Kingdom of the Serbs, Croats, and Slovenes (which became known as Jugoslavia) was formed early in 1919. However, in view of the inscription on the War Commemorative Medal, and the fact that collectors have always known and designated both medals as Serbian awards, they have been retained under this heading; also we understand that the certificates accompanying the award of these medals still bore the name of Serbia.

Siam (now Thailand)

Siam declared war on Germany 1917, after the USA had done so. Although the country was not actively engaged in the war as such, a Siamese Expeditionary Force served with allies in France in 1917–18.

EXISTING AWARDS

Order of the White Elephant (1861)
Order of the Crown of Siam (1869)
Dushai Mala Medal (with clasp for Conspicuous Bravery) (1882)

NEW AWARDS

Military Order of Rama   R

This order was instituted on 6 April 1918 by King Vajiravudh, or Rama VI (1910–1925), for exceptional military services, in four classes. It is named after King Rama I, founder of the dynasty.

The badge is a gold medallion enamelled red, with the gold figure of Parasu Rama (Rama I) defeating King Kartavirya.

The ribbon is black, with red side stripes.

Rama Medal   R

Instituted on 22 July 1918, the medal is oval, in silver. The *obv* shows Parasu Rama defeating King Kartavirya, while the *rev* has the crowned Royal cypher, RR, with the Siamese figure six between the letters.

The ribbon is black with 4mm red side stripes inset 2mm. When awarded for gallantry in action a clasp symbolising a thunderbolt is worn on the ribbon.

War Medal R

This medal was created in 1919 for members of the Siamese Expeditionary Force, and others, who had served in a theatre of war. It is in silver, 32mm in diameter, with the head of King Rama VI, left, with his titles in Siamese characters. The *rev* bears an inscription meaning *Commemorative Medal of the War of BE 2461* (= AD 1918). Suspension is by an ornate scroll suspender, with a dull red ribbon, 33mm wide, with a 4mm black stripe near each edge.

Victory Medal R

Not unexpectedly, the Siamese version of the Victory Medal departs from the western world's classical figure of a winged Victory, substituting a typically oriental figure of a four-armed deity sitting on a fabulous winged creature. The *rev* has four lines of sloping stylised Siamese characters (no doubt indicating 'The Great War for Civilisation') within an ornamental border.

The ribbon is the usual 'double rainbow' pattern.

United States of America

The United States of America did not enter the war until 6 April 1917, but its large, if belated, contribution was a major factor in the defeat of the Central Powers.

EXISTING AWARDS

* Medal of Honor (1861, Navy; 1862, Army)
* Certificate of Merit Medal (1905)

NEW AND AMENDED AWARDS

Medal of Honor

Both the Army and Navy Medal of Honor (as well as the Air Force variety, established in 1960), in their various designs, have always been basically of a five-pointed 'inverted' star pattern (ie. with a single point downwards), except for the period 1917–1942, when a gold cross *patée* with straight sided widening arms was used for the navy. This type was in fact authorised by Congress on 4 February 1919, and was applicable to Great War awards as the highest decoration for gallantry (for the army, however, the 5-pointed star type continued to be used). On each of the arms is an anchor; a wreath, showing between the arms encircles the octagonal central medallion which shows the American eagle and shield of arms; around is the legend, UNITED STATES NAVY – 1917–1918. The *rev* is plain. The normal ribbon was used – pale blue with 13 white stars, arranged; (from the bottom upwards), 1, 2, 3, 2, 3, 2, and the cross was worn on the left breast. The top suspender brooch was also of gold, with the word, VALOUR (on the army medal the spelling is VALOR).

For a subsequent award of the Army Medal of Honor ,a bronze oak leaf cluster was authorised in 1918. This consists of four oak leaves and three acorns, 13/32in in length (a smaller size is used when ribbons only are worn). No similar emblem was authorised for the navy.

Bronze Oak Leaf and Oak Leaf Cluster

A War Department Order of 12 January 1918 authorised the wearing of a bronze oak leaf on the ribbon, and ribbon bar, of the Distinguished Service Cross and the

Distinguished Service Medal. The manufacturers were requested to supply both single oak leaves and clusters, and it appears that the intention was for the single leaf to be worn on the ribbon bar, and the cluster on the ribbon of the decoration. A later War Department Order, of February 1919, cancelled this and substituted an oak cluster (for subsequent awards) on the ribbon of the Army Medal of Honor, the DSC and the DSM, and a miniature cluster for the ribbon bar (*fig. 6a*).

Fig. 6   U.S.A.: a – Oak leaves cluster; b – Victory
button; c – Service star; d – Cross *patée* on
Victory Medal ribbon.

Certificate of Merit Medal
This was an army award, which in 1905 replaced the Certificate of Merit instituted in 1874. It was awarded to any private soldier or NCO who distinguished himself 'by Merit and Courage' in action or in peacetime, and whom the President deemed worthy of the award.

The medal was discontinued by Act of Congress of 9 July 1918, but a recipient could surrender his medal for the newly instituted Distinguished Service Medal (In 1934 a further ruling enabled him to receive instead the Distinguished Service Cross).

Distinguished Service Cross   RP
Instituted by executive order of 2 January 1918 for award to army personnel, and confirmed by Congress on 9 July 1918, the DSC ranked next to the Medal of Honor, and was awarded only for combat service, for extraordinary heroism.

The bronze badge is a plain Greek cross with bevelled arms, each ending in a scroll ornament. In the centre is a laurel wreath on which is superimposed the American eagle with wings spread and raised; below is a scroll lettered, FOR VALOR. The *rev* is similar, but with the whole wreath showing, and the back of the scroll and eagle's wings.

The ribbon is dark blue with narrow red edges separated from the blue by a narrower white stripe.

The earliest examples of the DSC have oak leaves on the arms of the cross and the scroll is lettered, E PLURIBUS UNUM (From many, one). It is reported that only about a hundred of this type were awarded, and most of the examples now found are copies.

Distinguished Service Medal (Army)   R
This medal is the nation's highest award for 'exceptionally meritorious service to the government in a duty of great responsibility', and may be awarded both on active service or otherwise. It was authorised on 2 January 1918 and confirmed by Act of Congress on 9 July 1918.

The medal is $1^{1}/_{2}$in across, of bronze-gilt, with the national arms within a blue enamelled circle in gold, FOR DISTINGUISHED SERVICE – MCMXVIII. The *rev* has a scroll (for the recipient's name) superimposed on a trophy of flags and weapons. As the spaces between the design and the outer circle are pierced, the flags, etc., do just coincide with the eagle's wings on the *obv*.

Suspension is by a swivelling straight bar suspender, with a white ribbon, with broad red edges, and a narrow dark blue stripe between the white and red. For subsequent awards, oak leaves clusters are granted for wear on the ribbon.

Distinguished Service Medal (Navy)   R

Although the Navy DSM was not authorised until 4 February 1919, it was awarded retrospectively from 6 April 1917, on the same basis as its army counterpart.

The medal is of bronze-gilt, with *obv*, the American eagle in a blue enamelled circle lettered, UNITED STATES OF AMERICA NAVY. Outside the blue circle is a gilt border with a 'wave' pattern. The *rev* has the same outer border, and a trident within two laurel sprays; the blue circle is lettered, FOR DISTINGUISHED SERVICE.

Above the medal is a hinged white enamelled 5-pointed star with gilt ball finials. The star has a gold anchor, and rays between the angles. The *rev* on the star is plain.

The ribbon is deep navy blue with a narrow yellow central stripe. The first design of the medal, depicted in the *National Geographic Magazine*, December 1919, and in *Carnet de la Sabretache*, July–August 1920, but stated (by E. E. Kerrigan in *American War Medals & Decorations*) never to have been authorised for award, was in bronze, with a fouled anchor, with the sun setting (or rising) beyond the seas. Round the upper edge are the words, DISTINGUISHED SERVICE. The suspender was in the style of an eagle with expanded to form a straight line; by its feet was a scroll dated, 1917–18. There is no note of the *rev* design, so presumably this was plain. The ribbon was the same as that described above.

Navy Cross   R

Like the Navy DSM, the Navy Cross was authorised on 4 February 1919, originally as the navy's third highest decoration for acts of heroism in action and for other distinguished services (In 1942 it was given precedence over the DSM, making it a purely combat award, and the second only to the Medal of Honor, like the Army DSC).

The cross is very thick, of dark bronze, with arms curved outwards and rounded at the ends, with clusters of laurel leaves in the angles. The central medallion has an ancient sailing vessel, while on the *rev* are crossed anchors with, in the angles, USN. The ribbon is dark navy blue, with a narrow white central stripe.

A few British naval officers were awarded the Navy Cross for distinguished services during the Great War, but these are rare awards; they are recorded in the *London Gazette*.

Victory Medal   RP

Authorised in 1919, the US Victory Medal was awarded to members of the US armed forces for active service between 6 April 1917 and 11 November 1918, and for later service in Russia, up to April 1920.

Similar in style to those of the other allies, the *obv* has a standing figure of a winged Victory, facing, holding a sword and shield. The *rev* has the US shield surmounted by fasces; above is the legend, THE GREAT WAR FOR CIVILISATION, and below, six stars. On each side of the shield are ranged the names of the principal allies – FRANCE, ITALY, SERBIA, JAPAN, MONTENEGRO, RUSSIA, GREECE/GREAT BRITAIN, BELGIUM, BRAZIL, PORTUGAL, RUMANIA, CHINA. The ribbon is of the usual 'double rainbow' pattern.

Some thirty-eight clasps were authorised. The following fourteen are designated as battle clasps, narrow with a star at each end of the name: CAMBRAI, SOMME DEFENSIVE, LYS, AISNE, MONTDIDIER-NOYON, CHAMPAGNE-MARNE, AISNE–MARNE, SOMME OFFENSIVE, OISE-AISNE, ST MIHIEL, YPRES-LYS, MEUSE–ARGONNE, VITTORIO-VENETO, and DEFENSIVE SECTOR. There are five service clasps, also narrow but without stars: FRANCE, ITALY, SIBERIA, RUSSIA, and ENGLAND. These nineteen clasps relate mainly to the army, but the navy and marine corps were eligible for some of them. In addition there are nineteen wider clasps which apply only to the navy and marine corps: OVERSEAS, ARMED GUARD, ASIATIC, ATLANTIC FLEET, AVIATION, DESTROYER, ESCORT, GRAND FLEET, MINE LAYING, MINE SWEEPING, MOBILE BASE, NAVAL BATTERY, PATROL, SALVAGE, SUBCHASER, SUBMARINE, TRANSPORT, WEST INDIES, and WHITE SEA.

A five-pointed silver star was worn on the ribbon for each citation for gallantry in action not warranting a cross or medal (*fig. 6c*), while a similar bronze star was affixed to the ribbon (when ribbons only were worn) for each battle clasp but not for service clasps.

A bronze cross *patée* (incorrectly described in some US books as a Maltese cross) was worn on the ribbon by officers and men of the marine corps and naval medical corps who served with the American Expeditionary Force in France and were entitled to any battle clasp (*fig. 6d*).

For use in civilian clothes, Victory Buttons were issued to holders of the medal, in silver for men wounded in action and in bronze for others. The button consisted of a five-pointed star, lettered US in a circle, and superimposed on a laurel wreath (*fig. 6b*).

War Worker's Medal

Commandant V. Sculfort, in the July–August 1920 number of *Carnet de la Sabretache*, records this medal as instituted in 1918 on the proposal of the Commission of Control of War Labour, and later by the Secretary for Labour. He states that the medal was worn from a red, white, and blue ribbon (no details), with an enamelled bar, 44mm long. Four months' consecutive service in the war production qualified for a bronze medal, while for eight months' consecutive service, a silver medal was awarded. We have been unable to trace any further information or reference to this medal.

Silver Star

As forerunner of the Silver Star Medal (1932), the Silver Star was instituted by Act of Congress of 9 July 1918, to be worn on the ribbon of appropriate campaign medals (in this case the Victory Medal) by army personnel cited for gallantry in action not warranting the award of a Medal of Honor or DSC.

Originally known as the 'Citation Star', it consisted of a 3/16in five-pointed silver star. The award was made retrospective, so that not only citations in respect of the Great War, but those made during campaigns back to the Spanish–American War of 1898 were recognised.

Distinguished Flying Cross   RP

Although not instituted until 1926, and then primarily for 'heroism or extraordinary achievement while participating in an aerial flight, subsequent to 11 November 1918', the DFC could also be given for similar acts prior to that date if the man had been recommended for, but not awarded, the Medal of Honor, DSC, Navy Cross, or DSM.

The decoration is a bronze cross *patée*, 1½in across, with a four-bladed propeller superimposed, and with five rays between each arm, shaped up into a square format. The *rev* is plain.

The ribbon, which fits through a straight suspender bar, is dark blue with narrow white side stripes, and with a narrow red centre stripe flanked by narrower white stripes.

Subsequent awards to army or air force personnel are indicated by bronze oakleaf clusters, while small gold five-pointed stars are used by other service personnel.

Army of Occupation of Germany Medal R

From 12 November 1918 to 11 July 1923, US forces shared in the occupation of Germany and Austria, and this medal, instituted on 21 November 1941, which is directly connected with the Great War, is included although technically it falls just outside the period.

The medal, 1¹/₄in diameter, in bronze, has the bust of General Pershing, left, with four stars round the upper edge; behind the general's head is a sword, point upwards, with the dates, 1918, 1923, within laurel sprays. On the left is the name, GENERAL JOHN/J. PERSHING. The *rev* has the American eagle with wings expanded and turned down, standing on Castel Ehrenbreitstein; around is the legend, U.S. ARMY OF OCCUPATION, with three stars at the bottom.

The ribbon is black, with narrow white side stripes and very narrow blue (outer) and red (inner) edges. In the original design, which appeared in April 1942, these two edge colours were wavy stripes, but in September 1942 they were changed to normal straight stripes.

American Red Cross World War I Service Medal

For service at home during the war, a small medal was awarded, enamelled white with a red Geneva cross in a blue circle lettered, SERVICE – AMERICAN RED CROSS. This was for a minimum of 800 hours or six months' service. The ribbon was plain dark blue, but was changed to blue with one, two, three, or four narrow white stripes for each further six months' service. For foreign service a top suspension bar was awarded, blue with gold letters, FOREIGN SERVICE.

NOTE:

Apart from some awards for gallantry (including life-saving) and some polar medals, U.S. medals are not normally named, although some can be found impressed with a set of numbers. We understand that this is not a personal number of the recipient, but the serial number of the particular medal. Such numbered medals are sought after by U.S. collectors, as they are evidenced as having been actually awarded.

Some campaign, and other U.S. medals may be found with the name of the recipient engraved or impressed on the edge (or elsewhere, as appropriate); such medals, unless they are in the category of awards which are officially named on issue, have been privately named and unless fully documented, their value or desirability is not materially increased.

2

The Central Powers

Austria-Hungary

The history of Austria – *Oesterreich*, literally the eastern kingdom – goes back to the time of Charlemagne, at the end of the eighth century, when its ruler was given the title of *Markgraf* (Margrave) or Count of the Marches, in the Kingdom of Germany, later known as the Holy Roman Empire.

The Emperor Friedrich I, Barbarossa, made the country a hereditary duchy in 1156, while in 1453 it was raised to an archduchy. In 1493 Archduke Maximilian I became Emperor of Germany. This title continued until 1804 when the Emperor Franz II gave up his title of Emperor of Rome and King of Germany, and became Franz I, hereditary Emperor of Austria. Although Hungary had been under Austrian control since at least the 15th century, it was not until 1868 that the empire was decreed to be known as Austria-Hungary.

Ostensibly the instigator of the Great War, because of the murder of the Archduke Franz Ferdinand and his wife, on 28 June 1914 at Sarajevo, Austria-Hungary was the chief partner of Germany in the conflict.

In November 1918 the Emperor Karl abdicated, and Austria became a republic.

There were no contemporary separate awards for Hungary other than the Order of St. Stephen, but some Hungarian awards were instituted after the war when the country became an independent state (*qv*).

EXISTING AWARDS

Order of the Golden Fleece (1429/30)
Military Order of Maria Theresa (1757)
* Royal Hungarian Order of St. Stephen (1764)
* Imperial Austrian Order of Leopold (1808)
* Imperial Austrian Order of the Iron Crown (1816)
* Imperial Austrian Order of Franz Joseph (1849)
* Medal for Bravery (1789)
* Cross for Military Merit (1849)
* Medal for Military Merit – *Signum Laudis* (1890)
* Chaplains' Cross for Merit (1801)
* Gold and Silver Crosses for Merit (1849)
Marianer Cross of the Teutonic Order (1871)
War (General Service) Medal (1873–1916)
Order of Elizabeth and the Elizabeth Medal (for Women; 1898)

NEW AND AMENDED AWARDS

Royal Hungarian Order of St. Stephen
Although this was essentially an order for civil merit, Dr Klietmann records that in 1918, Field Marshall the Archduke Joseph was awarded the grand cross of this order 'with War Decoration and with swords'.

83

Order of Leopold and Order of the Iron Crown

From 13 December 1916 these orders could be awarded 'with swords' when won in action.

Order of Franz Joseph   R

In 1915 a special war ribbon was introduced – the ribbon of the Military Cross of Merit – red and white horizontally striped with red (inner) and white (outer) edges, in place of the statute ribbon of plain red. On 13 August 1916, new statutes and regulations were published, under which the war ribbon, as above, applied to all classes except the grand cross.

Medal for Bravery   RP

Since its creation in 1789, there had been several types of the *Tapferkeitsmedaille*, in gold (which for many years was issued in both gold and bronze-gilt) and silver, awarded to NCO's and men for bravery in action.

A third class, in bronze, was instituted on 14 February 1915. The medal, 31mm in diameter, was made of 50% copper and 50% gunmetal. The *obv* has the head of the Emperor Franz Joseph I, in field marshal's uniform, to right, with the inscription, FRANZ JOSEPH I V.G.G.KAISER V. OESTERREICH(Franz Joseph I, by the grace of God, Emperor of Austria). Under the bust is the engraver's name, TAUTENHAYN, in small capitals. The *rev* has the two-line inscription, DER/TAPFERKEIT (For Bravery), within two laurel branches tied at the base; below the lower part of the branches are six crossed flags, three to the left and three to the right.

The ribbon, 40mm has narrow red and white horizontal stripes, with 5mm red side stripes and 5mm white edges; it is, of course, made up in Austrian fashion, in a triangular shape, point downwards, with the medal fastened into lower folds.

On 29 November 1915, bars were authorised for second, third, and fourth awards of the same class of the medal, for all three metals. The bars, in rustless iron, are 8mm wide, with top lengths of 50mm, 40mm, and 30mm respectively, and are trapezoid in shape (to fit the triangular ribbon); they are spaced 2mm apart (*fig. 7a*).

After a reign of some 68 years, Franz Joseph died in November 1916, and was succeeded by the young Archduke Karl. Consequently a new type of medal was struck as from April 1917. The *obv* has the bust of the new Emperor, right, with the inscription (in Latin instead of German), CAROLVS D.G. IMP. AVST. REX BOH. ETC ET REX APOST. HVNG. (Charles, by the grace of God, Emperor of Austria, King of Bohemia, etc., and Apostolic King of Hungary). Below is the name of the designer, KAUTSCH. The *rev* has a laurel wreath, tied at the base and resting on a group of flags; in the centre is FORTITVDINI (For bravery).

From the autumn of 1917 the medal in gold was no longer made, being replaced by bronze-gilt (lettered BRONZE on the edge, also HMA – UNECHT, if struck in Vienna, or KB – NEM VALODI, if struck in Hungary, to indicate the base metal). It was intended to exchange these for gold medals after the war.

An order of 15 September 1917 extended the award to officers as regards the 'gold' and silver medals, and these were embellished by a gilt or silver ornamental K on the ribbon (*fig. 7b*).

Many copies exist of both the Franz Joseph and Karl Medals for Bravery; they are usually of lighter metal, in a rather poor style and without the designer's name under the bust.

Fig. 7 a – Austria: Bars to second (top), third, and fourth
awards of Medal for Bravery, Cross for Military
Merit, *etc.* b – Austria: Gilt or silver K on ribbon of officers'
Medals for Bravery. c – Brunswick: Service
emblem for Cross for War Merit.

Cross for Military Merit   R

This award, dating from 1849, had in its later years particularly a very complicated history. In 1860 the 'War Decoration' was added for distinction in action, consisting of a matt gilded laurel wreath appearing between the arms of the cross and well clear of the central medallion.

On 23 September 1914 the decoration was reorganised into three classes, the First Class becoming a *Steckkreuz*, or pin cross, 62mm across, with a 27mm central medallion and a plain *rev.* The white enamelled arms of the cross *patée* and the medallion have a red border, 3.5mm wide, while the laurel wreath (the *Kriegsdekoration*), when awarded, was in green enamel. In the centre is the inscription in gilt, in two lines, VER/DIENST (Merit). This class was awarded only to generals in command of army corps.

The 2nd Class, worn at the neck from the red and white horizontally striped ribbon, was 40mm across, with an 18mm medallion, and 2.5mm red enamel borders, while the laurel wreath was 3mm from the medallion. The 3rd Class was worn on the left breast and was 31mm across, with a 12mm medallion and 2mm red borders; the laurel wreath (if awarded) was gilt.

From 13 December 1916, the decoration could be awarded 'with swords', set diagonally between the arms of the cross, except for the 3rd Class, when crossed swords were worn on the ribbon. The award 'with swords' applies to crosses both with and without the *Kriegsdekoration*.

From 1 August 1917, subsequent awards of the 3rd Class were indicated by plain gilded bars or clasps, trapeze shaped, on the ribbon. These were 8mm wide, and varied in length, as described for the Medal for Bravery. If swords were awarded, these were soldered to the top bar.

A complicated difference is found in cases where the recipient of a lower class with *Kriegsdekoration* and/or swords received a higher grade without these embellishments. In such cases the badge of the higher grade had the wreath set close up against the central medallion instead of being clear of it, in green for the 2nd Class and in gilt for the 3rd Class; the earlier swords of the lower class appeared on the higher class in oxidised silver instead of gilt. Also from 8 February 1918, a further award of the 2nd Class *mit der Kriegsdekoration* was indicated by the addition of a 20mm green laurel wreath on the ring at the top of the cross. Yet another variation was the wearing of a 3rd Class cross differenced to indicate the 1st or 2nd Class, by a miniature of the higher class being worn on the triangular ribbon. That for the 1st Class was 19mm high (and a *Steckkreuz*); for the 2nd Class it was 18mm high, including an enamelled piece of 'ribbon'. When ribbons only were worn these miniatures were also worn on the ribbon strip.

Medal for Military Merit – *Signum Laudis*   R

Founded in 1890, for outstanding services in war and peace, this medal also used the red and white horizontally striped ribbon of the Medal for Bravery, when awarded in wartime to officers, or a plain red ribbon for non-military persons of rank. In peacetime the plain red ribbon was used in all cases.

On 1 April 1916 the Emperor Franz Joseph enlarged the decoration, instituting (as a higher class) the **Large Medal for Military Merit**, on the horizontally striped ribbon, as the highest award for merit. Known as the 'Gold Signum Laudis', the medal was of silver-gilt, 37mm across, with the laureate head of the Emperor, right, and titles, FRANCISCVS IOS. I D.G. IMP. AVST. REX. BOH. ETC. ET REX APOST. HVNG., all within a narrow wreath of laurel leaves. The *rev* has SIGNVM LAVDIS (A token of esteem) within branches of laurel and oak, tied at the base. Above the medal is the imperial crown with sprays of laurel. For awards in the face of the enemy, crossed swords in gilt were added to the ribbon, while in February 1917 bars were authorised for second and third awards; these were plain silver-gilt trapezoids, 50 x 9mm and 40 x 9mm respectively (to fit the triangularly folded ribbon). Where swords were awarded, these were soldered to the top bar.

With the accession of the Emperor Karl in November 1916, the design of all the *Signum Laudis* medals was changed to one with his head, and titles in Latin. Above the medals are two crowns, those of Austria and Hungary, resting on laurel and oak sprays. At first the *rev* of the crowns also showed the leaves, but later it was plain. The Large Gold Medal was originally issued in dull silver-gilt, but from early 1918 it was of bronze-gilt, and later of bronze. Similarly the small medal was produced at first in oxydised matt silver, later in silvered bronze, while the bronze-gilt medals later became just bronze. By the end of the war they were made of grey zinc ('war metal'), the higher grade being oxydised with silver. The bars for subsequent awards were of silver plated metal.

Chaplains' Cross of Merit

As with other decorations, the *Geistliches Verdienstkreuz* could also be awarded from 13 December 1916 with crossed swords (in gilt) on the ribbon, when won for services at the front. Up to 1917, the 1st Class crosses were made of gold, but thereafter silver-gilt was used; the 2nd Class crosses remained silver throughout. When awarded in wartime, the decoration had a 40mm white ribbon with three 8mm red stripes, 4mm apart, instead of the peacetime ribbon of plain white.

Gold and Silver Crosses for Merit   R

Originally instituted in 1849 as awards for civil merit, with a plain red ribbon, from 20 September 1914 a war service ribbon was authorised, using that of the Medal for Bravery – narrow red/white horizontal stripes with red and white edges. From 13 December 1916 crossed swords were added to the war ribbon for merit in action.

Iron Cross for Merit   R

This decoration, instituted on 1 April 1916 as a lower grade to the Gold and Silver Crosses for Merit, was to reward meritorious service by 'persons of the standing of soldiers and civil servant employees, without rank'. It was mainly given to medical corps, field railway corps, and military post office personnel. It could be awarded 'with crown and swords', or with either, on the ribbon of the Medal for Bravery (red/white horizontal stripes, with red and white edges) for war services, or on a plain red ribbon, with or without crown, for peacetime services; in fact, no awards were made on the red ribbon. The crossed swords, which were in gilt, were authorised on 13 December 1916, for services at the front.

The decoration is a cross *patée*, 35mm, of grey rustless iron, with convex ends to the arms. The central medallion, 18mm in diameter, bears the initials, FJ, in large capitals, within a circle lettered VIRIBUS UNITIS (By united forces – the Royal motto). The *rev* has the date, 1916, in the centre, in a stylised wreath. Above the cross, when so awarded, is the imperial crown, 20mm high, in gilt.

An order of 26 September 1917 extended the award to old soldiers and civil servants, born in 1865 or 1886, who had voluntarily remained in active service, while later the birth date was extended to 1867.

War Cross for Civil Merit

The Emperor instituted this decoration on 16 August 1915, in four classes, for outstanding meritorious services, the class of award being influenced by civilian rank or standing rather than by the degree of merit. These awards were all of the *Steckkreuz* type, pinned to the left side without ribbon.

The 1st Class badge is of silver-gilt, 64mm in diameter, being a cross with widening arms and with the ends engrailed in two curves, enamelled white with a broad border narrowly lined in the inside, both in gilt. The central medallion is oval, with FJI in large letters within a border inscribed, MERITO CIVILI TEMPORE BELLI – MCMXV (For civil merit in time of war – 1915). The cross is encircled by a wreath (described by Hessenthal & Schreiber, and also by von Falkenstein, as laurel, but in their illustrations it is clearly of oak, which is more usual for civilian and non-bravery awards). The wreath goes over the vertical and under the horizontal arms.

The three lower classes have similar insignia, but 44mm in diameter; that of the 2nd Class is of silver-gilt, while the 3rd Class badge, also enamelled white, is of silver with silver edges to the arms of the cross. The 4th Class is in bronze, without enamel (some writers say gilded bronze).

Karl Truppenkreuz   RP

This decoration, the Emperor Karl's Cross for the Troops, was instituted on 13 December 1916, for award to all service personnel, regular, militia, and volunteers, who had seen at least twelve months' field service before the enemy and who had participated in at least one battle. Thus it virtually replaced the War Medal, 1873–1916.

The cross, similar to the old Cannon Cross of 1813–14, was a grey 'war metal' straight-armed cross *patée*, 29mm across (examples in dark or very light coloured zinc are of private manufacture). The *obv* is lettered GRATI (top) PRINCEPS ET PATRIA (across the centre); below, in two lines, is CAROLVS/IMP. ET REX (Thanks – Sovereign and Fatherland – Karl, Emperor and King). The *rev* has, on the upper arm, the crowns of Austria and Hungary above the initial, C. Across the centre is VITAM ET SANGVINEM, and in base, MDCCCCXVI (By life and blood – 1916). Between the arms of the cross is a laurel wreath. Copies of the cross were produced early in World War II; these had a ring at the top at right angles (whereas the original cross had a loop, semi-circular in shape, in line with the top edge). This meant that the ring connecting the loop with the suspension was unnecessary and was omitted.

The ribbon is 40mm, red with 12mm edges horizontally striped red and white. It is also found 38mm wide, with 10mm edges.

Franz Joseph Cross

The old Emperor had wished to reward the services of officers who had worked closely with him during the war, but his death on 21 November 1916 prevented his giving effect to this. However, on 28 November 1916, his successor, the Emperor Karl, instituted the Franz Joseph Cross for this purpose.

This is a *Steckkreuz*, worn on the right side with a pin fastening and no ribbon, 56mm in diameter, being a Maltese cross but with shallow V ends to the arms. It is made of blackened iron, with borders of oxydised silver and gilt. The central medallion, 23mm, is black with the gilt monogram, FJI, and the surrounding inscription, MILITANTIBUS A LATERE MEO – MCMXIV-MCMXVI (For the warriors by my side, 1914—1916). Between the arms of the cross appears a gilt laurel wreath.

The cross is extremely rare, only about twenty–six having been awarded.

Medal for Wounded R

A special medal for the sick and wounded troops was established on 12 August 1917, and struck in grey 'war metal', 37mm in diameter.

The *obv* has the head of the Emperor Karl, right, with two laurel branches below. Above is his name, CAROLVS. The *rev* is simple, with just the central inscription in two lines, LAESO MILITI (to wounded warriors), and, in base, the date, MCMXVIII (it was not struck until 1918). The 40mm ribbon is basically a greyish brown with 5mm red edges. In this form it applied to those seriously ill but not wounded. For each wound, up to a maximum of five, red stripes were added, symmetrically placed, each 2mm wide including a pin stripe of black on each side.

Tyrol Commemorative Medal, 1914–18 RP

The Tyrol Parliament instituted this bronze-gilt medal, 34mm in diameter, on 7 February 1928, for all Tyrolese participants in the war and also for others who served in the defence of the Tyrol during 1915–18, including alpine troops of the German army. About 120,000 medals were issued.

The *obv* shows the Tyrol eagle; above is a small laurel wreath. The *rev* has the 7-line inscription in an oak wreath, DAS/LAND TIROL/DEN VERTEIDIGERN/ DES/VATERLANDES/1914–18 (The Province of Tyrol to the defenders of the Fatherland). Original medals have a tiny TJ below the dates.

The 39mm ribbon is red with 8.5mm white side stripes, each flanked by a 1mm green stripe and a 2mm white edge.

War Commemorative Medal RP

The 35mm bright bronze medal was instituted on 21 December 1932, for all ranks who served in the war. The *obv* has an eagle with wings open, but with feathers pointing downwards, and standing on a shield with the arms of Austria, *gules a fesse argent*. Below is the legend, FÜR ÖSTERREICH (For Austria). The *rev* has the dates, 1914–1918, in an oak wreath.

The ribbon, 40mm, is white with two 3.5mm red stripes 4mm apart and 1mm red edge stripes inset 2mm. On November 1933 crossed swords in gilt were added to the ribbons of front line troops, those who were wounded, and prisoners of war with an honourable record.

Elizabeth Cross

This silver cross, 40mm, for ladies, for meritorious services in various spheres of work, in religious, humanitarian, or philanthropic fields, would not appear to be eligible for inclusion here, but for the fact that it was largely awarded for war work of the type connected with its objects.

It was instituted on 30 April 1918 and attached to the Order of Elizabeth (1898). The four arms of the cross are each composed of three rays ending as the top of a *fleur de lis*. Rose branches fill the angles between the arms. The central medallion, which was struck separately and superimposed, has the crowned head of St. Elizabeth, right. The *rev* has the florid initial, E, in a circle of rose branches.

The ribbon is white, with carmine-crimson side stripes, 2.5mm wide and inset 2.5mm from the edge, made up into a double bow.

Decoration for Merit to the Red Cross

On 17 August 1914 (the 50th anniversary of the Geneva Convention) Emperor Franz Joseph instituted decorations for merit to the Austrian Red Cross, consisting of four grades and two medals. The highest grade was the Star of Merit, a Latin cross *patée* (ie. the lower limb is longer than the other three) with slightly rounded ends to the arms, enamelled red with a white border, 69 x 56mm. Between each of the arms are seven facetted rays, graded in size. The 20mm central medallion is white with a red Geneva cross, in a red circle lettered PATRIAM AC HUMANITATI (For Fatherland and humanity). The *rev* is plain silver except for the central medallion, which is white with the dates, 1864/1914, in a red circle.

There is a hinged pin at the top, fastening to a claw at the bottom of the lower arm. When awarded for wartime service, the badge carries a *Kriegsdekoration*, consisting of a wreath of oak (left) and laurel (right), encircling the arms of the cross but going behind the rays.

The badge of the 1st Class is similar, but 56 x 46mm, with a 17mm centre, and with a somewhat rectangular lug to take the flattened loop through which the ribbon runs; there are no rays between the arms, and the *rev* is enamelled red and white, again with the dates in the centre. The *KD* is a similar oak and laurel wreath, 43 x 35mm, superimposed on the cross. The ribbon is 50mm wide, white with two red stripes on each side. For men, the badge is worn at the neck, while for women the ribbon is made up in a bow, with a silver bow on the ring.

The third grade is that of Officer, who wears a cross of the same size, without ribbon, pinned to the left side. The *rev* is plain silver, with the years, 1864, 1914, engraved on the horizontal arms.

The fourth grade, or 2nd Class, badge, worn on the left breast with a 40mm or 37mm ribbon (triangular for men, in a bow for women), is similar to that of the 1st Class but smaller, 45 x 37mm.

The Medals, in silver and bronze, are oval, 44 x 36mm, and show two angels supporting a white shield with a red Geneva cross; above is a 5-pointed star with rays emanating, while below is PATRIAE/AC/HUMANITATI. The *rev* is plain except for the dates, 1864/1914. The *KD* consists of a 5mm oak and laurel wreath edging to the medal, which necessitates the central design being slightly smaller than on the medal for peacetime services.

Von Prochazka, in *Österreichisches Ordenshandbuch*, illustrates a badge of the 2nd Class with *KD*, with crossed swords on the ribbon. We have been unable to ascertain if this is correct, but it would certainly appear to be out of keeping with the spirit of the Red Cross movement.

Medal for Catholic Sisters

In 1917 an award was instituted for Sisters of Catholic Orders who had given meritorious service in Austrian military hospitals. It consisted of an oval matt silver medal, 50 x 37mm. The *obv* shows an angel offering a cup to a kneeling man, with the inscription (at right), ADORATIO-IMITATIO-EXPATIO-AMOR (Worship, imitation, atonement, love). The *rev* shows a sick person seeing a vision of Christ and the

Virgin Mary. The medal is worn from a bow of narrow white ribbon, about 15mm wide, with thin double red stripes (like a miniature of the previous ribbon).

Golden Cross of the Austrian Legion of Honour

This would appear to be a decoration of an ex-service men's organisation. It is listed by Von Prochazka, and a correspondent has sent me a photograph. It consists of a gilt cross *patée* with straight sides, 40–41mm across, with wide borders to the arms. The central medallion, 12mm, is lettered: PRO PATRIA (For the Fatherland), around a small star. A laurel wreath appears between the arms. The *rev* is plain, except that the medallion is lettered: ÖSTERR./1914–1918/EHRENLEGION. Prochazka shows the ribbon as 30mm, yellow with 5mm black side stripes, inset 1mm. My correspondent's example has a 37mm ribbon, plain violet, with a metal emblem of the Austrian eagle over the scroll lettered: ÖSTERREICH.

Bulgaria

The ancient kingdom of Bulgaria was conquered by the Turks in 1396, and only regained full independence in 1908, after thirty years as a principality tributary to the Sultan of Turkey.

Hoping eventually to acquire Macedonia, the wily King Ferdinand negotiated with both sides, and eventually decided to throw in his lot with the Central Powers. In consequence, Bulgaria declared war on Serbia on 12 October 1915.

EXISTING AWARDS

* Order for Bravery in War (1879 or 1880)
  Order of St. Alexander (1881)
* National Order of Merit (1891, Civil; 1900, Military)
  Order of Merit – 'Pour le Mérite' (1881/1883)
  Medals of Merit (1883)
* Soldiers' Cross for Bravery (1879)

NEW AND AMENDED AWARDS

Order for Bravery in War

During the war insignia were issued with, first, 1915 on the base of the outer circle of the central medallion. Later types are found with dates on the upper and lower arms of the cross, thus: 1915, 1917.

King Ferdinand amended the 3rd and 4th Classes of the order in 1915, making a first and second grade of each class. The 1st Class of the order could also be awarded 'With Skulls', 'With Brilliants' or 'With Skulls and Brilliants', but we have not been able to ascertain the date of introduction of these embellishments.

National Order of Merit

During the war the order could also be awarded with the war decoration, consisting of a wreath round the central medallion, and with the ribbon of the Order for Bravery, pale blue with silver thread side stripes, instead of the statute ribbon of yellow with black (inner) and white (outer) edges.

Soldiers' Cross for Bravery   P

A new model was introduced in 1915, similar to the previous type, being a 35mm Bath cross but without ball finials, with crossed swords in the angles. The *obv* centre was a rampant lion, crowned, with the surrounding legend (in cyrillic letters), ZA CHRABROST – 1915 (For bravery). The *rev* has the Bulgarian crown and Royal monogram, with the legend indicating Principality of Bulgaria (as it was when the decoration was founded) and the date of institution, 1879. As before, the ribbon was pale blue with silver thread side stripes inset 3mm.

War Medal, 1915–18 RP

The War Medal was somewhat belatedly instituted on 9 December 1933, by King Boris III, for all ranks who served in the war.

It is in bronze-gilt, 32mm in diameter, with the arms of Bulgaria, a lion rampant, with a crown above the shield, crossed swords behind, on sprays of laurel and oak. The *rev* has the dates, 1915–1918, within an unusual 'wreath' of sprays with roses at the base, barley ears at the top, and with oak leaves (left) and laurel leaves (right) in the middle.

The ribbon for front-line combatants is 38mm, made up in triangular from, with a 22mm red centre and white/green.white edges, the green stripes being 3mm wide. For other combatants, the ribbon has a narrow white centre stripe, while for home service the narrow centre stripe is black.

The medal was also fairly widely awarded to many personnel of Bulgaria's allies.

Georgia

Georgia, under Russian domination since 1783, cannot strictly be considered as a member of the Central Powers, but in her continual struggle for independence, she was greatly assisted by Germany in achieving this.

The Georgian Legion, a volunteer army officered by Germans and supported by the German Caucasus Expedition, was founded in 1915 and was largely responsible for the ultimate Declaration of Independence on 28 May 1918. However, it was a short lived freedom, as Georgia became a Soviet province in February 1921.

Order of Queen Tamara

Late in 1915 this military decoration for merit was instituted by the first commander of the Georgian Legion, Lieut. Horst Schliephack, and named after Queen Tamara, also known as St. Tamara of Georgia who reigned from 1184 to 1212.

The insignia is designated as a 'badge', consisting of a breast star, in one class (according to Dr. Klietmann, but Wehrlich quotes three classes). The eight-pointed rayed star appears in various sizes, 71, 72, and 88mm in diameter, and various finishes, depending on the manufacturers, but it is believed that many unofficial examples are on the market. The star is usually in silver (or silvered), but may be found in gilt; the central medallion shows the head of Queen Tamara within a circle inscribed, in ancient Georgian letters, the equivalent of GEORGIAN LEGION 1915. The centre background is sometimes enamelled in blue or white, while the circle may be blue with silver or gold lettering. The portrait of the Queen is from the only existing picture of her – a painting in a monastery near Tiflis.

The star is worn on the left breast. When ribbons only are worn, the badge is represented by a ribbon with a narrow black and red horizontal stripes and wide red edges.

In addition to awards made from early in 1916, an order by the Minister of War, dated 13 December 1918, decreed that officers and men of the German troops in the Caucasus, who remained after 4 November 1918 in Georgia, had the right to wear the

Order of Queen Tamara. In all some 300 officers and 2500 men received the decoration, but as badges could not be made locally, recipients had to buy them in Germany.

With the return of Georgia to Russian domination in 1921, the order became defunct.

The German Empire

Germany, the dominant partner in the alliance of the Central Powers, entered the war on 1 August 1914, by declaring war on Russia, followed by declaring war on France the following day.

Strangely enough, the German Empire, *das Deutsche Reich,* had no orders, decorations, or medals, either existing or new, for services in the Great War, except the *Helvetia Benigna* medal and, perhaps, the Cross of Merit of the Military Carrier Pigeon Organisation, although a number of special badges, *Abzeichen,* were instituted (worn pinned to the uniform): even the Cross of Honour (the War Commemorative Medal) was instituted in the early days of the Third Reich.

On the other hand, the German States had many awards, old and new; in the main these were awarded to their own troops, although very many cases occurred of awards to other Germans, particularly the Iron Cross, which was officially a Prussian decoration but was widely awarded by the King of Prussia (who also happened to be the Emperor of Germany and supreme head of the armed forces) to several million Germans and their allies. Thus groups of decorations may be found with the Iron Cross coming *after* the decorations of the recipient's own state, ie. among the 'foreign' awards, but it is more usual to find it given precedence over all other awards, including orders.

EXISTING AWARDS

None

NOTE:

By an Order from the Kaiser dated 16 November 1916, all orders and decorations originally issued in real gold were henceforth to be made of silver-gilt.

NEW AWARDS

The Helvetia Benigna Medal

The two leading authorities on German awards (Hessenthal and Schreiber, in their book *Die Tragbaren Ehrenzeichen des Deutschen Reiches*, and Dr K-G Klietmann, in *Deutsche Auszeichnungen*, vol. 2) both allocate this award to the *Deutsches Reich* (German Empire), although it would appear that it was instituted on 15 March 1917 by the Royal *Prussian* Ministry of War.

It was awarded to Swiss men and women, and to a few Germans resident in Switzerland, who had looked after Germans interned in that country. The medal, in fine silver, was originally made up with a diameter of 60mm, and depicted a female figure – Helvetia (Switzerland) – standing in front of a panel bearing the arms of Switzerland, distributing food, etc., to German soldiers, with a background of Alps. At left and right base are the dates, 1914, 1917. At the top is the inscription, HELVETIA BENIGNA (Kind Switzerland).

The *rev* has the legend, DAS DANKBARE/DEUTSCHLAND/ZUR ERINNERUNG/AN DEN/WELTKRIEG (Grateful Germany, in remembrance of the World War), within two tied olive branches; at the top is the Swiss cross but shaded for red (ie. the Red Cross), with nine rays emanating from it.

This medal was not intended to be worn, but later a smaller model was made, 34.5mm in diameter, with a ring for wear by men, from the watch-chain, etc., or with a brooch for women. There was no ribbon.

Apparently only 25 of the large medals were awarded, but we have been unable to trace the number of small medals; it is unlikely that any large quantity was awarded.

Cross of Merit of the Military Carrier Pigeon Organisation

Like the previous medal, Dr Klietmann allocates this decoration to the *Deutsches Reich* although founded by the Royal Prussian Ministry of War, but Hessenthal & Schreiber list it under Prussia.

It was instituted on 17 December 1917, for award to members of the German Military Carrier Pigeon Breeders Association who, under considerable difficulties, had maintained the supply of carrier pigeons needed for military purposes.

The cross, 39mm across and made of grey iron, is a Greek cross with slightly rounded ends to the arms, which are 14mm wide. The central medallion shows the head of the Kaiser, right. Each arm of the cross bears an oak spray within a wide border. The *rev* is in low relief and shows a scene of trench warfare; over this is the inscription, FÜR/VERDIENSTE/UM DAS/MILITAER/BRIEFTAUBENWESEN (For merit concerning the Military Carrier-pigeon Organisation), with a pigeon flying above; on the lower arm is a soldier in a dugout holding a pigeon.

Suspension is by a ring, with a blue watered ribbon, 30mm wide, of the same colour as that of the Order of the Crown of Prussia. It is reported that 469 crosses were awarded between 13 October 1918 and 8 October 1919, thus the decoration is somewhat rare.

Cross of Honour for the Great War, 1914–18   P

One of the last acts of President Hindenburg, only a few months before his death, was to institute the *Ehrenkreuz des Weltkrieges* on 13 July 1934, in three categories – for frontline fighters, for other troops and serving personnel, and for widows and parents of the fallen, of those who died from wounds, or who died as prisoners of war.

Since the Nazi regime, known as the Third Reich, dated from 1933, this must technically be considered as an award of that regime, although it does not bear the swastika or other Nazi emblem. But for all practical purposes we can include it under the heading of the German Empire, as it relates solely to the 1914–18 war.

The first category included those who had served in a battle or siege, or other action on land, sea, or in the air, while the second included all German subjects who were engaged in war service of Germany or her allies. In 1938 the entitlement was extended to Austrians and Sudeten Germans and in the following year to Memellanders. Various subsequent decrees up to September 1944 made further extensions of eligibility to Czechs and other 'associated people' who had served in the war (not always voluntarily, presumably) on the German side.

It was originally intended to strike the crosses in bronze, but on the grounds of expense, this was changed to iron, bronzed for combatants and other troops, and blackened for widows and parents, although crosses for all three groups are found made of bronze or *tombak* (an alloy of zinc and copper).

The cross, which measures between 37mm and 38mm across, is virtually a cross *patée*, but while some examples show slightly curved arms, others have the arms quite straight as they widen. The combatant's cross has the dates in the centre, 1914,

1918, within a wreath of laurel, and with swords saltirewise in the angles. The cross for other troops is similar, but with an oak wreath and no swords, while that for widows and parents is the same as for other troops but of blackened iron. The reverse is plain.

The ribbon is normally 30mm wide, or watered silk (but one finds it in 28mm or thereabouts); for the first two categories it is black, with a red centre stripe and white side stripes (as for the 1870–71 War Commemorative Medal). For widows and parents the ribbon is white, with a red centre stripe and black side stripes.

Various figures have been quoted for the numbers awarded, but with the various later awards under extended eligibility, it is impossible to be accurate. A reasonable estimate seems to be something over 6,000,000 combatants' crosses, just over 1,000,000 for other troops, and approaching 1,000,000 for widows and parents.

Badges for the Wounded P

In March 1918 pin-on badges were authorised for wounded soldiers, in the form of bracteate oval metal 'plaques', approximately 38 x 43mm in black for one or two wounds, silvered for three or four, and gilt for five or more wounds.

The badge shows a steel helmet, left, on two crossed swords, all within a laurel wreath.

A similar set of badges for the navy, but somewhat rounder, were instituted in June 1918. These showed two crossed swords over an anchor, all within a studded cable border.

Both types have a granulated or 'pock-marked' field. They are worn on the left side, below the Iron Cross, 1st Class, or similar decorations.

ANHALT

In 1606 the principality of Anhalt was divided into four duchies – Anhalt-Dessau, Anhalt-Zerbst (which became extinct in 1793), Anhalt-Plotsgau or Köthen, and Anhalt-Bernburg. In 1863 these became the Duchy of Anhalt, which existed until November 1918, when it became a *Freistaat*, or Free State, within the framework of the Weimar Republic.

EXISTING AWARDS

The House Order of Albrecht the Bear (1836)
Medal of Merit of the above Order

NEW AWARDS

The Friedrich Cross RP

Duke Friedrich II instituted the decoration which bears his name, by decree of 12 December 1914, for officers, military officials, non-commissioned officers, and other ranks, for distinguished service in the field or at home, during the war.

The decoration is a cross *patée*, 37mm across, of bronze, dark toned but lighter toned examples are found. The central medallion, which has a gothic capital F for the founder, is surrounded by an oak wreath which lies over the horizontal arms and under the vertical ones. The top arm has a crown of five demi-arches, while the lower arm bears the date, 1914.

The *rev* is almost plain, except for the narrow raised border line to the arms and the large central medallion (which occupies the *rev* of the areas taken up by the *obv* medallion and the oak wreath). The centre has the inscription, FÜR/VERDIENST/

IM/KRIEGE (For merit in the war).

The field of the cross on both *obv* and *rev* is pitted or 'granulated'. Suspension is by a ring. The ribbon, 30mm wide, is of watered dark green silk (in the distinctive Anhalt green shade), with 2mm red edges when the decoration was won in action, but with 2mm white edges for other awards.

Dr K-G Klietmann (in *Deutsche Auszeichnungen*, vol. 3 – *Anhalt*) reports that a *Steckkreuz*, or cross with a back-pin exists (similar to the 'first class' of some other decorations), like the normal cross but slightly convex; the *rev* is, of course, plain with a pin and catch. It is possible that it was intended to amend the statutes to make a provision for a higher class of the decoration, which may have been forestalled by the abdication of the Duke in November 1918, but because of the intention a Berlin firm certainly made a supply of them. Dr Klietmann also reports that copies of the Friedrich Cross exist, both from the period just after (and possibly during) World War I, and after World War II. Unfortunately no details of the copies are given.

The Marie Cross   R

On 10 January 1918, Duke Friedrich II instituted a cross of merit for women, for wartime nursing services, care of the wounded, and similar work. The decoration, named after his wife, the Duchess Marie, is known as the *Marien-Kreuz*, and consists of a bronze cross *pommée* (with oval 'knobs' to the arms of the cross), matt silvered, 35mm across. Like the Friedrich Cross, the field of the cross is granulated, with a narrow polished rim to the outer edges and to the central medallion. The latter bears on the *obv* the combined initials, M, F (Marie, Friedrich); the upper arm of the cross has a small crown, while on the lower arm is the date of foundation, 1918. The *rev* of the medallion shows the arms of Anhalt – a shield divided vertically (*per pale*), showing on the dexter side (left, as the viewer sees it), half an eagle with wing raised, and, on the other side, the gold and black bars and diagonal rue crown of Saxony.

The ribbon, made up in the usual bow form for women, is 26mm wide, of watered Anhalt green silk, with two white stripes on each side, 1mm wide, 1.5mm apart, and inset 3mm.

BADEN

The Grand Duchy of Baden dates from 1806, before which it was ruled by a *Markgraf* (Count of the Marches or borders) or a *Kurfürst* (Elector). It became a Free State in November 1918, but is now joined with Württemberg.

EXISTING AWARDS

* Karl-Friedrich Order of Military Merit (1807)
  Order of Berthold I (1877)
  Order of the Zähringen Lion (1812)
* Karl-Friedrich Medal for Military Merit (1807)
* Cross of Merit of the Order of the Zähringen Lion (1889)

NEW AND AMENDED AWARDS

Karl-Friedrich Order of Military Merit

This order, founded in 1807 for officers, had one new feature introduced during the Great War, namely the provision of 7 November 1917, that when ribbons only were worn, a green enamelled laurel wreath should be worn on the ribbon of the order. The reason for this was to distinguish the ribbon of the order from that of the Cross of

Merit of the Zähringen Lion when won in action (*qv*). The ribbon is in three equal stripes of yellow, red, and yellow, with narrow white edges.

Karl-Friedrich Medal for Military Merit
By an order of 7 November 1917, the ribbon (which is the same as that of the Karl–Friedrich Order), when worn without the medal, should bear a gold (gilt) or silver wreath, according to the metal of the medal. This was to distinguish it from other similar ribbons.

The medal is rare as only 1282 silver medals were awarded from 1914 to 1918, and none in gold. Silver medals continued to be struck at the State Mint and Karlsruhe up to 1936, from the original dies, as replacements for lost medals. After World War II cast copies were also made, but 39.4mm in diameter, weighing 30.57 grammes (against 40.3mm and 34.96 grammes for the original medals).

Cross of Merit of the Order of the Zähringen Lion
The cross was instituted in 1889 and affiliated to the Order of the Zähringen Lion, as a distinction of honour, with an orange-yellow ribbon with 3mm green side stripes.

On 25 September 1914 a new regulation enabled the cross to be awarded as a decoration for special merit in action, with the ribbon of the Karl-Friedrich Order, ie. yellow-red-yellow with narrow white edges.

An order of 13 November 1917 provided that, when ribbons only were worn, a 12mm crowned F should be affixed to this ribbon when it related to the Cross of Merit, thus making it equivalent to the addition of 'swords' as seen on many orders and decorations indicating the winning of an award in action. Just over five hundred crosses were awarded with this ribbon during the war.

Cross for Voluntary War Assistance   R
On 24 December 1915 the Grand Duke instituted a cross, virtually a revival of a similar award created in the Franco-Prussian War, for merit in voluntary nursing, and similar services.

Similar in shape to the Prussian Iron Cross, 39mm across, this bronze-gilt cross has a crown on the upper arm, while the lower arm has the arms of Baden (shaded for gold with a red *bend*); the dates, 1914, 1916, appear on the left and right arms respectively (one wonders if, in December 1915, the Germans thought that the war would be over in 1916, in the same way that we mistakenly dated our first medals for the Boer War, 1899–1900).

The central medallion has a Geneva cross, shaded vertically for red. The *rev* is plain except for the crowned ornamental F in the medallion. When awarded for merit at the front, an oak wreath appears between the arms of the cross, clear of the central medallion. The cross was also made in white metal, presumably towards the end of the war.

The 30mm ribbon is lemon yellow with 7mm red side stripes and 1mm white edges.

The War Merit Cross   R
Instituted on 9 September 1916, this cross was a mark of distinction for those who had rendered meritorious service to the army and the general welfare during the war. It is a Bath cross, but without ball finials to the arms of the cross, 37mm in diameter, in bronze-gilt (also in white metal gilt). The 15mm silvered medallion has, on the *obv*, a crowned griffin looking left and holding the shield of the arms of Baden. The *rev* has a crowned, ornamental F. A wreath appears between the arms of the cross, close against the medallion.

The ribbon, 30mm, is red with 3.5mm yellow side stripes and 2.5mm white edges.

The Medal of Merit

In September 1866 a medal of merit, in gold and silver, was instituted by Grand Duke Friedrich I, with a plain yellow ribbon. This was originally called the Civil Medal of Merit, but later became known as the General Decoration of Honour.

During the Great War it was frequently awarded, in silver-gilt (later in white metal gilt) and in silver (later in white metal), to NCO's and lower ranks for military merit, and in such cases it had the ribbon of the Karl-Friedrich Order (*qv*).

BAVARIA

Bavaria had existed as a duchy for close on a thousand years before it became a kingdom in 1806, when the reigning duke and elector became King Maximilian–Joseph I. With the abdication of King Ludwig III in November 1918, Bavaria became a Free State within the Weimar Republic.

EXISTING AWARDS

Military Order of Max-Joseph (1797)
* Order of Military Merit (1866)
* Cross of Military Merit (1866)
* Cross of Merit for Voluntary Sick Nursing (1901)
* Medal for Military Merit (1794/1849)

NEW AND AMENDED AWARDS

Order of Military Merit   R

Dating from 1886, this order had a full range of classes, with various ribbons, and, as an existing order, does not really come into our scope, except that by a decree of 10 November 1914, a special ribbon was authorised for military officials and other recipients of the order 'with swords', not actually in the army. This was in five equal stripes of black-white-blue-white-black, except for the 2nd class, which was black–blue–white–blue–black.

Owing to the shortage of precious metals, from the end of 1916 insignia which had previously been made of gold were now made of silver-gilt.

Cross of Military Merit

At the outbreak of war the badges of the three classes of the cross were made of copper, the first class being gilt, the second silvered, and the third class, toned copper (the first two classes having the centre enamelled). Towards the end of the war, the cross was made of a zinc alloy with a grey hue. Also, in the interests of economy, the width of the ribbon was reduced from 35mm to 30mm.

Order of Military Hygiene   R

King Ludwig III founded this order on 16 October 1914, for medical officers who had distinguished themselves in the care of the sick and wounded on the field of battle or in field hospitals. The order was awarded in two classes, and replaced the Military Hygiene Decoration founded in 1812.

The badge consisted of a white enamelled cross with widening arms, 43mm across, in gold for the first class (changed to silver-gilt towards the end of the war) and silver for the second class. The central medallion, in gold (or silver-gilt) for

97

both classes has, on the *obv*, the crowned cypher, L, on a blue ground, within a white circle, gold edged, with the date, 1914, at the top between scrolls; below are stylised laurel branches. The *rev* has the legend, FÜR/VERDIENSTE/IM/KRIEGE, in gold on blue, the outer circle having stylised laurel branches. The ribbon, 40mm, is that of the Military Max-Joseph Order, black with white inner and pale blue outer stripes, and a white pin-stripe edge. Originally the badges of both classes were worn on the left breast, but shortly after the foundation of the order the first class was designated to be worn at the neck, consequently an additional flattened ring was added to take the neck ribbon.

King Ludwig Cross
RP

On 7 January 1916 the King instituted the *König Ludwig-Kreuz*, as a mark of recognition of voluntary work of special merit at home, for the troops or for other welfare work.

Originally made of black iron and later of bronze, the cross was finally made of zinc, blackened. It measures 42 x 38mm, with slightly widening arms and slightly rounded outer edges. The oval medallion, 23 x 19mm, has the head of the King, left, on the *obv*, while the *rev* has the foundation date in two lines, 7.1./1916, on a background of the Bavarian lozenges.

The ribbon for men is 35mm wide, with the 19mm centre in horizontal stripes of blue and white, and 8mm blue edges. For women, the ribbon is 27mm wide (15mm centre), made up a bow.

Crosses with the same obverse and a similar reverse, the latter bearing the dates, 1868/1918, or 1818/26. v./1918, are not war awards but are, respectively, the Jubilee Cross for officers and NCO's of the 62nd Austrian Infantry, known as 'Ludwig III, König von Bayern' Regiment (to celebrate the 50th year of the regiment), and the Commemorative Cross for the Members of the Parliamentary Chambers (to celebrate the centenary of the Bavarian constitution). Both crosses were worn with a white ribbon with pale blue side stripes and very narrow blue edges; the Jubilee Cross ribbon was made up in triangular Austrian fashion.

a

b

Fig. 8   Bavaria: Cross of Merit for Voluntary Sick Nursing,
a – Crown and 1914 bar, for special merit; b – 1914 bar

Cross of Merit for Voluntary Sick Nursing – Bar: 1914
Instituted by Prince Regent Leopold in 1901 as an award for meritorious nursing services, both in war and in peacetime, this matt silver rounded cross, with a red Geneva cross on the central medallion, carries a date bar when awarded for war service.

From 8 July 1915 it was awarded with a bar, 32 x 5mm, bearing the year date, 1914 (*fig.* 8b). In cases of special merit the cross was awarded 'with crown', and a 20mm silver crown, showing five arches, was worn on the ribbon, in which case the date bar, 1914, was reduced to 20mm (and worn below the crown) (*fig.* 8a). Such awards were rare up to 1918, totalling only some 33, but immediately after the war about 200 were given, in 1919–20.

The ribbon for this cross was 35mm wide, described as of cornflower blue, with 6mm white side stripes, inset 1.5mm.

Medal for Bravery

In 1914 the title of the Medal for Military Merit was authorised to be changed to *Tapferkeitsmedaille* – Medal for Bravery – the name by which it was already popularly but unofficially known. This is the date by the authoritative writer, Georg Schreiber, both in his book, *Die Bayerischen Orden*, and *Die Tragbaren Ehrenzeichen des Deutschen Reiches*, but Dr Klietmann gives the date of the changes as 2 March 1918.

The medal had always been awarded in gold and in silver, but from the end of 1916 silver-gilt replaced gold in the higher class.

Although originally instituted in 1794, and renewed in 1849 (and thus not eligible for inclusion in detail), by virtue of the change in title, we have decided to include the description.

The medal is 34mm in diameter and the *obv* shows the bust of the renewer, left, in general's uniform, with his titles, MAXIMILIAN JOSEPH KOENIG VON BAIERN. The *rev* has a crowned lion standing to left, *regardant*, holding a shield in the left fore-paw and a sword in the right. The shield has the arms of Bavaria, *lozengy bendy* with an oval inescutcheon showing crossed swords and a crown.

The 35mm ribbon is black with white (inner) and blue (outer) edge stripes, with 1mm black outside edges.

BRUNSWICK

The duchy of Brunswick was a very ancient one, the country having been conquered by Charlemagne and was subsequently governed by counts and dukes. With the Napoleonic conquests, Brunswick was included in the kingdom of Westphalia in 1806, but was restored to the duke in 1815.

With other German states, Brunswick became a Free State in November 1918, and is now part of Niedersachsen (Lower Saxony).

EXISTING AWARD

Order of Henry the Lion (1834)

NEW AWARDS

Cross for Military Merit   RP

Originally founded in December 1879, this award was discontinued and was renewed on 18 August 1914. It was given, albeit sparingly, to sergeants and lower ranks for repeated and special acts of bravery.

The silver-gilt cross is of Bath type, but with very shallow V ends to the arms and no ball finials, plain with double lined edges. The 15mm central medallion bears the legend, KRIEGS–/ VERDIENST, with laurel branches below. On the *rev* are the crowned intertwined initials, EA (Ernst August). The ribbon is the same as that of 1879,

38mm wide, red with 5mm gold-yellow edges, like the ribbon of the Order of Henry the Lion.

Cross for War Merit

Duke Ernst August instituted this cross on 23 October 1914, originally in one class only, as an award junior to the Cross for Military Merit. The bronze cross is similar to the Prussian Iron Cross in shape, 30mm across, with the initials, EA, in the centre; at the top of the upper arm is a 5-arched crown, and at the bottom of the lower arm, 1914. The two lateral arms have oakleaf sprays. The *rev* has the inscription in gothic letters, **Für/Verdienste im/Kriege**.

The 30mm dark blue ribbon has 3mm yellow side stripes, inset 2mm, when awarded to combatants. From 17 November 1915 awards to non-combatants were made using a similar ribbon but with the colours reversed.

On 20 March 1918 the Duke instituted a first class of the decoration (the original award becoming the second class), for those who had already won the lower award and deserved further recognition.

The first class cross was in bronze, 40mm across, of the same design as the *obv* of the 2nd class, and with a plain *rev* which has the brooch pin for wear on the left side, without ribbon.

A special emblem was introduced on 20 March 1918 for combatant recipients of the 2nd class who had less than two years' unbroken field service. The emblem, worn on the ribbon of the decoration, is of oxydised bronze (or matt silver), 30mm tall x 23mm wide, with two sprig pins for fixing. It shows the salient horse of Brunswick, facing left, in a laurel wreath with crossed swords at the base and a five-arched crown above. (*fig.* 7c).

Cross of War Merit for Women

This award for special merit in nursing the wounded and similar philanthropic work, was founded on 13 September 1917. There was only one class, consisting of a dark bronze cross, 31mm across, with slightly widening arms, curved inwards at the ends; in the centre are the large figures, 1914. Between the arms of the cross is 4mm wide circle, 19mm in diameter; this bears the script initials, EA (Ernst August) at the upper left and lower right points, and VL (Victoria Luise) at the upper right and lower left. Outside the cross, above each of the pairs of initials, is a small 5-arched crown. The *rev* has the same details of design except that the arms of the cross carry the inscription, in four lines of gothic characters, **Für/aufopfernde Dienste/im/Kriege** (For devoted service in the war).

The ribbon, 30mm is sulphur yellow, with 3mm dark blue centre stripe and side stripes, 8.5mm apart and 2mm inset from the edge.

The Duchess Victoria Luise, wife of Duke Ernst August, was the daughter of the Kaiser.

THE FREE HANSE TOWNS – BREMEN, HAMBURG, AND LÜBECK

The Hanseatic League, dating from the middle ages, was originally formed by a number of port towns for mutual protection against Danish and Swedish pirates. By the end of the 14th century over a hundred cities were involved, but by 1630 only Bremen, Hamburg, and Lübeck retained the name of Hanse Free Towns, a status which had been recognised for centuries.

EXISTING AWARDS

None

NEW AWARDS

The Hanseatic Cross RP

The Hanse Free Towns of Bremen, Hamburg, and Lübeck, which instituted a joint medal in 1815 for the war against Napoleon, also created crosses of merit for the Great War, for serving or former members of the 75th Infantry Regt. (Bremen), 76th Regt. (Hamburg), and the 162nd II Battn. (Lübeck), for crews of the warships, *Bremen*, *Hamburg*, and *Lübeck*, for inhabitants of the three towns serving in other units, and for those serving in voluntary nursing auxiliary units in the three towns.

The crosses, all similar in design except for the coat of arms in the centre of the *obv*, were authorised by the governing bodies of the three towns, in Lübeck on 21 August, in Hamburg on 10 September, and in Bremen on 14 September 1915.

The design is a St. George cross, 40mm across, but with slight inward curves on the ends. It is of silvered copper-bronze, with the *obv* strongly enamelled in deep red with underlying radial lines and a narrow silver edge. The central medallion, 17mm, bears the appropriate arms; for Bremen, red with a diagonal silver key, wards at the top, pointing upwards; Hamburg is also red, with a triple-towered castle in silver, while Lübeck has a gilt centre with a black double-headed eagle with a small shield in the centre, horizontally divided, white over red.

The *revs* are all alike, plain silvered, with the central medallion lettered in gothic letters, **Für Verdienst** (curved, around the top of the medallion) /im/ **Kriege/1914** (For merit in the war).

The cross has a ring soldered at the top, in line with the edge of the cross; a small connecting ring links it to the 13mm ribbon ring. The ribbons are all red and white, 30mm (but other widths are found); for Bremen it has five white and four red stripes; Hamburg has 8mm red side stripes, inset 2mm from the edge; Lübeck's ribbon is half white, half red.

HESSE

During the middle ages Hesse was ruled by a Landgrave (a count of sorts). In 1567 it was divided into Hesse-Kassel and Hesse-Darmstadt, the former becoming an electorate in 1803, while the latter was elevated to a Grand Duchy in 1806. Hesse–Kassel was annexed by Prussia in 1866, while Hesse-Darmstadt retained its status until November 1918, when it became a Free State.

EXISTING AWARDS

Order of Ludwig (1807/1831)
Medals of the Order of Ludwig, for Merit (1850)
Order of Philip the Magnanimous (1840)
Order of the Star of Brabant (June 1914)
General Decoration of Honour (1843)

NEW AWARDS

Military Medical Cross

Originally instituted in August 1870, for the Franco–Prussian War, the *Militär Sanitätskreuz* was discontinued in 1876. It was reinstated on 12 August 1914 by

Grand Duke Ernst Ludwig for meritorious service in the medical branch of the army, and also for nursing services and transport of the wounded.

Holders of the 1870 cross who qualified for a Great War award received a bronze bar, 40 x 6mm, with the date, 1914.

The 1914 cross was first made of copper-bronze, but in January 1918 this was changed to coppered zinc. It is 45mm wide, with straight widening arms, the ends of which are shaped like a gothic arch. The motif is repeated on the arms of the cross. There is no central medallion; the *obv* has three lines of inscription in gothic characters: **Für/Pflege der Soldaten/1914**. The *rev* has the design of the 1870 cross, with a crowned L in the centre, and the date in gothic characters on the four arms, **Den/25ten/August/1870**.

Two ribbons were in use; the war ribbon for merit by medical officers, NCO's, and men, was 36mm wide, bright blue with 7mm red side stripes, inset 2mm from the edges (this was the ribbon of the General Decoration of Honour when awarded for bravery); and for other awards the ribbon was carmine red with 4mm silver side stripes, inset 2mm. From early 1918 narrower ribbons, 25mm wide were used.

Decoration of Honour for War Welfare Work
The Grand Duke created this award on 17 September 1915, for merit in war welfare work and for officers and other ranks in the medical services, for military merit but not in action.

The decoration is a bronze medal, 24mm in diameter, with the *obv* having a stylised 3-arched crown above the initials, ELE (looking like ECE, and indicating Ernst Ludwig, Elenore). The *rev* has the legend, **Für/Kriegsfür-/sorge** (For war care), in a laurel wreath bound at top and bottom.

The ribbon, 30mm wide up to January 1918, is carmine with 4mm white side stripes, inset 2mm; after January 1918 a 25mm ribbon was used.

War Decoration of Honour
The *Kriegsehrenzeichen*, a variation of the previous decoration, was instituted in June 1916, for merit in cases where the award of one of the higher decorations was not appropriate. The medal, 24mm in diameter, has the same *obv* as the previous medal, while the *rev* has the inscription, **Kriegs-/ehren-/zeichen**, within a wreath.

Originally made of bronze, from May 1918 coppered 'war metal' (a type of zinc) was used. The ribbon is the same as that for the previous medal.

Das Kriegerehrenzeichen
The name of this award does not translate easily into English, but TROOPS' DECORATION OF HONOUR is reasonably accurate. It was established by the Grand Duke Ernst Ludwig on his silver jubilee, 13 March 1917, for outstanding bravery by his Hessian troops in the front line. It consists of a black lacquered laurel wreath, in which are the entwined initials, EL, with a 3-arched crown above; at the base, binding the wreath, is a small panel with the figures, 25; these are all in silvered metal and pierced within the wreath. The badge has a pin on the *rev*, and is worn on the left side. It measures 46mm high by 38mm wide.

HOHENZOLLERN

The small Principality of Hohenzollern, absorbed into Prussia, was virtually only of importance in that the ruling house of Prussia and Germany emanated from Hohenzollern-Sigmaringen.

EXISTING AWARDS

The Princely House Order of Hohenzollern (1841)
Medal of Honour (1842)
Cross of Merit (1910, attached to the House Order)
Bene Merenti Medal (1910)

No amendments to existing awards or new awards were made during 1914–18.

NOTE:
The insignia of the Princely House Order are very similar to those of the (Prussian) Royal House Order of Hohenzollern, using the same ribbon – white with a narrow black centre stripe and slightly wider black side stripes. The badges of the former show, in the central medallion, the Hohenzollern white and black quartered shield, crowned, with the surrounding inscription: FÜR TREUE UND VERDIENST (For loyalty and merit). Those of the Royal Order have the shield placed on the breast of the Prussian eagle, while the surrounding inscription is the family motto: VOM FELS ZUM MEER (From the mountains to the sea).

LIPPE

Lippe, sometimes referred to as Lippe-Detmold from its capital, Detmold, to distinguish it from Schaumburg-Lippe, was a constitutional principality until November 1918, when it joined with Schaumburg-Lippe to form a Free State.

EXISTING AWARDS

The House Order of Lippe (1869)
Cross of Merit and Medals of Merit affiliated to the House Order
* Order of Leopold (1906)
* Medals of the Order of Leopold (1908)
Order of Bertha (1910. For women)
* Medal for Military Merit (1832)

NEW AND AMENDED AWARDS

Order of Leopold
In 1916 the design of the badges was altered. The blue enamelled Bath cross, which previously had a white central medallion with the red rose of Lippe, now had a red centre with a swallow, in a green circle lettered: FIDELITER SINE TIMORE (Loyal without fear) 1906, superimposed on a silver heraldic rose. In each of the angles of the cross is a large script capital L.

Medals of the Order of Leopold
From 1916 the gold (silver-gilt), silver and bronze medals could be given 'with swords' for war service awards.

Medal for Military Merit
The *Militär-Verdienst-Medaille* was originally founded in 1832, and in 1908 it was decreed that awards for merit in action should be distinguished by crossed swords on the ribbon.
As from 17 December 1914 the design was amended, with crossed swords

103

incorporated in the *obv*. The bronze medal, 36mm in diameter, has the entwined script Royal cypher of Fürst Leopold IV, with a crown above, with surrounding legend, DEM MILITAIR-VERDIENSTE, all within two oak branches with crossed swords in the base. The *rev* has the Lippe rose (not unlike our Tudor rose) within two laurel branches tied at the base. Suspension is by a ring.

The ribbon, 41mm wide, is red with 5mm yellow side stripes, inset 1.5mm.

War Cross of Honour for Heroic Deeds

Instituted on 8 December 1914, this bronze-gilt cross, rather like the Iron Cross in shape, 45mm across, has the Lippe rose in the centre, encircled by a laurel wreath, 23mm across and about 3.5mm wide, and with pierced inner angles to the cross. On the upper arm, outside the wreath, is the crowned initial, L; the left and right arms have the inscription, in two lines, FÜR/HELDEN (above) MÜTIGE/TAT (below); at the base of the lower arm is the date, 1914.

The *rev* is plain, with a pin for fixing to the left side of the tunic.

Cross for War Merit R

This was instituted at the same time as the previous item, and is of very similar design, in bronze-gilt, but only 41mm across, and with the usual ring suspension. The *obv* has the Lippe rose in the centre, with the crowned L above the wreath and the date, 1914, below, but the wide arms are plain.

On the *rev* the wreath shows only between the arms of the cross; the arms bear the inscription, in seriffed capitals (with the first and last words near the top and bottom edges) FÜR/AUSZEICHNUNG IM/KRIEGE (For distinction in war).

There are two ribbons, 34mm wide; for combatants it is yellow with 3mm red side stripes and 3mm white edges; for non-combatants it is white, with similar red and yellow edges.

War Medal of Honour R

Founded by Fürst Leopold IV on 25 October 1915, for men and women, at home or in enemy country, for merit in welfare work, especially in nursing, etc., this bronze–gilt medal is octagonal in shape, 33mm across. The *obv* has a representation of the Cross for War Merit, extending to the horizontal and vertical edges. The *rev* has the 4-line inscription, TREU BEWÄHRT/IN/SCHWERER ZEIT/1915 (Proved faithful in difficult times).

Two ribbons were used, of the same designs as those for the Cross for War Merit, but narrower, 25mm wide; for merit in enemy country, it is yellow with 2mm red side stripes and 3mm white edges, while for merit at home it is white, with red and yellow edges.

SCHAUMBURG-LIPPE

Schaumburg became a county in 1033, and was transferred in 1640 to Philip of Lippe, becoming a principality in 1807. It joined with Lippe-Detmold in November 1918, to form a Free State.

EXISTING AWARDS

The House Order of Lippe (1869)
* Gold and Silver Cross of Merit (1869)
Gold (silver-gilt) and Silver Medals of Merit (1869)

NEW AND AMENDED AWARDS

Gold and Silver Cross of Merit
The Gold Cross of Merit was made of gold (10 grammes) up to 1916, but in 1917 silver-gilt crosses (30 grammes and 20 grammes) made their appearance.

Medal for Military Merit   R
This medal, in silver and 30mm in diameter, originally dates from 1850, was awarded in 1870-71, and was reinstituted in August 1914. The *obv* has the entwined florid initials, GW (Georg Wilhelm, the original founder), with a three-arched crown above, within two laurel branches tied at the base. On the *rev* are two laurel branches, tied, with the inscription, FÜR/MILITAIR-/VERDIENST, in seriffed capitals above crossed cavalry swords.

The ribbon is 38mm wide, red with 8mm light blue side stripes near the edges. For merit in the face of the enemy, crossed antique swords, 35 x 10mm, in silver, were worn on the ribbon. On 25 October 1914, for cases of merit in nursing, welfare, etc., it was decreed that an octagonal silver emblem, 15mm in diameter, should be worn on the ribbon, with a red Geneva cross on white within a narrow black edge line (*fig.* 9a).

a   b   c

Fig. 9   a – Schaumburg-Lippe: Medal for Military Merit;
b – Saxe-Coburg-Gotha: 1914 bar to Medal of Merit;
c – Schwarzburg: 1914–15 emblem for Cross of Honour.

Cross for Faithful Service   P
On 18 November 1914 Fürst Adolph reinstituted the *Kreuz für Treue Dienste* (which had originally been created by Fürst Adolph Georg as the commemorative cross for 1870–71), intended primarily for officers and men of the regiments of which he was colonel-in-chief: the 2nd Kurhessischen Hussars, Regiment No. 14 of the Cavalry Division, the Westphalian Jäger Battn. No. 7, and the Rhenish Hussars Regt. No. 7.

The 35mm bronze-gilt cross has straight arms, slightly turned outwards at the ends (rather similar in shape to the British Military Cross but with wider arms). In the centre of the *obv* is an ornamental A with a small 5-arched crown above; the four arms of the cross bear the inscription in squat seriffed letters, FÜR/TREUE DIENSTE/1914. The *rev* is plain, polished. Suspension is by ring, but the cross was also occasionally awarded with a pin on the *rev* (and no ribbon) for wear as *Steckkreuz*; these latter were mainly given to royalty.

When awarded to combatants the 39mm ribbon was dark cornflower blue with a 4.5mm white centre stripe and similar side stripes inset 1mm from the edge; non–combatants received the cross with a white ribbon with 3mm red side stripes and lightish blue edges.

MECKLENBURG

The House of Mecklenburg claims descent from Genseric the Vandal, dating back to the 5th century A.D. In later years it became a dukedom or duchy, and in 1701 was divided into the two duchies of Schwerin and Strelitz. In 1805 the two states were elevated to grand duchies, but with the abdications of November 1918, they joined to form the state of Mecklenburg.

EXISTING AWARDS

The House Order of the Wendish Crown (1864 – a joint order shared by the houses of Mecklenburg-Schwerin and Mecklenburg-Strelitz)
* Medal of Merit (1904 – Mecklenburg-Strelitz)
Friedrich Franz-Alexandra Cross (1912 – Mecklenburg-Schwerin)

NEW AND AMENDED AWARDS

(1) MECKLENBURG-SCHWERIN

Cross for Military Merit   RP
This award was revived on 28 February 1915, and dated back to 2 August 1914 (having been originally instituted in 1848, and revived on several occasions, but discontinued).

The cross, 42mm across, is of cannon bronze, gilt, of a shape similar to the Prussian Iron Cross. The first class badge, worn as a *Steckkreuz* with pin (and no ribbon) was originally double sided and flat; the *obv* had the seriffed letters, FF (Friedrich Franz IV, Grand Duke) in the centre, crowned, and the date, 1914, at the bottom; the *rev* had the inscription on the arms, FÜR/AUSZEICHNUNG IM/KRIEG (For distinction in war). Later the first class badge was one-sided, with a curved surface.

The second class badge was the same as the original first class, but with a ring suspension. When awarded to women, however, a smaller cross was used, 33mm across.

During the war a change was made (the date for which I have not been able to ascertain) by which the original 'FF' *obv* became the *rev*, and the inscription now becoming the *obv*.

The normal ribbon for the second class badge was 36mm, pale blue with 3mm yellow side stripes and 3mm red edges (as the ribbon of the Mecklenburg Order of the Wendish Crown), but when awarded for special merit in philanthropic war work, the ribbon was red with 3mm light blue side stripes and 3mm yellow edges. The ribbon for the women's cross was made up into the form of a bow, and was 26mm wide, carmine red, with 2.5mm light blue side stripes and yellow edges.

Friedrich Franz Cross   R
Grand Duke Friedrich Franz IV instituted this decoration which bears his name, on 1 August 1917, as an award for special merit for both men and women who, in their daily work or in voluntary services, materially assisted in furthering the war effort.

The bronze-gilt cross, 41 x 32mm, has the lower arm longer than the upper one, which in turn is longer than the horizontal arms. The central medallion, 12mm in diameter, has two stylised F's, back to back. At the top of the upper arm is a tiny representation of the Wendish Crown, while at the bottom of the lower arm is the date, 1917. The arms of the cross are plain on the *rev*, while the *rev* medallion depicts the Cross for Military Merit (*qv*).

From the bottom of the lower arm spring laurel sprays which bend outwards towards the horizontal arms and then inwards towards the upper arm, level with the small crown.

The ribbon, 26mm wide, has yellow and red horizontal stripes, with 3mm yellow side stripes and 3mm pale blue edges.

(2) MECKLENBURG-STRELITZ

Cross for Distinction in War

Grand Duke Adolph Friedrich VI revived, on 11 August 1914, the decoration, *das Kreuz fur Auszeichnung im Kriege*, originally instituted in 1871 for all ranks but later discontinued.

The 40mm cross *patée* was made of silver until 1916, when it was changed to silvered bronze, which later was replaced by a lead alloy. The central medallion, 20mm diameter, has the ornamental initials, AF, interlaced with a 5-arched crown above, within a laurel wreath (in the outer circle); at the bottom of the lower arm is the incuse date, 1914. The *rev* has the three line inscription in the medallion, TAPFER/UND/TREU (Brave and loyal); another *rev* has the inscription, in two lines, FÜR/TAPFERKEIT (For bravery); this type was awarded only to those of princely rank.

The ribbon, 29mm wide, for conbatants is pale blue with 3mm yellow side stripes and 3mm red edges; for non-combatants it is carmine red, with 3mm pale blue stripes and 2mm yellow edges.

On 1 January 1915 the cross as described above became designated as the 2nd Class of the decoration, and a 1st Class was created on the same day. The cross, in the same size, has a pin fastener, as *Steckkreuz*, and was made of silver until 1917, but of silvered metal thereafter. Three types exist; one has FÜR/TAPFERKEIT in the centre, and the date, 1914, on the lower arm; a second type has the crowned cypher, AF, also with the date below; the third variety has TAPFER/UND/TREU in the centre and no date. The decree instituting the award describes it as the first of these three types, but Dr Klietmann, of Berlin (who is the leading authority on German awards) assures us that the other two are contemporary and genuine, although he has been unable to verify this since the state records were destroyed near the end of World War II.

A smaller version of the 2nd Class cross, 33mm across, was authorised on 17 June 1915, for awards to women, with the *obv* inscription, TAPFER/UND/TREU. Like the 1st Class badge, it was made of silver until early in 1917, when it was changed to silvered metal. The ribbon, made up into a bow for wear on the left shoulder, is 30mm wide, carmine red, with 2.5mm pale blue side stripes and 2.5 yellow edges.

Medal of Merit

The Grand Duke introduced a new design for this 30mm medal, on 1 January 1915, to replace the original design dating from 1904. It was issued in silver-gilt (the first type was in silver), later changing first to bright copper, and, towards the end of the war, to dark oxydised metal with a matt finish. The new design showed the bust of the Grand Duke, left, in uniform, with the surrounding titles, ADOLF FRIEDRICH VI – GROSSHERZOG VON MECKLENBURG – STRELITZ. The *rev* has the inscription, FÜR/VERDIENST, within two laurel branches.

The 28mm ribbon is carmine red with 5mm yellow side stripes and 3.5mm pale blue edges.

Adolf-Friedrich Cross

On 17 January 1917 the Grand Duke instituted an iron cross for men and women, to reward special merit in work and industry of all kinds furthering the war effort. In design it is similar to the Bavarian Ludwig's Cross, 40 x 38mm, with an oval medallion, 23 x 20mm.

The stubby arms are straight sided, widening slightly outwards, with shallow convex-curved ends. The *obv* has ornate interlaced initials, AF, with a 5-arched crown above, all within a laurel border.

The *rev* is lettered, FÜR/WERKE/DER/KRIEGSHILFE/1917 (For services in aiding the war).

The ribbon is 26mm wide, with five yellow and four carmine red stripes, and 1.5mm pale blue edges.

OLDENBURG

Like some other German states, Oldenburg has had a varied history, being annexed to Denmark in 1448, then ceded to Russia in 1773, but soon afterwards became a duchy under Duke Friedrich August. It was seized by Napoleon in 1811, but after his downfall Oldenburg regained independence and became a Grand Duchy. The Grand Duke abdicated in November 1918, and Oldenburg became a Free State.

EXISTING AWARDS

* The Order of Duke Peter Friedrich Ludwig (1838)
  Cross of Honour of the above order (1838)
  Red Cross Medal (1907)

NEW AND AMENDED AWARDS

Order of Duke Peter Friedrich Ludwig

This order, which has the designation of *Haus-und Verdienstorden* (House Order and Order of Merit), had a special augmentation authorised on 21 October 1918, for recipients of the order 'with swords' who also had received another order 'with swords' or the *Pour le Mérite*, consisting of the addition of two laurel branches flanking the cross, over the swords and the horizontal arms.

Friedrich August Cross   R

On September 1914 Grand Duke Friedrich August instituted the cross which bears his name, as a decoration for meritorious service, in two classes; the first class was only awarded to holders of the 2nd class, and, as a *Steckkreuz*, was worn in addition to the 2nd class.

The 1st class badge, 45mm across, was a black iron cross *patée*, with the initials, FA, on the 22mm central medallion. The top arm bears a crown, while the lower arm has the date, 1914. Between the arms of the cross, and clear of the medallion, is a laurel wreath. There is, of course, no ribbon.

The 2nd class badge is similar, but smaller, 39mm, with a 19mm central medallion. The *rev* is similar to the *obv* but without inscription. Suspension is by the usual ring.

On 20 September 1918 an augmentation was authorised for merit at the Front, consisting of a black iron bar, 34 x 6mm, lettered, VOR DEM FEINDE (In the face of the enemy), to be worn on the ribbon.

The ribbon for combatants is 35mm, a rich deep blue, with 5.5mm red side stripes; for non-combatants and for merit at home, it is red with 5mm blue side stripes, inset 1.5mm.

Medal for War Merit

The *Kriegsverdienstmedaille* was instituted on 21 November 1916, for women helpers over the age of 15, caring for the wounded, etc., and who had served for at least one year. On 9 May 1917 eligibility was extended to men and women equally, for meritorious service in industry connected with the war.

The medal is oval, 35 x 28mm, of black iron. The *obv* shows the head of the Grand Duke, left, with the surrounding inscription, FRIEDRICH AUGUST GROSSHERZOG VON OLDENBURG. The *rev* has only the four-line legend, in *sans serif* capitals, FÜR/TREUE DIENSTE/IM/WELTKRIEGE (For faithful service in the world war), with a small cross ornament of five dots at the top and bottom.

The ribbon, 30mm, is red with three blue stripes, 4mm wide and 8mm apart; for women, it is made up into a bow.

PRUSSIA

The most powerful of the German states, Prussia dates its history back to early times, when the lands of the Venedi were conquered by the Borussi, from whom the country acquired its name. Its history of military might and power, was closely tied up with the Teutonic Knights. The House of Hohenzollern came to power in 1415, as Margraves and Electors of Brandenburg, and ruled until 1918. Prussia became a duchy in 1618 and a kingdom in 1701. In 1871 the King of Prussia became Emperor of Germany, but with the Kaiser's abdication in November, 1918, Prussia became a Free State.

EXISTING AWARDS

Order of the Black Eagle (1701)
* Order *Pour le Mérite* (1667/1740)
* Order of Merit of the Crown of Prussia (1901)
Order of the Red Eagle (1705/1792)
Royal Order of the Crown of Prussia (1861)
Royal Hohenzollern House Order (1841/1851)
Order of Louisa (1814 – for women)
* Military Cross or Merit in Gold (1864)
* General Decoration of Honour (1814)
Military Decoration of Honour (1814)
* Red Eagle Medal (1835)
* Medal of the Order of the Crown (1888)
* Red Cross Medal (1898)
Soldiers' Medal of Merit (1835)

NEW AND AMENDED AWARDS

Order Pour le Mérite
A small change was made in the suspension on the badge early in 1915. For many years part of the V of the upper arm was filled in with gold sector, plain with a narrow raised edge and pierced to take the flattened loop through which the ribbon passes. But early in 1915 this sector was replaced by a narrow ornamental arched loop connecting the two sides of the V, similar to that in use in the 18th century.

In view of the change from gold to silver-gilt, in accordance with the Kaiser's order of 16 November 1916, there should be three types of badge for the Great War period – sector type in gold, loop type in gold, and loop type in silver-gilt, but it would seem that the sector type is also found in silver-gilt.

It might perhaps be mentioned that according to the statutes, the eagles between the arms should be *uncrowned* (which seems to have been an unexplained mistake, especially as on the Grand Cross, introduced in 1886, the eagles are crowned, as in the arms of Prussia). Certainly most of the badges have the uncrowned eagles, but examples exist with crowned eagles, including some of the 1810 period; modern examples with crowned eagles can only be regarded as incorrect copies.

NOTE:
The correct ribbon should be 57mm wide, black, with 7.5mm silver side stripes, inset

2mm (although in practice a narrower ribbon, about 30mm wide was used, for convenience of fitting under the uniform collar). The stripes were basically white, with thirty silver threads, showing in two staggered sets of fifteen, in 3mm warps. Modern copies of the decoration are often found with a 57mm black ribbon with 10mm side stripes containing fourteen silver threads, in two staggered sets of seven, in 1mm warps Apart from the incorrect width of the stripes, the effect is quite different, but collectors may have to use this ribbon, as the genuine weave may now be unobtainable.

Order of Merit of the Crown of Prussia

This very high award, instituted in 1901 in a single class with a blue sash with wide gold thread side stripes, and ranking between the Order of the Black Eagle and the Grand Cross of the Order of the Red Eagle, was occasionally awarded to generals, during the war, 'with swords'.

The Iron Cross   RP

It is not always realised that the Iron Cross – *das Eiserne Kreuz* – was a purely Prussian decoration (until Hitler revived it in 1939, as a German order); furthermore, it was not a permanent decoration like the Victoria Cross, but was discontinued after each of the wars during which it was awarded. Thus, after two earlier periods of award – for the war against Napoleon, 1813–15, and the Franco-Prussian war of 1870–71 – it was necessary for Kaiser Wilhelm II, in his capacity as King of Prussia, to reinstitute the Iron Cross, which he did on 5 August 1914.

There were three classes – Grand Cross, 1st Class, and 2nd Class, as on the two previous issues. The Grand Cross was awarded only four times (apart from one which the General Staff requested the Kaiser to assume for himself), and one of these, awarded to General Field Marshal von Hindenburg in December 1916, was augmented in March 1918 by the addition of an 8-pointed breast star, 84mm (one writer says 88mm), silver-gilt, with an Iron Cross, 1st Class, superimposed. As various writers differ in their quotations of the sizes of most insignia, and the Grand Cross of the Iron Cross is no exception; Hessenthal & Schreiber give the size as 63mm, while others quote figures varying from 58mm to 62mm. Similarly, ribbons are found in slightly varying widths, but Hessenthal & Schreiber give 57mm, unwatered black, with 10mm white side stripes, inset 3mm from the edge. The badge was worn at the neck.

The design of the decoration is a black painted iron cross *patée* (not a Maltese cross, as so often described – this has deep V cuts in the end of each arm, while the cross *patée* has straight ends to outward curving arms), set in a silver rim, 4.5mm wide (the inner 2mm being raised and the outer 2.5mm, flat). The *obv* has the seriffed capital, W in the centre, with the Royal crown above, on the upper arm , and with 1914 on the lower arm. The *rev* has the original design with, on the upper arm, the crowned initials, FW; in the centre are three oakleaves on a stem with acorns, and on the lower arm, the original foundation date, 1813.

The first class badge is a one-sided, plain silver-backed cross (with a vertical pin and claw), approximately 42mm in diameter, but minor variations occur. The *obv* has the black painted iron centre, set in a silver frame, and design as the *obv* of the Grand Cross. Sometimes the cross is flat, but more usually it is slightly convex, and occasionally a screw 'nut and bolt' stud fitting may be found instead of the pin. Semi–miniatures of 36mm or somewhat less, are sometimes seen; these are known as 'Prinzen' size crosses, and are supposed to be as awarded to the young royal princes, but could well be undress or evening wear crosses.

The details of the badge vary slightly according to the manufacturer, which is not surprising as a very large number were issued. The figures vary considerably, but Dr Klietmann gives 163,000 up to November 1918, and a further 55,000 up to 1924, making 218,000 in all.

The Iron Cross, 2nd Class, is also about 42mm in diameter, and like the Grand Cross, is a black cross set in a silver rim. The *obv* is the same as that of the two higher classes, and the *rev* as that of the Grand Cross. Suspension is by a thin silver ring. As with the 1st class, there is some minor variation in design, and occasionally one finds examples made all in one piece, blackened in the centre, with a *silvered* rim, probably made towards the end of the war or in early post-war inflation period.

The ribbon for awards to combatants is 30mm wide, black, unwatered, with 5mm white side stripes, inset 2mm from the edge; the ribbon for non-combatants reverses these colours – white, with black side stripes' this latter ribbon is sometimes referred to, even in some German publications, as the 'civil Iron Cross ribbon', but this is completely incorrect, as the Iron Cross was essentially a military decoration. However, many of the recipients of the white–ribboned cross were civilians, usually military officials serving with the armed forces, and some earned their cross 'not in action with the enemy'. I have even seen the white ribbon in Grand Cross width described as 'Grand Cross of the Iron Cross civil', but this is impossible, as the Grand Cross could not be awarded other than for fully military achievements; however, this ribbon did exist, and would have been worn by a Military Senior Official (civilian) who had been decorated with one of three Prussian orders (Red Eagle, Crown, or Hohenzollern Orders), 'with swords' or won in action, in a grade carrying a badge worn at the neck.

While the ribbon actually used on the Iron Cross, 2nd Class, was 30mm wide, as described above, the width used for the ribbon as worn through the buttonhole of the tunic was usually less than this, 25-27mm.

An order or 4 June 1915 instituted a bar for recipients of the 1870 Iron Cross, 2nd Class, who qualified for a further 2nd Class award in the Great War. This consisted of a silver bar, 33 x 7mm, with a miniature Iron Cross, 13 x 13mm, superimposed (*fig.* 10a). The bar was fitted with two sprigs for fixing to the ribbon, above the 1895 jubilee oakleaves, which themselves are worn on the ribbon just above the cross. The bar applied only to the second class; unlike a somewhat similar bar authorised in 1939, no provision was made for a bar to the first class.

Dr Klietmann gives the figures for awards of the Iron Cross, 2nd Class, as follows: up to 9 November 1918, approximately 5,000,000 plus some 3,000 with the white ribbon; from 9 November 1918 to 1924, about 196,000 plus some 10,000 with the white ribbon. These make a total of approximately 5,209,000 but estimates vary considerably. The late awards, made after the war, were presumably retrospective issues; Hessenthal & Schreiber have a note that 'the awards of the Iron Cross, interrupted in 1920, was resumed in 1923, and on 31 May 1924 was finally discontinued'.

Fig. 10   a – Prussia: 1914 bar to 1870 Iron Cross;
b – Saxony; Bar to Friedrich August Medal and Carola
Medal when awarded to women.

In recent years, as with many other German awards, both of Imperial times and of the Third Reich, copies of the Iron Cross have been flooding the market for collectors of German militaria. Some of these are rather crude in design and would hardly fool even a beginner, but others are dangerous and difficult to detect, particularly since some of the genuine crosses made towards the end of the war and up to 1924, were of poorer standards than the earlier ones. It is impossible to describe these differences, since several types of copies exist, and the collector is advised, if in doubt, to make a comparison with a known genuine example.

The Red Eagle Medal (Medal of the Order of the Red Eagle)
This medal was instituted in 1883; from September 1916, it was issued in zinc-gilt instead of copper-gilt, also the crown above the medal and the medal itself were struck all in one piece, instead of separately as previously.

The ribbon, 25mm wide with 5.5mm red-orange side stripes, 1.5mm inset, is often found (as is that of the order itself) in a wartime weave in which the side stripes are a deep reddish brown.

Medal of the Order of the Crown
As with the previous item, from September 1916, the medal was made in zinc-gilt instead of copper-gilt.

Military Cross of Merit in Gold
Dating from 1864, this high decoration for 'other ranks' for merit in action against the enemy, was awarded in gold prior to 1914, but from that year it was given in silver-gilt.

General Decoration of Honour
The *Allgemeines Ehrenzeichen* was issued in silver up to August 1918, after which it was in grey 'war metal', owing to the shortage of silver.

The Prussian Red Cross Medal
The 2nd Class, in silver and enamel, and the 3rd Class, in bronze, of this award (of which the 1st Class was, in fact, not a medal but a *Steckkreuz*), were circular medals, 33mm across, up to September 1916. But as from that date, by Order of 23 May 1916, the 3rd Class was not only successively struck in iron (1916–17), grey 'war metal' (1917–18), and white metal (1918–20), but was 'cam' shaped, 37 x 33mm,

with a solid triangular lug incorporated at the top of the medal. This was pierced for a small connecting ring linked to the usual suspension ring.

Cross of Merit for War Aid   RP

On 5 December 1916 this grey 'war metal' Bath cross (without ball finials), the *Verdienstkreuz für Kriegshilfe*, was instituted as a decoration for special merit to the Fatherland's war aid activities, for men and women, without distinction of station or rank. The first award was made to General-Field Marshal von Hindenburg.

The cross is 42mm in diameter, with a 20mm central medallion, lettered in the upper half, FÜR/KRIEGS-/HILFSDIENST, with, below, a curved pair of oak branches. The *rev* medallion has the entwined ornamental initials, WR, crowned. Suspension is by a ring, with a smaller link ring and a pierced sector in the V of the top arm of the cross. The 30mm unwatered ribbon has six black and five white stripes, with 1mm red edges. Like the Iron Cross, awards continued up to 1924, when the decoration was finally discontinued.

REUSZ

The Principality of Reusz consisted of a Senior Line and a Junior Line, who traced their ancestry back to Ekbert, Count of Osterode, in the 10th century. The Emperor Sigismund conferred the princely dignity on the reigning house in 1426. All the ruling Princes of Reusz were named (or took the name) of Heinrich (Henry).

EXISTING AWARDS

* Cross of Honour (1869)
* Gold Medal of Merit (1869 – affiliated to the Cross of Honour)

Cross of Honour

The ribbon for this award was plain amaranth red (crimson-purple), but from 9 January 1915 a special ribbon, 35mm, gold-yellow with 3.5mm red (inner) and 3mm black (outer) side stripes, inset 1mm, was authorised for awards *without swords* but given for wartime merit.

Dr Klietmann reports that on one solitary occasion, on 4 April 1918, the officer's cross was awarded bearing the date, 1914.

Gold Medal of Merit

The ribbon for this medal was also plain amaranth red, but from 9 January 1915 this was designated as the ribbon for peacetime merit; for war merit the ribbon was to be as described above for the Cross of Honour without swords.

Cross for War Merit

The *Kriegsverdienstkreuz* was instituted by Fürst Heinrich XXVII on 23 May 1915, in a single class, for officers, NCO's, and men, who held the Iron Cross, 1st Class, or who had distinguished themselves by bravery in action. The uniface *Steckkreuz*, worn below the Iron Cross, 1st Class, is 45mm across, in silver. The arms of the cross *patée* are enamelled black, with a narrow silver edge; the horizontal members bear the raised silver figures, 19–14. The central medallion, 18mm, is silver, with the crowned cypher, an antique H with XXVII below, in raised symbols. Two green laurel branches, tied at the base, encircle the cross, over the lower arm, under the horizontals, and with the tips over the top arm.

Medal for Devoted Service in Wartime

Fürst Heinrich XXVII founded this medal on 10 November 1915, to reward meritorious service in the field of philanthropic work in connection with the war. The bronze medal, 33mm in diameter, has for the *obv* a 5-line inscription in tall *sans serif* capitals, FÜR/TREUES WIRKEN/IN/EISENER ZEIT/1914 (For faithful effort in iron times), within an oak wreath. The *rev* has the crowned cypher, an antique H over XXVII.

The 30mm ribbon is gold-yellow, with 2.5mm red (inner) and similar black (outer) side stripes, inset 1mm.

The Waldorf-Astoria *Orden* – a usually authentic album of cigarette cards – states (card No. 269) that this medal was an award for women and girls, but Hessenthal & Schreiber (No. 1408) definitely quote it as being awarded to both men and women; we feel that the latter version is more likely to be correct.

THE KINGDOM OF SAXONY

After a long history as a fierce and warlike people, the Saxons were completely subdued by Charlemagne, c 765. Saxony became a duchy in 880, an electorate in 1180, a kingdom in 1806, and a Free State in 1918.

EXISTING AWARDS

Military Order of St. Henry (1736)
St Henry Medal (1796 as Medal for Military Merit; 1829 as St. Henry Medal)
Order of Albrecht (1850)
Order of Merit (1815) and Cross of Merit (1876)
Albrecht Cross (1876)
Cross of Honour (1876)
* Friedrich August Medal (1905)
* Commemorative Cross for Voluntary Sick Nursing (1870/1912)
* Carola Medal (1892)

NEW AND AMENDED AWARDS

Friedrich August Medal

Dating from 1905, for award to personnel not above the rank of *Feldwebel* (sergeant-major), or the civilian equivalent in official status, for meritorious service in war or peace, this medal could, from 22 May 1916, be awarded with a bar lettered WELTKRIEG 1914–16 (World War), for special merit at home. For men the bar was rectangular, 32 x 8mm, with rounded corners, and in the same metal as the medal, ie. either in silver or in bronze. For women the bar was an oakleaf (*fig.* 10b), exactly like the bars to the British Crimea Medal (from which it was obviously copied).

During 1918 the bronze medal was medal of coppered iron.

Commemorative Cross for Voluntary Sick Nursing

This cross, *das Erinnerungskreuz für Freiwillige Krankenpflege im Kriege*, was instituted on 1 March 1912 (after being discontinued from its original foundation in 1871, for the Franco-Prussian War), but on 11 October 1915 its title was changed to Cross of Honour – *das Ehrenkreuz für ...* etc. The *rev* was now dated 1914/1915 or 1914/1916.

Cross of Honour for Voluntary Welfare Nursing in War

On 31 March 1916 the previous decoration was re-named, with *Wohlfahrtspflege* replacing *Krankenpflege*. The *rev* was dated 1914/1916, 1914/1917, or 1914/1918.

Carola Medal

On 26 February 1915 a new design was introduced for the *rev* of this medal, with a 5-line inscription, GESTIFTET/FÜR/HILFREICHE/NÄCHSTEN-/LIEBE (Instituted for benevolent charity), within two branches of rue. Bars for war merit, rectangular for men and an oakleaf for women, both lettered, WELTKRIEG 1914–16 (as for the Friedrich August Medal), were authorised on 15 September 1915. For gold and bronze medals the bars were yellow brass, while for the silver medal it was of 'new silver' (presumably white metal). The bars are fixed to the ribbon by two sprigs.

War Merit Cross   P

King Friedrich August III founded this award on 30 October 1915, being a cross *patée* but with an elongated lower limb, 41 x 35mm (excluding the lug at the top). It was made of darkened bronze, with a bright outer edge, and a central medallion, 9mm in diameter. The *obv* bears the bust, left, of the founder, and the inscription, FRIEDRICH AUGUST, KÖNIG V. SACHSEN. On the top arm is a small crown, while at the base is the date, 1915. Between the arms of the cross, and clear of the medallion, is a laurel wreath, while at the top of the cross is a small ornamental lug, pierced for the suspension ring. The *rev* has the crowned cypher, FA, in ligate script; on the horizontal arms is the inscription, WELT-KRIEG (World War).

The cross is worn at the neck, from a 35mm grassgreen ribbon with 6mm white side stripes and thin yellow edge stripes narrowly edged on both sides with pale blue; this design cleverly combines the ribbons of two of the orders of Saxony – in the centre, the Order of Albrecht, and at each edge the ribbon of the Military Order of St. Henry.

SAXE-WEIMAR-EISENACH

The Grand Duchy of Saxe-Weimar-Eisenach dates from 1815, but it traces its history back to Johann Friedrich, Elector of Saxony, in the 16th century. Grand Duke Wilhelm Ernst abdicated in November 1918, and the country became a Free State. In 1920 it was absorbed into the Free State of Thuringia.

EXISTING AWARDS

House Order of Vigilance or of the White Falcon (1732)
Cross of Merit (1878)
* General Decoration of Honour (1902)

NEW AND AMENDED AWARDS

General Decoration of Honour

A small alteration was made to the *rev* at the beginning of the war, by adding the date, 1914, below the inscription, DEM VERDIENSTE (For merit).

The various grades appeared in different metals during the war, the 'gold' award came in silver-gilt, and later in gilt metal alloy; the silver medal was made originally in silver, but later in silvered alloy, while the bronze medal deteriorated to bronze alloy.

Wilhelm Ernst War Cross

The Grand Duke Wilhelm Ernst instituted this award on 10 June 1915, for members of the Grand Duke of Saxony Infantry Regiment (and also for those who had been transferred to other units) who had won the Iron Cross, 1st Class. The decoration is a white enamelled cross *patée*, edged gilt, 46mm across, with green laurel sprays crossing the horizontal arms and just overlapping the top arm; antique swords are set diagonally between the arms of the cross, and under the laurel sprays. In the centre is a gilt-rayed medallion, 20mm, with a white, gold lined, falcon (of the House Order), 24mm wide, thus its wings extend beyond the medallion. The *rev* is blue enamel, gilt edged, with the gilt monogram, WE, crowned; on the lower arm is the date, 1915. There is no ribbon as the cross was worn, like the Iron Cross, 1st Class, as a *Steckkreuz*, on the left side.

Decoration for Merit for Women

On 15th August 1915 the Grand Duke and the Grand Duchess, Feodora, jointly instituted the *Ehrenzeichen für Frauenverdienst im Kriege*, on the centenary of the Saxe-Weimar Women's Union. The first distribution of the medal took place in March 1918.

The decoration is an oval medallion, 48 x 36mm, in silvered 'war metal' (ie. zinc; it was intended to issue a silver medal, but war shortage prevented this). The *obv* has the heads, right, in low relief, of two Grand Duchesses, Feodora (in front) and Maria Paulowna. The surrounding inscription reads, round the upper half, FEODORA – MCMXV – MARIA PAVLOWNA – MDCCCXV. The lower half reads, GROSSHERZOGINNEN V. SACHSEN (Grand Duchesses of Saxony). The *rev* has the crowned cypher of entwined letters, EWF (Ernst Wilhelm – Feodora); below, in two lines, XV AUGUST./MCMXV. An inscription round the edge (from 10 o'clock downwards and round to 2 o'clock) reads: FRAVEN-VERDIENST-IM-KRIEGE.

At the top is an ornamental ring. The ribbon is 36mm wide, red, with 3mm green side stripes and 5mm white edges.

Cross for Merit in the Homeland During the War Years, 1914–18 R

Another decoration with a long title was instituted on 27 January 1918 – *das Verdienstkreuz für Heimatsverdienste während der Kriegsjahre 1914–18* – for special merit on the home front. It consisted of a grey 'war metal' (zinc, but it was also made in iron) cross, 48 x 42mm, with slightly widening arms, rounded at the ends. The lower arm is longer than the other three. The central medallion, 18mm, bears on the *obv* the head of the founder, left. Above the cross is a 5-arched crown with the suspension ring through the orb. The *rev* of the medallion has the three-line legend, FÜR/HEIMAT-/VERDIENST (For Homeland merit); at the base of the lower arm is the foundation year, 1918.

The ribbon, 31mm, unwatered, has a 13mm red centre, with three 3mm side stripes green (inner), yellow (centre), and black (outer).

SAXONY – DUCHIES

The associated duchies of Saxe-Altenburg, Saxe-Coburg-Gotha, and Saxe–Meiningen, all trace their ancestry back to the 15th century Elector Ernest, when the sons of the Elector Frederick II divided the states between them. The senior line then became known as the Ernestine Line. The duchies issued their own decorations and medals, but shared the common Saxe-Ernestine House Order. The duchies became Free States in 1918, and were absorbed into the Free State of Thüringen in 1920.

EXISTING AWARDS

* The Ducal Saxe-Ernestine House Order (1833)
* Cross of Merit and Medals of Merit in Gold and Silver, associated with the above order (1833)

Saxe-Ernestine House Order

Unlike most orders of the German States, this one continued to be awarded until November 1935.

An unusual amendment was introduced on the suggestion of the Duke of Saxe–Altenburg, when the 2nd class cross of the order could be awarded bearing the date, 1914, on the lower limb (*fig.* 11a), for distinguished military service *behind the lines*. Subsequently the crosses bore the dates, 1914 on the upper arm, and 1915, 1916, 1917, or 1918, on the lower arm; crosses are also found with both dates on the upper arm, ie. 1914/18.

Fig. 11   a – Saxe-Ernestine House Order: 1914 embellishment for House Order;
b – Saxe-Altenburg: 1914 bar to Medal of Merit;
c – Saxe-Altenburg: 1914–15 oakleaves for Duke Ernst Medal.

Cross of Merit of the Saxe-Ernestine House Order

The third type of this decoration, current in 1914, is a silver Bath cross, 37mm across, with or without swords between the arms, with a 17mm medallion showing, *obv*, the head of Ernest the Pious, left, within a wide oak wreath, cross-tied at the cardinal points. The *rev* has the arms of Saxony – horizontal bars with a diagonal stripe (*bend*) representing the Crown of Rue – surrounded by the motto, FIDELITER ET CONSTANTER (Faithfully and firmly). From autumn 1914, for war merit in the homeland, the date, 1914, appears on the *obv* upper arm; then followed in later years, 1915, 1916, etc., on the lower arm.

In Saxe-Coburg-Gotha only, a larger cross was introduced in 1916, 42mm across, with larger swords. This cross was also issued with the dates on the arms, as applicable, for war merit at home.

SAXE-ALTENBURG

EXISTING AWARDS

* Medal of Merit of the Saxe-Ernestine House Order (1833)
* Duke Ernst Medal (1906)

NEW AND AMENDED AWARDS

Medal of Merit of the Saxe-Ernestine House Order

Each of the duchies had its own version of the Medal of Merit, with several varieties of design over the eighty-odd years.

For merit at home during the war, a bar in silver-gilt or silver (according to the metal of the medal itself) was awarded, 27 x 10mm, bearing the date in large figures, **1914** (*fig.* 11b), with a top and bottom border of conventional rue (as in the Order of the Rue Crown).

Duke Ernst Medal

On 31 August 1915, Duke Ernst II authorised the award of a bar on the ribbon, bearing the date, **1914**, for special merit in voluntary nursing and welfare work.

For military merit crossed swords on the ribbon were authorised, while for a second award a crown was added.

The medal was normally awarded with a 31mm sky blue ribbon, with 6mm lemon side stripes inset 1mm (these are colours of the ruling house of Wettin), but it could also be awarded in special cases with the so-called 'war ribbon', being that of the Medal for Bravery, 32mm green with 4mm white centre stripe and side stripes, inset 2mm; there is usually a very narrow white edge, but this is due to the weave and is not part of the design.

The suite who accompanied Duke Ernst in the field were awarded the medal with a ribbon decoration of three silver oakleaves, the central leaf bearing the dates, 1914/15 (*fig.* 11c). If awarded for service in action, crossed swords on the ribbon were also given.

Duke Ernst Medal, 1st Class, With Swords

In place of the Duke Ernst Medal with swords, a new decoration, in the form of a *Steckkreuz* – a pin-fastened cross worn on the left side, like the star on an order – was introduced on 29 June 1918. Existing holders of the former medal could exchange it for the new one. The cross, of matt silver, 47mm across is of the *patée* type with a large central medallion, 33mm, with the head of the Duke, right, with the surrounding inscription, ERNST II HERZOG VON SACHSEN-ALTENBURG. Between the arms of the cross and near their ends, clear of the medallion, is an oak wreath over which (and between the arms) are crossed antique swords.

The *rev* of the medallion has the crowned cypher, E II, in a laurel wreath, but the remainder is plain.

Recipients had to be citizens of Saxe-Altenburg or members of the Thüringen Infantry, 153 Regt., and holders of the Iron Cross, 1st Class.

Medal for Bravery   R

To reward bravery by NCO's and men, the Duke instituted the Medal for Bravery on 20 February 1915. It was also given to those who had won the Iron Cross, 2nd Class. The medal, 30mm in diameter, was successively made of bright bronze, bronze zinc alloy, coppered zinc alloy, and 'war metal' of grey zinc. The *obv* shows a cross *patée* extending to the edge of the medal. In the centre is a shield with a half-round base, with the arms of Saxony (see Cross of Merit of the Saxe-Ernestine Order); on the top of the cross is a crown, while the horizontal arms bear the divided date, 19–14.

The *rev* has the crowned ducal cypher, E II. Suspension is by a thin ring through an eye soldered at the top of the medal, with a 32mm ribbon, at first grass green, but later bright green, with a 4mm white central stripe and similar side stripes, inset 2mm. There is usually a very thin white edge, but this is due to the weave and is not part of the design.

SAXE-COBURG & GOTHA

EXISTING AWARDS

* Medal of Merit of the Saxe-Ernestine House Order (1834)
* Oval Silver Duke Carl Eduard Medal (1905)

NEW AND AMENDED AWARDS

Medal of Merit

As with the Cross of Merit of the House Order, the gold (silver-gilt) and silver Medal of Merit could be awarded from 22 May 1915 with a bar, 26 x 8mm, bowed at the top, with the date, **1914** (*fig.* 9b), later **1914–15, 1914–16**, etc., for war merit in the homeland. It could also be awarded with swords for war merit in action, to recipients of the Iron Cross, 2nd Class. Some examples have the swords behind the dated bar, as in *fig* 9b, while others have them just above the bar.

The ribbon was that of the Saxe-Ernestine House Order, originally in a rich crimson-purple with a green side stripe near the edge, narrowly lined with black on the inner side, but in the later part of the war crimson-purple became a shade of lilac–red; some examples also have a lighter green for the side stripe. No doubt these differences were merely due to difficulties in getting correct dyes for ribbon manufacture.

Carl Eduard War Cross

Duke Carl Eduard founded this decoration on 19 July 1916, for members of the 6th Thüringen Infantry, 95 Regt. (also for officers, NCO's and men of this regiment who had been transferred to other units) who had been awarded the Iron Cross, 1st Class. Hessenthal & Schreiber report that only 87 were awarded, so genuinely awarded examples are quite rare, but specimens, either unissued or made for collectors, are not uncommon.

The silver cross, of Bath pattern but without ball finials, is 42mm across, with a 19mm central medallion bearing the crowned ducal cypher, CE, in antique capitals. A green enamelled laurel wreath, 30mm in diameter, is superimposed clear of the medallion.

The *rev* has the arms of Saxony in the circle, with the motto, FIDELITER ET CONSTANTER (Faithful and steadfast). There is no ribbon as the badge is a *Steckkreuz*, with a pin fastening.

Oval Silver Duke Carl Eduard Medal

This award for merit was instituted in 1905 in two classes, and was originally a circular medal, with a 25mm ribbon in the basic colours of the arms of Saxony, half black, half yellow. In 1911 it was changed to an oval medal, 39 x 33mm, with a crown above, 14 x 20mm.

On 22 May 1915 a date bar was authorised for war merit in the homeland, and date bars and swords for war merit in action, as for the Medal of Merit, (*qv*).

Decoration for Merit in the Homeland

On 19 July 1918 the duke instituted the *Ehrenzeichen für Heimatsverdienst*, for award without distinction of sex, rank, or civil standing, for merit in furthering the war cause on the home front. It is of the same design as the Oval Silver Carl Eduard Medal, but in dark bronze, with the bust of the Duke, right, in the uniform of the Prussian Guards. The surrounding inscription reads, CARL. EDUARD. HERZOG. V.

SACHSEN. COBURG. GOTHA. The *rev* has the arms of Saxony with the inscription above, FUER VERDIENST (For merit)

The ribbon is 25mm, black with adjacent side stripes of orange (inner, 2.5mm) and green (outer, 1.5mm), and a narrow black edge. The decoration is quite scarce.

War Commemorative Cross, 1914–18

In the summer of 1918 this cross *patée* was instituted, in dark oxydised copper. In the centre is the date, 1914, with the crowned ducal cypher, CE, above and a laurel branch below. The *rev* has the shield of Saxony in the centre. The ribbon is the same as the previous, black with orange and green side stripes.

According to Dr Klietmann, only a small number were awarded, and thus the cross is quite scarce.

SAXE-MEININGEN

EXISTING AWARDS

* Medal of Merit of the Saxe-Ernestine House Order (1833)

NEW AND AMENDED AWARDS

Medal of Merit

The Saxe-Meiningen variety of the Medal of Merit was similar to those of the other duchies, in gold (silver-gilt) and silver, 35mm in diameter, but with the head of Duke Bernhard, left, with the inscription, BERNHARD HERZOG ZU SACHSEN MEININGEN.

The *rev* depicts the reverse of the Cross of Merit of the Saxe-Ernestine House Order, with the motto, FIDELITER ET CONSTANTER.

In December 1914 a bar, 23 x 10mm, with the date, **1914**, was authorised for war merit on the home front, while in the Spring of 1915 a bar with crossed swords was instituted for awards won in action.

Cross for Merit in War   RP

This cross was instituted for officers on 7 March 1915, for special merit. It is an attractive decoration, 39mm in diameter, consisting of a bronze cross *patée* with curved ends to the arms, and with a conventional coronet (as in the Order of the Rue Crown) between each arm. The central medallion has the founder's initial, B. The cross is surrounded by an oak wreath, cross-tied at the cardinal points. The *rev* has the arms of Saxony in the centre, while the outer circle bears the inscription, FÜR VERDIENST IM KRIEGE 1914/15. An unusual feature is the *umlaut* on the U; instead of the usual two horizontal dots above the letter, they are vertical and appear within the U. Above the badge is a large 5-arched crown, 22mm tall. Later in the war the decoration was made in grey zinc.

The ribbon for combatants was 40mm wide at first, but later 30mm, black with yellow side stripes and white edges with small green squares. For non-combatants it was black with 6mm yellow side stripes, 3mm white outer side stripes, and 3.5mm green edges.

A few special awards were made, without ribbon, as *Steckkreuz*, with a pin fastening.

Medal for Merit in War   R

Also instituted on 7 March 1915, for NCO's and men, was the Medal for Merit in War, very similar to the Cross, 39mm in diameter, but not pierced between the arms of the cross and the wreath, ie. it is solid metal. There is no crown above the medal, but a small crown appears on the top arm of the cross.

The ribbons are the same as those for the Cross for Merit in War, and later awards of the medal appeared in grey zinc instead of the earlier bronze.

Cross of Merit for Women

The Duchess Charlotte instituted the *Kreuz für Verdienst von Frauen und Jungfrauen in der Kriegsfürsorge* on 3 March 1915, as an order for women, for special merit in war work.

The decoration is similar to the Cross for Merit in War, but 30mm in diameter, with a crown above, 17mm tall. In the medallion are three C's intertwined, while the surrounding wreath is of laurel. The *rev* is similar to the Cross for Merit in War.

The early crosses were in bronze, but later in grey zinc. The ribbon is unusual, being a double bow of two 15mm ribbons, one being half green, half white, with 1mm edges of the opposite colour, while the other is half black, half white, also with counterchanged edges. In some exceptional cases a 30mm ribbon was used, as for non-combatant recipients of the Cross for Merit in War.

SCHWARZBURG

The counts of Schwarzburg were the ruling family since the middle ages. In 1552 the two sons of Count Günther divided the estates into Schwarzburg-Rudolstadt and Schwarzburg-Sondershausen. The former became a principality (*Fürstentum*) in 1697, the latter in 1710. When the Sondershausen ruling line died out in 1909, the two principalities were both ruled by Fürst Günther of Schwarzburg-Rudolstadt. After becoming a Free State in 1918, Schwarzburg became a part of the Free State of Thüringen in 1920.

EXISTING AWARDS

* Schwarzburg Cross of Honour (1853, Rudolstadt; 1857, as an order for both states)
* Medal of Honour (1857, associated with the Cross of Honour)
* Medal of Merit (1899)
* Recognition Medal (1899)

NEW AND AMENDED AWARDS

Schwarzburg Cross of Honour

Although the first three classes could be awarded 'with swords' for merit in action since 1870/71, this distinction was not added to the 4th class until 21 August 1914.

On 19 January 1915 an oakleaves spray was introduced for special merit in war. This consists of three oakleaves, about 22mm high, in gilt, with the dates, 19–14–15, so arranged with the 19 high on the central leaf, and 14 at an angle and lower, on the left leaf, and the 15 similarly placed on the right (*fig.* 9c).

Medal of Honour

The oakleaves spray, as above, was also introduced on 19 January 1915 for the gold (silver-gilt) and silver Medals of Honour, made in the appropriate metal. This was, in fact, instituted on the 25-year jubilee of the reign of Fürst Günther, for special merit.

Medal of Merit

The gold (silver-gilt) and silver Medals of Merit date from 1899, originally for arts, science, commerce, agriculture, etc., but were extended on 21 August 1917 to reward merit at home for the war effort, with a ribbon bar, **1917**.

The ribbon for arts, science, etc., was 26mm ultramarine blue with a 3.5mm white centre stripe and similar white edges, but from 1 January 1918 it was awarded with a plain deep blue ribbon, which was, in fact, the one used previously by Schwarzburg–Sondershausen.

Anerkennungs-Medaille

The title of this medal does not easily translate into English, except as Recognition or Commendation Medal, and was given for good services. It had been instituted in 1899, in Schwarzburg-Rudolstadt, and was similar to the previous medal, but in silver or bronze, with the head of the prince on the *obv*, but with two entwined G's, crowned, on the *rev* (instead of DEM/VERDIENSTE). As with the previous medal, a bar, **1917**, was authorised, and the ribbons were, first pale blue with white centre stripe and white edges, and from 1 January 1918, plain dark blue.

Silver Medal for War Merit

Originally created for the Franco-Prussian War, 1870/71, and then discontinued, this award was re-instituted on 21 August 1914 for *Feldwebels* (Sergeant-majors) and lower ranks. At first in silver, but later in silvered metal, but later in silvered metal, this 40mm medal has the entwined cypher of two G's, with crown above, and 1914 below (described by Hessenthal & Schreiber on the plates as the *obv* and in the text as the *rev* – the former is probably correct), while the other side has VERDIENST/IM/KRIEGE (Merit in war), in a wreath of laurel branches, tied at the base.

The 28mm ribbon, for merit in the face of the enemy, was dark blue, with 3mm yellow edges and centre stripe; for war merit but not in action, it was dark blue with 3mm yellow side stripes, 0.5mm inset. For military auxiliaries the ribbon was plain dark blue.

Anna Louisa Award of Merit

Fürst Günther instituted this award for women on 19 February 1918, for outstanding war work. It is an oval medal, 40 x 32mm, in matt oxydised silver. The *obv* has the entwined cypher, AL, with crown above, and 1918 in a curved panel below. The border, with oak branches in the base, is lettered, VERDIENST UMS VATERLAND (Merit towards the Fatherland). The *rev* is plain.

For merit in wartime the ribbon was 28mm, dark blue with 3mm yellow side stripes, 0.5mm inset. In October 1918 a peacetime ribbon appears to have been authorised, dark blue with narrow white/orange/white edges. Some authorities state that this ribbon was not authorised and was never made, but the author has a small piece, 25mm wide, with three 1mm edge stripes, through the kindness of Dr Klietmann, who states that just one metre was made for the Schwarzburg Chancellery.

WALDECK

The principality of Waldeck, associated with Pyrmont, was established in 1682. After becoming a Free State in November 1918, it was absorbed into the Free State of Prussia in 1929.

EXISTING AWARDS

* Cross of Merit (1857)
* Cross of Honour (1899)
* Gold Medal of Merit (1899)
* Silver Medal of Merit (1878)

(The last two were associated with the Cross of Merit, which was virtually an order rather than a decoration).

NEW AND AMENDED AWARDS

Cross of Merit
By an order of March 1915, crossed swords set between the arms of the cross, were authorised for awards won in action.

Cross of Honour
As above, crossed swords were authorised in March 1915. The normal ribbon for this award was the same as that for the Cross of Merit – 33mm, orange-yellow with 3mm red (inner) and black (outer) edge stripes, inset 1mm. The ribbon for awards 'with swords' was altered to 33mm, white with 2mm yellow (inner), red (central), and black (outer) edge stripes, inset 1mm.

Gold Medal of Merit
The Gold Medal, made in silver-gilt from 1899 to 1917, became gilt alloy in the latter year. Crossed swords, for awards won in action, were authorised on 27 March 1915, and these were set above the medal. The ribbons were the same as those for the Cross of Honour, but 26mm wide. The gilt alloy medals are thicker than the earlier silver–gilt ones.

Silver Medal of Merit
As for the former medal, crossed swords above the medal were authorised from March 1915. From 1917 silvered alloy replaced silver, and the alloy medals are thicker than the silver ones.
  The same ribbons were used as for the previous medal.

Friedrich-Bathildis Medal
Fürst Friedrich instituted this award on 24 December 1915, for recognition of wartime merit at home for men and women, in the fields of philanthropy and auxiliary war work.
  The medal is in bronze, 38mm in diameter, and shows two heads, left, of the Fürst and Fürstin; the inscription is, left, FRIEDRICH . BATHILDIS, and, right, F.u.F.z.W.u.P. (Prince and Princess of Waldeck and Pyrmont). The *rev* has a 5-line inscription in a 23mm stylised wreath of palm leaves, with a heart at top and bottom: FÜR/TREUES/WIRKEN/IN/EISENER ZEIT/1915 (For loyal effort in hard times).
  Suspension is by a long lug at the top of the medal, with a 36mm ribbon, red with 3mm gold thread (inner) and black (outer) edges.

WÜRTTEMBERG

Like most of the other German states, Württemberg has a long history dating back to before the middle ages. It became a duchy in 1494 and an electorate in 1803. The Elector Friedrich assumed the title of King in 1805. In 1918 the country became a Free State.

EXISTING AWARDS

Order of the Crown (1818)
Order of Friedrich (1830)
* Order of Military Merit (1759 as Mil. O. of Carl; since 1806 as Order of Military Merit)
Order of Olga (1871)
* Medal for Military Merit (1794)
* Cross of Merit (1900)
Karl Olga Medal (1889)

NEW AND AMENDED AWARDS

Order of Military Merit   R
Prior to 25 September 1914 the ribbon was plain dark blue, but on that date it was changed to yellow with 6.5mm black side stripes, 2mm inset, and in special cases the order could be awarded with a crown above the cross.

From 6 November 1917, when the ribbon only was worn it carried a small gilt wreath, enamelled green, thus distinguishing the ribbon from that of the Medal for Military Merit.

Medal for Military Merit
As with the previous order, on 25 September 1914 the ribbon was changed from plain dark blue to yellow with black side stripes (Hessenthal & Schreiber give the date of the change as 8 April 1914). Late in the war the width of the ribbon was reduced to 26mm with 4mm black side stripes.

The medal was awarded in two classes, gold and silver. In the early part of the war the gold medal was made in 14ct gold, and the silver medal in good quality silver, but later the gold was reduced to 8ct, and the silver to one-third silver and two-thirds alloy.

From 30 November 1917 the ribbon of the gold medal, when ribbons only were worn, was distinguished by a gilt wreath. The gold medal was automatically awarded to recipients of the Iron Cross, 1st Class.

Cross of Merit
Established in 1900, and the highest decoration prior to the institution of the Wilhelm's Cross, the Cross of Merit could be awarded 'with swords' from 29 January 1915 to holders of the Iron Cross who were of Württemberg nationality. The swords are placed saltirewise between the arms of the cross.

Wilhelm's Cross   R
On 13 September 1915, King Wilhelm II of Württemberg instituted the *Wilhelmskreuz* as a decoration, ranking above the Cross of Merit, for men who had given specially meritorious service during the war. It was awarded in four categories – with swords and crown; with swords; for war merit on the home front; and for special merit in public welfare.

The cross 'with swords and crown' is a *Steckkreuz*, ie. worn without ribbon, with a back pin. It is of dull oxydised bronze, a cross *patée* with convex ends to the arms. The central medallion, 22mm, has a gothic monogram w, in an oak wreath. On the lower arm is the date, 1915. Between the arms are crossed antique swords and above the cross is a 5-arched crown. The *rev* is plain.

The cross 'with swords' is similar in design but without the crown above; instead it has a small crown on the top arm of the cross. The *rev* has a two-line inscription, KRIEGS/VERDIENST (War merit) in a closed wreath of oakleaves. The ribbon, 34mm wide, is yellow with 3mm black side stripes and 1.5mm black edges, with a 4mm yellow stripe between.

When awarded for merit on the home front, the cross is similar but without the swords, while that for special merit in public welfare does not have 1915 on the lower arm and the *rev* has no inscription. Both have the ribbon already described.

These last three crosses, according to a note in Hessenthal & Schreiber, are fitted with a vertically pierced (*von oben nach unten gelochte*) eye or lug, to which the ribbon ring is connected by a small link ring; they tell us that copies of the cross exist with a poorer arrangement, in which the ribbon ring is linked directly to the eye on the top of the cross. The descriptions are somewhat obscure, and as we have not had the opportunity of seeing both types, the note is quoted only for what it appears to be worth.

Charlotte Cross   R
King Wilhelm II instituted the *Charlottenkreuz* on 5 January 1916, in honour of Queen Charlotte, for merit in nursing the sick and wounded, or in general war welfare work at home or in the field.

The matt silver cross *treflée*, 40mm across, has a 13mm central medallion with the entwined initials, CW. The *rev* has the date, 1916, in a circle. During the latter part of the war, the cross was made in an alloy of 50% silver.

The 33mm ribbon is yellow with two black side stripes, 1.5mm (inner) and 3.5mm (outer), inset 1.5mm. For women recipients it is made up in bow form.

Turkey

The Turkish Ottoman Empire, ruled by Sultans, dated from 1299 AD. For some years prior to 1914, Germany had been making her influence felt in Turkey, and German officers had been training the Turkish army. Following a treaty of alliance signed on 1 August 1914, Turkey entered the war on the side of the Central Powers on 28 October 1914, when Enver Bey made a naval attack on Odessa without a declaration of war.

EXISTING AWARDS

   Nichan-i-Imtiaz (Order of Merit) (1879)
* Order of the Mejedie (1852)
* Order of Osmanieh (1862)
* Imtiaz Medal (Medal for Bravery) (1883)
* Liakat Medal (for Merit) (1891)
   Red Crescent Medal (1912)

NEW AND AMENDED AWARDS

Order of the Mejedie: Order of Osmanieh
From 1915 these orders could be awarded 'with swords' to military personnel.

Imtiaz Medal

This medal, associated with the order, Nichan-i-Imtiaz, and dating from AH1300 (AD1882/3), was awarded for bravery and distinguished service. During the Great War it carried swords (sabres, with hand guards) below a bar with (AH) date **1332** (1914/15 AD) (*fig.* 12a). Recipients were also automatically entitled to the War Medal (*qv*).

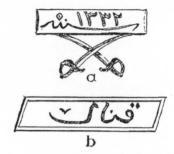

Fig. 12   Turkey: a – War service bar to Imtiaz and Liakat Medals;
b – Engagement bar to the War Medal.

Liakat Medal

Awarded for merit, the Liakat Medal was also given with crossed sabres (as above) during the Great War, and recipients were similarly entitled to the War Medal

War Medal   P

Much has been written about this decoration, which has been variously (but erroneously) described as the Turkish Star, the Gallipoli Star, the *Eiserner Halbmond* (Iron Crescent), etc. It has also been erroneously described as of two classes, one for officers, in enamelled silver, and one for other ranks, in painted base metal. We understand, from a letter from the Turkish Ministry of Defence and from the researches of Dr K-G Klietmann (of Berlin), that the War Medal is a decoration (not a general service award), instituted on 1 March 1915, for distinguished war service, in a single class. Recipients of the Imtiaz Medal or Liakat Medal were entitled to receive it, and it could be awarded to personnel of the army, navy, and nursing services, both of Turkey and its allies, for bravery and war merit.

The decoration as issued, is an iron, zinc, or other base metal, five-pointed star, point uppermost, approximately 55mm across, with flattened ball finials, crudely enamelled or lacquered red. In the centre is an upturned crescent enclosing the toughra or sultan's sign-manual, above the date, 1333 (1915 AD). The crescent, toughra, date, and the narrow edges of the star are unpainted. The *rev* is plain with a poor pin fastener.

The badge was worn pinned to the left side, without ribbon, but from a photograph of Mustafa Kemal Pasha (Kemal Ataturk), it would appear that he wore his on the right side, owing, no doubt, to the large number of insignia on the left side. A ribbon was authorised for wear in the 2nd buttonhole (like that of the Prussian Iron Cross) or on a ribbon bar. This is 30mm wide, red with 5mm white side stripes, inset 2mm, for combatants, and with the colours reversed for non-combatants.

Other varieties of the War Medal are found, of a better style of manufacture, and were undoubtedly privately made to meet the requirements of recipients, particularly officers. These are usually of silvered metal, properly enamelled red, with a narrow silver edge (which is sometimes slightly ornamented); some have the crescent, toughra, and date superimposed, while others have them integrated with the star itself. Unlike the poor originals, these copies (which are certainly made for wear, and not just specimens for collectors) are often slightly convex and have a better pin fastening. One variety is possibly British made since the *rev* is lettered 'B.B. & CO.'on the pin bar. Dealers' lists often describe these better specimens as '1st Class' or 'Officers' badges'. but it must be accepted that they are merely better-style copies for those who chose to buy them.

It should be noted that various editions of Taprell Dorling's *Ribbons & Medals*, from page 59 of Part II (first published in July 1918) to page 338 of the 1974 edition, give the date on the star as '333' (and illustrated thus in the 1918 edition), and also incorrectly indicate that the decoration was worn with the ribbon attached to the pin.

From correspondence from several collectors, published in Spink's *Numismatic Circular* during 1974/75, it appears that larger-sized stars exist, measuring 80-85mm across, against the 56mm of both poor quality original and the silvered metal and enamel, better quality star often encountered (although some examples of both are known measuring 52-54mm in diameter). These would seem to be unofficial insignia, probably made for foreign recipients, to enhance their appearance.

Also from this correspondence, it appears that at least three battle bars or clasps exist, but again it is not known if they are official; two were found on the ribbon attached to an old Turkish uniform of the Great War period, and would appear at least to have been contemporary. The bars (*fig.* 12b) are in white metal, of parallelogram shape, 41 x 9mm, inclined to the right, with a narrow border and inscriptions in Turkish indicating (we understand) respectively, CHANAQ QILA (Fort of Chanaq; equivalent to what we call the Dardanelles or Gallipoli actions), and QAFQAS (Caucasus);a third one, from another source, reads SINAQ (Suez). We have also heard of (but have not seen) a bar alleged to read the equivalent of 'The Canal'. These bars are for the attachment, not to the medal, but to the ribbon as worn diagonally from the buttonhole.

Dr Klietmann, in an article in *The Medal Collector* (May 1961) reports that some German ribbon bars have a metal crescent on the ribbon, but this is unofficial. Incidentally, in this article, which is a full survey of this award, Dr Klietmann does not mention any battle clasps.

Ukraine

In their struggle for independence, the Ukrainian National Republic, proclaimed on 20 November 1917, signed a separate peace with the Central Powers at Brest Litovsk on 9 February 1918, although a Ukrainian Legion had been fighting for Austria throughout the war. They had then asked Germany and Austria for assistance against the Russian Bolsheviks.

A number of decorations and other insignia were instituted, some of them long after the war, but most of these must be regarded as unofficial or semi-official. Also many of them relate to actions occurring after the Great War, but the one described below appears to be authentic and relevant.

Cross of the Legion of the Ukrainian Sich Riflemen (1914-18)
The legion was formed from Ukrainians in Galicia, in August 1914, to fight with the Austrian 2nd Army (For details of their history, see *The Medal Collector* for May 1965).

The cross, which comes in two sizes (the larger, 44mm across, for parade wear, and the smaller, 37mm, for formal wear) is in bronze-gilt and blue enamel. It consists of a narrow Greek cross, ornamented with diamond-shaped motifs on each arm; at each extremity is a large diamond with ball finials on its three outer corners; these diamonds are inscribed (in old Slavonic letters), У, С, С, 1914 (UKRAINSKICH SICHOVICH STRILTSIV – Ukrainian Sich Riflemen). The arms of the cross are joined by what can be described as four T's, forming a diagonal cross with their vertical members and a diamond-set square with their cross members (*fig.* 13).

Fig. 13   Ukraine: Cross of the Legion of the
Ukrainian Sich Riflemen.

There seems to be some doubt about the ribbon, but we understand that it was probably in yellow and blue horizontal stripes, with yellow edges; these are, of course, the Ukrainian colours.

All members of the legion were entitled to the decoration.

NOTE:
The Combatant's Cross of the Ukrainian Sich Riflemen (1918–20) was apparently created by a veterans' organisation in 1940, during the German occupation of Poland, and although it relates partly to activities during the last part of the Great War and to immediately subsequent events, it does not appear to be eligible for inclusion here. Details will be found in *The Medal Collector* for May 1965.

3
The Neutral Countries

Denmark

The ancient kingdom of Denmark, together with the other Scandinavian countries, remained neutral or non-belligerent during the Great War. No medals or decorations were awarded or instituted by the Danish government in connection with the war except the Slesvig Medal of 1920, but the Danish Red Cross issued one, described below.

Slesvig Medal, 1920   R
Following a promise made in 1864, but rejected by the Prussian victors, that a plebiscite should be held to determine whether the population wished to return to Denmark, such a plebiscite was held after Germany had lost the 1914–18 war, and this was supported by the British and French governments. There was an overwhelming majority and Slesvig was returned to Denmark. During the plebiscite the 1st Battn. Sherwood Foresters and the 22nd Bn. Chasseurs Alpins served in Slesvig and the medal was awarded to all ranks.

Instituted on 15 April 1920, the medal is in silver, 28mm in diameter. The *obv* has the head of the King, right, with the name and title, CHRISTIANUS X REX DANIAE. The *rev* bears the two-line inscription, SLESVIG/1920, under a 5-pointed star, within two branches of oak tied at the base.

The ribbon is 27mm wide, in three equal stripes, red, white, red.

Danish Red Cross Medal for Aid to Prisoners of War   R
This medal was instituted on 16 August 1919, and was approved by King Christian X for award to those who gave aid over a long period to prisoners of war during 1914–19. The medal is rare, as only 566 were awarded.

The decoration consists of a silver laurel wreath, 34mm in diameter, and 6mm wide, bound at the top (the binding incorporates the lug which holds the suspension ring). Inside the wreath is a red enamelled Greek cross; the quadrants between the angles of the cross and the wreath are pierced. The *rev* has a four-line inscription on the cross: 1914/DANSK KRIGS/FANGEHJAELP/1919 (Danish aid for prisoners of war).

The ribbon is 27mm wide, white with 8mm red edges.

The Netherlands

The Netherlands remained neutral throughout the Great War, and thus had no campaign or victory medals. Troops were, however, mobilised in case of attack.

Mobilisation Cross, 1914–1918   RP
On 2 February 1924 the National Committee *Herdenking Mobilisatie*, 1914 (Commemorating the Mobilisation) instituted the *Mobilisatiekruis* for (a) all those who had worn an official Dutch uniform during the period, August 1914 –

November 1918; also all regular and reserve personnel of all categories who had served under arms at home or in overseas territories, on land or at sea, and (b) all civilians who served under the military control, replacing servicemen, on recognised duties of defence, guard duties, etc.

The cross, 32mm in diameter, is of bronze with convex ends to the arms, and bundles of arrows between the arms as symbols of the power of unity. The top and bottom arms of the cross show, respectively, 1914 and 1918, while the horizontal arms have AUGUSTUS, NOVEMBER. The *rev* bears the words, MOBILISATIE-VREDE-EER (Mobilisation, peace, honour).

The ribbon, 30mm wide, is Nassau blue with narrow red, white, and blue edges (3 x 2.5mm), the red stripe being on the left on each side; the sets of edge stripes are separated from the blue centre by a 1mm white stripe.

By an Army Order No. 396 of 26 November 1924, Queen Wilhelmina authorised the cross to be worn in uniform, after long service medals and before foreign awards. Recipients had to purchase their crosses, but these cost only 46 cents (at that time, approximately 3.75p).

The White Mobilisation Cross, 1914–1918

This cross, normally in German silver (but examples are found in proper silver), has the same *obv* as the previous item, but the *rev* has the words MOBILISATIE – WAARDEERING (Mobilisation – appreciation), and the ribbon, 27mm, is white with 7.5mm edges of red, white, and blue, as before.

It was instituted on 10 September 1927, for those who had given specially meritorious voluntary service. Like the bronze cross, it could be worn in uniform.

NOTE:
There is a similar cross with an orange-yellow centre to the ribbon, with the red/white/blue edges, which often confuses collectors. This is the Cross of Merit of the *Nationale Bond 'Het Mobilisatiekruis'* (National Union of the Mobilisation Cross), instituted 11 August 1939, and awarded for service to the Union.

Amsterdam Burgerwacht Medal, 1918   R

Struck in silver and in bronze, 41mm in diameter, this medal was worn at the neck, on a red/black/red ribbon (the colours of Amsterdam), by officers of the Amsterdam Burgerwacht – similar to our Home Guard.

The *obv* shows a member of the Burgerwacht, armed, with the surrounding inscription, TER VERDEDIGING DER VOLKSVRIJHEID (In defence of the liberty of the people). The *rev* has the crowned arms of Amsterdam with the legend, VRIJWILLIGE BURGERWACHT, 1918 (Volunteer Civic Guard).

The silver medals worn by the commanding officers have the arms of the city enamelled (red, black, red vertical stripes, with three white diagonal crosses on the black stripe), while those of Sector Leaders and Under Sector Leaders were not enamelled.

The edges were engraved, HOOFDBESTUUR, SECTOR-COMMANDANT, or ONDER–SECTOR-COMMANDANT, respectively.

Amsterdam Burgerwacht Medal of Honour, 1918   R

The medal, 41mm in diameter, was struck in silver-gilt, silver, or bronze. The *obv* has the crowned arms of Amsterdam, with the inscription, VRIJWILLIGE BURGERWACHT, 1918. The *rev* has an inscription within a stylised wreath of oak and laurel leaves, IN DANKBARE/HERINNERING/AANGEBODEN AAN …/ VOOR/KRACHTIGEN STEUN EN/ GROOTE MEDEWERKING/VERLEEND AAN/DE AMSTERDAMSCHE/BURGERWACHT (Presented to … in thankful memory for vigorous support and co-operation given to the A'dam Civic Guard).

The ribbon, like that of the previous item, is in three equal stripes, red, black, red. The recipient's name was either engraved or impressed, and some examples are known with the arms enamelled.

Amsterdam Burgerwacht Cross for Ex-Mobilised Men, 1923   R

This bronze cross, 35mm diameter, was instituted in 1923 for members of the Burgerwacht who were mobilised during the Great War.

The arms of the cross have 'cut off' corners, and are lettered, DRAAGT (left), ELKANDERS (bottom), LASTEN (right) (Bear each other's burdens). The central medallion has, within a stylised laurel wreath, an armed soldier, with tower and houses in the background; the *rev* is plain. The ribbon is pale blue, with narrow yellow/white edges. There is a bronze bar on the ribbon, lettered, TER VERDEDIGING DER VOLKSVRIJHEID (In defence of the liberty of the people), with engraved dates of the recipient's service, 1914–1915, 1914–1916, 1914–1917, or 1914–1918; in the last case the bar also has a crown.

Fort Honswijk Medal, 1915

This bronze medal, 28.7mm in diameter, is unofficial, but was struck for about 300 men who formed the garrison of Fort Honswijk, in Gelderland, and part of the North Holland Water-Line – one of the Dutch lines of defence.

The *obv* has two crossed cannon and two crossed rifles, under which is the inscription, 'WIJ HANDHAVEN' – BEZETTING-FORT-HONSWIJK ('We maintain'. Garrison, Fort Honswijk). Around is an inscription is old Dutch, adapting a line from the national anthem, HET VATERLANDT GHETROUWE ZIJN WIJ TOT IN DEN DOET (We are loyal to the Fatherland unto death). The *rev* has a central inscription, TER HERINNERING AAN HET EERSTE BEZETTINGSJAAR, 1914–1915 (In memory of the first year of occupation), around which is *N. H. WATERLINE** STAAT VAN OORLOG* (North Holland Water–Line, state of war).

The 27mm ribbon has a wide centre stripe of blue with 4mm red (outer) and 1.5mm white (inner) edges. The medal is also known without a ring for suspension.

Fort Honswijk Reunion Cross, 1934

In addition to the medal described above, some 286 of the recipients received a memorial cross at a reunion of the garrison in 1934, also an unofficial award.

The bronze cross, 41 x 41mm, is a Bath cross, with ball finials to the points, and with a laurel wreath between the arms, clear of the central medallion. In the shallow angles of the ends of the arms is a scallop-like ornament. The arms are lettered, PLICHT (top), TOE/WIJDING (left), ZELFVER/LOOCHENING (right), KAMERAAD/SCHAP (bottom) (Duty, devotion, self-denial, comradeship). The central medallion shows the main gate of the fort, with HONSWIJK above; the arms of the *rev* are lettered, HULDE EN/DANK VAN (top), VOORM./BEZETTING (left), VAN FORT/HONSWIJK (bottom), 1914/1915 (right) (Homage and thanks of the former garrison, etc.). In the centre is WIJ HANDHAVEN – REUNIE 1934.

The ribbon is 31mm wide, blue with a narrow silver-grey centre stripe and 1.5mm similar side stripes, inset 1.5mm.

One cross was struck in gold for the former Fort Commandant, Lt. Col. A. Captijn.

NOTE:
It is fully appreciated that these unofficial awards should not really be included, especially as there are many such from other countries which have equal claims, but in the case of these Dutch awards little, if anything, has been written about them, and since collectors who have heard of them frequently asked for details, they have been included.

4

The Emergent Nations

Czechoslovakia

Czechoslovakia became an independent state on 28 October 1918, comprising the Czech state of Bohemia, Slovakia, Silesia, Moravia, and Carpathian-Ruthenia.

NEW AWARDS

War Cross   R
A decree of 7 November 1918 instituted the War Cross for military bravery between 27 July 1914 and 28 October 1918. A further decree of 7 July 1919 extended the period, to include subsequent operations against the Poles, at Teschen in January 1919, and against the Hungarians, in Slovakia in June 1919.

The unusual design, in bronze, of four interlaced circles symbolises the union of the newly-liberated areas (for some reason, Carpathian-Ruthenia seems to have been omitted); at the top is the double-tailed rampant lion of Bohemia; to the left is the chequered eagle of Moravia; to the right is the Silesian eagle; at the base are the three mountains and double-barred cross (as the Cross of Lorraine) of Slovakia (*fig.* 14a). The *rev* has the entwined letters, čs, in a design of linden, or lime, leaves. For crosses awarded to Silesians, who were of Germanic origin, the lime leaves were intended to be replaced by oak leaves, but were probably never issued.

The ribbon is red, narrowly edged with white and with three narrow white stripes, all with a pin-stripe of red.

The cross was awarded in a somewhat similar manner to the French Croix de Guerre. For a Unit Citation in an Army Order a spray of lime leaves was worn on the ribbon, while for a Unit Citation in an Army Corps or Divisional Order a single lime leaf was worn. Originally there was no emblem to indicate an individual citation, but a decree of 22 June 1919 instituted a silver star for an Army Order citation and a bronze star for one in an Army Corps or Divisional Order. If entitled to both types, sprays or leaves were worn above stars on the ribbon.

Medal of the Revolution   R
On 1 July 1918 the Provisional Government in Paris created a medal for all volunteers of the Czechoslovak army who enlisted before the date of the proclamation of the Provisional Government, and for others, nationals or allied subjects, who had rendered military or political services in assisting Czechoslovakia's gaining her independence.

The medal is in the form of a bronze-gilt Greek cross but with curves replacing the angles of the arms, with a nude horseman on a prancing horse, left, holding a flag. Behind the cross is a circular riband, almost at the outer edges of the arms, lettered, VZHURU/NA/STRAZ/SVOBODNY/NARODE (Keep good watch, you free nations). The *rev* shows an allegorical winged female figure holding above her head a stone block or panel inscribed, ZA/ZVO/BODU (For liberty), which she is about to hurl onto the snakes at her feet. The encircling riband bears the dates, 1914, 1918 (*fig.* 14b).

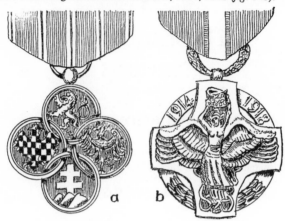

Fig. 14   Czechoslovakia: a – War Cross;
b – Medal of the Revolution *rev.*

Above the medal is a large oval wreath, for the 38mm red ribbon with a 5mm white central stripe flanked by 1mm blue stripes.

Bars are fixed by sprigs on the ribbon, in respect of actions, etc., and we have a note of the following: for Czechs fighting in Russia – ZBOROV, BACHMAČ. SIBIŘ, and Č.D. (The Čzech Brigade); for those serving with the French – ALSACE, ARGONNE, PERONNE, and L.E. (Foreign Legion); for those fighting with Italian units – DOSS'ALTO and PIAVE, and for those in Serbia – SERBIE. In addition, a small emblem with the number of the regiment in which the recipient served was worn on the ribbon.

Order of Liberty
This order was instituted in August 1918 by the Council of Soldiers in the Czechoslovak-Russian Army. Only two nominal awards were made, both post-humously, to two officers, one Russian and one Czech, but no actual insignia were issued. However, it appears that a ribbon, red-black-red in equal stripes, was manufactured and sold as that of the Order of Liberty.

Jan Žižka Medal or Medal of the Order of Liberty
This decoration was founded by the same Council of Soldiers as the previous item, in 1918, for acts of bravery by Czechoslovakian Corps in Siberia. It was awarded to 22 officers and men of the 6th Foot Regiment. The Provisional Government in Paris did not confirm either the Order of Liberty or this medal (although it was allowed to be worn), and so General Šefánik instituted the Order of the Sokol in lieu.

There were three classes, distinguished by bronze stars on the ribbon – two for first class, one for second, and no star for the third class (which was awarded for exceptional military services other than in action), but only the second and third classes were awarded, and only twenty-two medals in all.

The medal, 36mm in diameter, is of bronze, silvered. The *obv* has the portrait of Jan Žižka of Trocnov (a 15th century patriot), left, while the *rev* has the circum-scription, ČESKOSLOVENSKÉ VOJSKO (C-S Army); below, the medal is numbered, and in the centre, in a spray of lime leaves, is ZA SVOBODU (For liberty).

Suspension is by two silvered chains to either a wide or narrow bar, with a ribbon of appropriate width, red with narrow black velvet stripes sewn on.

Order of the Sokol

Werlich, in his *Orders and Decorations of all Nations*, shows this decoration as the Order of the Falcon; *Sokol* is the Czech word for falcon, but it is such a well-known word in Czech national culture that we prefer to retain it rather than to translate the title of this order.

The Provisional Government, established in Paris, confirmed this order in October 1918, for officers of the Czechoslovak Expeditionary Corps in Siberia under General Štefánik. Like the Jan Žižka Medal, this unofficial order was tolerated and was worn by entitled recipients.

The decoration is a 40mm cross of five arms (one pointing downwards) with widening arms, curved at the ends to form a broken circle, enamelled blue with white edges. The central medallion, in the same colours, has three mountains with four birds flying above (*fig.* 15a). The *rev* is white with the monograms, čs, in blue between gilt laurel branches and the date, 1918.

Fig. 15 a – Czechoslovakia: Order of the Sokol;
b – Slovakia: "Substitute" Cross for the Great War,
1914–18, 1st Class.

Above the cross is a small wreath of lime leaves, as a suspension ring, and if awarded 'with swords', these are worn crossed on the wreath. The ribbon is red with a narrow white centre stripe and narrower white side stripes.

Victory Medal   RP

The bronze medal has a winged Victory with head turned, left, and arms raised, holding an olive branch and a sword, point downwards. The *rev* has a shield with the crowned lion rampant, double-tailed, of Bohemia charged with the escutcheon of Slovakia; to left and right are narrow ribands inscribed, 1914, 1919, while ten lime leaves surround the shield. The outer edge circle is lettered, SVĚTOVA VALKA ZA-CIVILISACI (The world war for civilisation). The usual 'double rainbow' ribbon is used. Two types of the medal exist, one in dark bronze with the signature of the artist, O ŠPANIEL, and the other in light bronze and without the signature.

Order of the White Lion   R

Although not instituted until 7 December 1922, as an award for foreigners only, this order was granted retrospectively for services during the war, in connection with the gaining of independence and the formation of the Republic of Czechoslovakia.

There were five classes – grand commanders, grand officers, commanders, officers, and knights – following the usual routine, the first wearing the badge from a sash over the right shoulder, also a star on the left breast; the second and third classes wore a neck badge and (for the second class) a breast star; the fourth and fifth classes wore the badge on the left breast, with a rosette on the ribbon of the fourth class.

The badge is a cross of five arms, each with three points and ball finials. The arms are enamelled deep red, with a lime leaf between each. In the centre of the cross is the Czech lion rampant, crowned and double-tailed, with the shield of Slovakia on the shoulder. The *rev* has the monogram, ČSR, in a circle bearing the motto, PRAVDA VITEZI (Truth prevails). The five arms, enamelled red, each bear the shield of one of the provinces – Bohemia, Moravia, Silesia, Slovakia, and Carpathian-Ruthenia. Above the cross is a wreath of lime leaves, bearing two crossed swords for military awards and palm leaves in other cases.

The ribbon is red with white side stripes. The breast star of the two highest classes has silver rays with a central medallion of the Czech lion with the surrounding motto, PRAVDA VITEZI.

Commemorative Cross for Volunteers, 1918–19

This cross was instituted in 1938 for those who participated in the actions in Slovakia against the Hungarian troops of Bela Kun.

It consists of a bronze cross *patée*, approximately 36mm across, with a narrow edging to the arms; a central shield bears the two-tailed Czech lion. The *rev* has the central inscription, V TĚŽKYCH DOBACH (In hard times), with the dates, 1918, 1919, at the top and bottom respectively. Two types of cross are recorded, one having the details rather more sharply struck.

The ribbon, usually unwatered but a watered variety may be found, is pale blue with red side stripes narrowly edged with white.

Commemorative Medal for the Battle of Zborov, 1917

In 1947 this medal was issued on the 30th anniversary of the Battle of Zborov, in Russia. It is in silver, and shows the head, left, of the first President of Czechoslovakia, Thomas Masaryk, wearing the peaked cap associated with him. At the sides is the motto, PRAVDA VITEZI (Truth prevails). The *rev* is lettered, ZBOROV 1917–1947, with the colours of the three foot regiments who fought against the Germans in the battle.

The ribbon is red, with the central third in the colours of the Russian Cross of St. George – orange with three black stripes.

Commemorative Medal for the Battle of Bachmač, 1918

In 1948 a bronze medal was issued on the 30th anniversary of the Battle of Bachmač in 1918. The *obv*, lettered BACHMAČ, shows a half-length figure of a soldier, right, with a rifle. The *rev* is inscribed: PAMETNI MEDAILE, 1918, 1948 (Commemorative Medal); below is a lime leaf spray over a scroll.

The ribbon is that of the red and white striped War Cross (1918), the central third being orange with three black stripes, as with the previous medal.

Slovakia

Cross for the Great War, 1914–1918   R

Under German Nazi influence. the puppet Slovak government instituted, in September 1942, 'substitute' medals and decorations to replace those earlier awarded to Slovak citizens by 'foreign' governments – meaning ones under which Slovaks had served the before the formation of, or during the early days of, the post-war state of Czechoslovakia – but excepting those of Germany and Austria (which were considered as 'friendly', not 'foreign').

One such award was the little-known Cross for the Great War, for details of which we are indebted to the second volume of *Orders, Decorations, Medals, and Badges of the Third Reich*, by David Littlejohn and Col. C. M. Dodkins, and to Mr Vaclav Měřička, of Prague.

This is a straight-armed cross *patée*, struck in both gilt and silver, enamelled black, with the dates, 1914, 1918, on the horizontal arms, while the Slovak Cross – one vertical and two horizontal members – appears on both the top and bottom arms. Between the arms of the cross are crossed swords (*fig.* 15b).

There were three classes of both the gilt and the silver cross, identified by their ribbons; these are all basically white *moiré*, with narrow black stripes, as below. On the ribbon is a pair of flatly crossed swords with a miniature of the cross in its appropriate metal superimposed; this emblem is worn not only on the ribbon bar, but also on the full ribbon with the decoration attached.

Gilt Cross,	1st Class -	3 black stripes (For those who had any of the highest Austrian or German Orders).
	2nd Class -	2 black stripes (For those with lower classes of these orders).
	3rd Class -	1 black stripe (For those with only one order, or the Austrian Cross for Military Merit and the Gold or Silver Medal for Bravery).
Silver Cross,	1st Class -	3 black stripes (For those with the Bravery Medal and *Signum Laudis* in silver).
	2nd Class -	2 black stripes (For those with the Karl Truppenkreuz and the Bronze Medal for Bravery).
	3rd Class -	1 black stripe (For participants with no decoration).

Owing to the very complicated system, the decoration was subsequently withdrawn.

Estonia

Under the terms of the Treaty of Brest Litovsk, Russia renounced the provinces of Livonia, Estonia, and Finland, on 3 March 1918, although Estonia had already declared herself an independent state a week earlier, on 24 February 1918.

NEW AWARDS

Order of the Cross of Liberty   R
This order was established on 24 February 1919, a year after Estonia had gained her independence (although Guadagnini, in *Storia degli Ordini Equestri*, gives the year of institution as 1920). It was in three grades, each grade having three classes; the first grade was for war merit, the second for bravery, and the third for civil merit.

The badge is a Latin cross *potent*, ie. with a т (or crutch) end to each arm, and with the lower limb slightly longer than the others. The cross is edged in gold, with a thin gold centre stripe to each arm, couped. The first grade cross is enamelled white and has a black medallion, with a gold rim; the second grade is enamelled black, with a red medallion, while for the third grade the cross is blue with a white medallion.

When awarded to military personnel, the medallion bears an antique E above the arm holding a short sword, while awards to civilians have a larger E, but no arm or sword (*fig.* 16a). It is difficult to sort out all the varieties, and examples which have appeared in auction sales seem to vary in size, eg. 45 x 28mm, 40 x 31mm, and 36 x 30mm, while some appear to be in black iron, without the gold border or thin centre stripes. Also details of the *rev* are scanty; Werlich does not mention the *rev*, some auction sale descriptions mention just the date, 1919, while others give it as 21.II.1919.

The ribbon varies with the grade, and all are in the Estonian national colours; for the first grade it is black, with white (inner) and blue (outer) edges; for the second grade it is blue, with white (inner) and black (outer) edges; for the third grade it is white, with black (inner) and blue (outer) edges.

War of Liberation Medal, 1918–20 R
This bronze medal, 28mm in diameter, shows a soldier standing, right, guarding his family and home; at the right are the words, KODU KAITSEKS. The *rev* has crossed swords and a laurel branch, with 1918–1920 above and a scroll below, lettered, EESTI WABADUSSÕJA MALESTUSEKS.

The ribbon is in equal thirds, blue, black, blue, made up in triangular form, Austrian fashion. The medal can be found with a small bow in the same colours, on the lower point of the ribbon; this indicates that the recipient was wounded in action.

This medal is probably the same as the Independence Medal, 1918 (listed in the first edition of this book), as we understand that 'liberation' and 'independence' are indicated by the same word in Estonian, the title of the medal being *Eesti Wabadussõja Malestusmärk*. The medal formerly described as the Independence Medal, 1918, with the arms of Estonia on the *obv*, and the date, 24.II.1918, on the *rev*, now appears to be the Medal of the Order of the Arms of Estonia, instituted in 1936 to commemorate the proclamation of independence (hence the date on the *rev*), and was awarded in recognition of national constructive work, military and civil. Thus both the order and the medal fall outside the scope of this work.

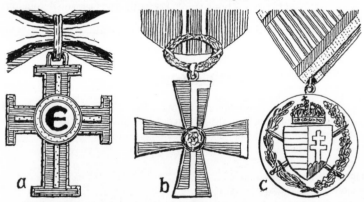

Fig. 16   a – Estonia: Order of the Cross of Liberty, Civil, 3rd Grade;
b – Finland: Cross of Liberty, Civil, 4th Class;
c – Hungary: War Commemorative Medal, for Combatants.

White Cross of the Civic Guard
This decoration was instituted on 19 June 1929 for members of the Civic Guard who had given distinguished or meritorious service, and was widely awarded to officers

and men who took part in the War of Liberation.

It was in three classes, worn on the left breast, but we only have a description of the 3rd Class. Measuring 46 x 39mm, it is a gold edged, white enamelled Latin cross (ie. with the lower arm longer) with V cuts in the ends. In the centre is a silver eagle looking right, with wings expanded but drooped, holding a sword and supporting a yellow shield with the three blue lions *passant guardant*, the arms of Estonia. The eagle is superimposed on a gold sword, point downwards. The *rev* has a white central medallion with the date, 11.XI.1918, the date of the founding of the Civic Guard.

The ribbon, 37mm, is cornflower blue with 5mm yellow side stripes edged on each side with 1mm, and inset 2mm.

Finland

For eight centuries Finland had been alternating under Swedish and Russian rule, and now, with the overthrow of the Czarist regime, she fought for and gained her independence, following the Treaty of Brest Litovsk in March 1918, between Germany and the Russian Bolsheviks.

NEW AWARDS

Cross of Liberty R

This, the first Finnish decoration (later to become the Order of the Cross of Liberty) was instituted on 4 March 1918, the day after the signing of the Treaty of Brest–Litovsk, on the suggestion of General Mannerheim, to reward bravery and meritorious service in the War of Independence. It was in two divisions – military, with swords, and civil; it could also be awarded with brilliants, or with Red Cross (for medical personnel).

There were five classes: grand cross, for lieutenant-generals and above; 1st class, for colonels; 2nd class, for captains; 3rd and 4th classes, for subalterns and other ranks, for bravery in the field. A breast star of five points (originally with two points uppermost) was worn by recipients of the grand cross.

The badge is a gold St. George cross, enamelled white for the grand cross, 1st and 2nd classes, with a gold swastika superimposed so that the vertical and horizontal arms are in the centre of the arms of the white cross, while the short right-angled ends occupy half the ends of the white arms. In the centre is a blue circle with an heraldic double white rose. (The swastika is obviously, in view of the date, unconnected with the emblem of the later German Nazis). The *rev* is plain white enamel, except for the date in gold, 1918.

Above the cross is an oval gold laurel wreath, and when awarded 'with swords', this is embellished with two arms in armour, each holding a sword. Medical personnel would be awarded the 4th class, with a Geneva cross superimposed in the centre, on the rose.

The sash ribbon for grand cross, 102mm wide, is yellow with a 3mm red stripe inset 2mm from each edge. For the 1st class badge (worn at the neck) and the 2nd class, narrower ribbons were used, 41mm and 31mm respectively, of the same colours and design. For the 3rd and 4th classes, the ribbon was also 31mm wide, red with two white central stripes, each 2mm wide and 4.5mm apart.

The badges of the 3rd and 4th classes with swords were similar in design to the above, but of blackened iron, with the swastika and rose in silver-gilt for the 3rd class and in silver for the 4th class. The dates on the *rev* are of the same material as the swastikas. For the civil division of the 3rd and 4th classes (without swords) the crosses were of blue enamel with silver-gilt or silver embellishments. At this period the same ribbon was used as for the military division (*fig.* 16b).

Medal of Liberty   R

Associated with the Cross of Liberty, and instituted at the same time, was the Medal of Liberty, in two classes, also for subalterns and other ranks, for bravery in the field. The first class was in silver and the 2nd class in bronze, 29mm in diameter. The *obv* has the head of the crowned Finnish lion, left, brandishing a sword in its raised paw. On the edge is (at top) URHEUDESTA, and (at bottom) FOR TAPPERHET (For Bravery – in Finnish and Swedish). The *rev* has a laurel wreath enclosing the inscription, SUOMEN/KANSALTA/1918 (From the people of Finland).

The ribbon, 31mm wide, is blue for the 1st class, with 1.5mm white side stripes inset 2.5mm; for the 2nd class it is red with 4mm yellow side stripes, inset 1mm (in practice the red edge is usually wider).

Order of the White Rose   R

The order was created on 28 January 1919 by General Mannerheim, with the statutes being confirmed on 16 May 1919, in five classes: commander grand cross, commander 1st class, commander 2nd class, knight 1st class, and knight 2nd class. Associated with the order are two decorations entitled Finland's White Rose Badge and Finland's White Rose Medal, the latter in two classes (*qv*).

The badge is a gold St. George cross (silver for knight 2nd class), enamelled white, with a crowned head of the Finnish lion, left, brandishing a sword, in each angle of the cross. The small central medallion is blue enamel but almost completely filled with a white heraldic rose. The *rev* is plain.

When awarded 'with swords' for bravery in the field, two crossed swords were set above the cross (later they were placed *in saltire*, under the lions in the angles).

The ribbon is a rich dark blue, 110mm wide for the sash of grand cross, 52mm for the commanders' neck ribbons, and 32mm for the knights. Commanders grand cross and 1st class also wore a breast star, silver, five-pointed; that of the grand cross has the three intermediate rays (between the five main clusters of seven rays) in gold. Originally the stars had two points uppermost, but in August 1936 this was changed to one point uppermost. The central medallion is similar to that of the badge, with a black outer circle lettered in gold, ISÄNMAAN HYVÄKSI (For the good of the Fatherland). Awards 'with swords' have crossed swords on the stars.

Finland's White Rose Badge (or Decoration)   R

This decoration was originally, in effect, a sixth class of the order, being awarded to under-officers after fifteen years of irreproachable service. It was of the same design as the knight's badge of the order, but wholly of silver (later the rose was enamelled white in a blue circle).

From 28 December 1920, the White Rose Decoration was decreed by the President to be reserved for award to ladies for distinguished service.

The ribbon is plain dark blue, as for the order, 32mm wide.

Finland's White Rose Medals   R

Instituted with the order were the medals, 1st class in silver and 2nd class in bronze. According to the statutes these should be 30mm in diameter, but in practice this is usually 32mm. The *obv* is fully occupied by the badge of the order, while the *rev* has a crossed oak spray and sword, with the sun's rays filling the top half of the medal. The lower half bears the inscription, ISÄNMAAN HYVÄKSI, as on the breast star of the order (*qv*). The ribbon is that of the order, plain dark blue.

The medal was awarded to under-officers for five years' (bronze) or ten years' (silver) service. When awarded for gallantry in action, the ribbon carried a bar engraved with the name of the campaign or action in which it was won.

War of Liberty Commemoration Medal R

On 10 September 1918, the Finnish government resolved to strike a commemorative medal for all who participated in the war to secure the country's independence.

The medal, 30mm, is of iron, with the *obv* showing the Cross of Liberty; in each of the upper angles is an armoured arm holding a sword (as in the suspender of the Cross of Liberty, military division), while in the lower angles is the year, 19–18. The *rev* has the arms of Finland – a crowned lion rampant standing on a curved sword and holding a sword in its raised paw.

The ribbon was originally plain dark blue, as for the Order of the White Rose, but on 3 July 1919, Mannerheim decided to alter this for the sake of distinction, to dark blue with 9mm black side stripes. On the same date it was authorised that in cases of award for bravery, the ribbon should bear a silver heraldic rose, while, at the recipient's own expense, he could add one or more of eleven bars with the names of the actions in which he had participated; these are: OESTERBOTTENS, FILPULA, TAMMERFORS, SATAKUNTA, SAVOLAX, KARALIAN FRONT, VIBORG, LEMPAALA-LAHTIS, KOUVOLA-KOTKA-FREDRIKSHAMM, PELLINGE, and SYD FINLAND.

Sharpshooter's Decoration

At the instigation of the women of Finland, a decoration was instituted in 1918 for members of the Finnish Sharpshooters' Battalion. This battalion was formed in Germany during the war, attached to the 27th Prussian Jäger Battn., and served during the Finnish civil war until the Nationalist Party's victory.

The award was confirmed by the Ministry of Defence on 24 February 1919. The badge is an oxydised silver cross *patée*, with a green laurel wreath over the horizontal arms and behind the vertical arms. Superimposed are the figures in gilt, 27. The *rev* is plain, engraved with the recipient's army number. The decoration was worn without ribbon, on the left side.

NOTE:
A considerable number of unofficial and semi-official medals and decorations were created in Finland, many of them of a regimental or 'old comrades' nature, but are outside the scope of this work.

Hungary

After the end of the Great War, Hungary broke away from Austria, becoming a republic in 1919 and a regency in 1920.

No existing awards are shown, as the new Hungary must virtually be regarded as an emergent nation; also Hungarians had been eligible for Austrian orders and decorations.

NEW AWARDS

World War Commemorative Medal with Helmet and Swords, for Combatants RP

The Regent, Admiral Horthy, instituted this medal on 26 May 1929, 36.5mm in diameter, in matt silvered metal. The *obv* has the shield of Hungary surmounted by the crown of St. Stephen (distinguished by the cross on the top being askew); behind the shield are crossed swords, all on branches of laurel (left) and oak (right) (*flg.* 16c).

The *rev* has a steel helmet above the dates, 1914–1918. Above is the legend, PRO DEO ET PATRIA (For God and Fatherland); below are two tied laurel sprays.

The ribbon is made up in triangular form, with narrow green and white horizontal stripes, and red (inner) and white (outer) edges, both 5mm wide.

World War Commemorative Medal for War Participants and Home Service (non-combatants) R

Instituted at the same time as the previous medal, of the same size and metal, the *obv* is similar but without the swords behind the shield. The *rev* has just the dates, 1914–1918, in the same surrounding legend and laurels.

The ribbon is white with red (outer) and green (inner) side stripes, each 5mm wide, 2mm apart, and inset 2mm.

Hero's Badge

On 10 August 1920 the Regent instituted this award as a decoration for offlcers and other ranks who had specially distinguished themselves in war and had been decorated. The award entitled the recipient to preflx his name with the title, *Vitez* (Hero), to wear the badge, and to a grant of land, etc.

The badge, oval, 57 x 38mm, has a blue ground, with the arms of Hungary and St. Stephen's crown above. On the centre line of the shield is a sword, point upwards (although some examples have the sword pointing downwards). The border consists, in the lower flve-eighths, of a green oak branch (left) with red acorns, and (right) golden ears of corn, Other examples exist, 58 x 40mm, 60 x 35mm etc.

There is no ribbon, and the badge is worn on the left side.

War Invalid's Badge

The Regent created this emblem on 31 March 1931, for those wounded or invalided, either during the Great War or in later actions. The badge is in bronze, circular, 22mm in diameter; in a laurel wreath are the letters, HR (*Hadirokkant* = War Invalid); above is the crown of St. Stephen, making the total height, 29mm.

There is no ribbon and the badge is worn on the left side.

Commemorative Medal for War Orphans

We have a note of a ribbon with this title, red, with white, green, white edges and a narrow white centre stripe, but no details of the medal itself have been traced.

Latvia

Latvia had a tough struggle for independence after centuries of foreign domination, but the new republic was founded on 18 November 1918. As with other emergent countries, the newly established awards were given for services, partly during the Great War and partly immediately afterwards, in connection with Latvia's gaining her independence.

NEW AWARDS

Military Order of Lacplesis (the Bear Slayer) R

This order was instituted on 11 November 1919, when Latvia was at the most dangerous and heroic hour of her struggle for independence. It was in three classes, and was awarded, without regard to rank, for bravery in the face of the enemy outside the normal call of duty, and for successful deeds of heroic leadership. For Latvians the second and first classes could only be awarded, respectively, to those who already held the class below. The first class, equivalent to grand cross, was worn from a sash, with a breast star; the second class badge was worn at the neck, and was smaller (47mm), while the badge of the third class was again smaller, and was worn on the left breast.

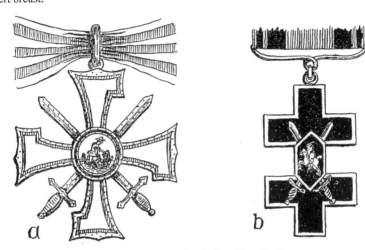

Fig. 17   a – Latvia: Order of Lacplesis
b – Lithuania: Order of the Cross of Vytis.

The badge can only be described as a swastika *patée*, enamelled white with a red border, fimbriated gold; the central medallion shows the legendary Latvian hero, Lacplesis, slaying a bear. Gilt crossed swords appear in the angles (*fig.* 17a). The *rev* has the date of foundation; the order was sparsely awarded, and an example which appeared in an auction sale in 1969 had the number 6 impressed on the *rev.*

The ribbon is seven equal stripes, four white and three deep red. The star of the first class is of eight major rays and eight lesser rays, with smaller rays filling in the spaces; superimposed is the badge.

Medal for the War of Independence, 1918–20
The ribbon for this medal is deep red with a white centre stripe. It has been difficult to get details of the medal itself, but we believe it to be shield-shaped, silvered bronze, 35 x 25mm, enamelled red, with a right arm holding a sword, and three white 5-pointed stars; at each side are clusters of oakleaves; at the top is a scroll lettered PAR TEVZEMI with the dates, 1918, 1920, on the scroll ends at left and right respectively.

War Commemorative Medal   R
A medal was issued in 1928 to those who had participated, ten years earlier, in the war for liberation. It is in bronze, 35mm in diameter, with a soldier guarding the frontier. The *rev* has a 4-line inscription, PAR LATVIJU 1918–1928 (For Latvia).

The ribbon is red with blue side stripes, narrowly edged in yellow on both sides, and with narrow yellow edges. On the ribbon are bronze crossed swords.

Lithuania

Lithuania, with a history going back to the middle ages, gained her independence by proclaiming a republic on 16 February 1918, although her struggles continued for several more years.

NEW AWARDS

Order of the Cross of Vytis   R

This, the highest military award of Lithuania, was instituted on 23 November 1918, in three classes. The badge is a Slavonic cross, with two horizontal members (rather like the Cross of Lorraine, except that the two horizontal arms are of equal length). The cross is of iron, with silvered edges. In the centre is a black hexagonal plaque with a warrior on horseback. When awarded for gallantry in action, crossed swords are set behind this plaque but within the confines of the cross itself (*fig.* 17b). The *rev* has the inscription, at the top and on the upper horizontal arm, in sloping script, *Uz Narsuma* (For valour); in the centre, in three lines, is the date of foundation, 1918/XI/23; on the lower horizontal arm is a space for the number of the badge (or possibly the recipient's number?), prefixed by a sloping capital *N*. An example in an auction sale in 1970 was impressed with the number, 20.

The ribbon is red with two black stripes near each edge, the inner one being wider than the outer.

Medal for Volunteers in the Independence Campaign 1918–20   R

This medal was issued in November 1928, on the tenth anniversary of the armed forces of the republic, and was awarded to the 'Founding Volunteers', some 2000 in all, including about 100 women and 100 American Lithuanians.

The *obv* shows a hand holding a swords, the blade breaking a chain, and the blade of another sword with the same blow. The *rev* has the dates, 1918–1920, at the top, over the word, SAVANORIUI, with a spray of oak and laurel below.

The ribbon is green, with a centre stripe and edges of red, narrowly flanked on each side with yellow.

Poland

Once a powerful kingdom, Poland suffered repeated partition in the 18th century and was then under German, Austrian, and Russian rule. She became an independent republic on 11 November 1918.

NEW AWARDS

Order of Military Bravery – Virtuti Militari   R

Originally instituted by King Stanislaus in 1792, the first *Virtuti Militari* existed for only a couple of months. It was restored at intervals, until, in 1831, it became reduced to a Russian decoration of a commemorative nature.

The newly independent Poland re-created the order on 1 August 1919, in five classes: grand cross (including a breast star in silver, with eight groups of rays), awarded to commanders-in-chief who had won a decisive victory or had conducted a gallant defence; commander's cross, awarded to generals for similar but lesser achievements; knight's cross, for officers and other ranks who had already won the gold cross, for a further act of bravery in action; gold cross, for a similar further award to a holder of the fifth class, the silver cross, for conspicuous gallantry in action.

The badge is a Leopold cross with ball finials, in gold (silver for 5th class) and black enamel. The four arms were lettered, VIR/TUTI/MILI/TARI (For military bravery), while the central medallion had the white Polish eagle within a laurel wreath. The *rev* had the inscription, HONOR I OJCZYZNA (Honour and Fatherland).

The ribbon is a rich deep blue with wide black side stripes.

Cross of Valour RP

The Council of National Defence instituted this award on 11 August 1920, for acts of bravery on the field of battle. It is a Leopold cross in bronze, 44mm across, with three of the arms inscribed, NA (top) POLU (left) CHWALY (right) (On the field of glory), while the lower arm has the date, 1920. Instead of a central medallion, the cross has a shield with the Polish eagle. The *rev* centre has a vertical sword in an oak wreath, while the horizontal arms are lettered, WALE/CZNYM (To the brave).

The ribbon is amaranth crimson with white side stripes. For each subsequent award a bronze bar was worn on the ribbon – a narrow straight strip with conventional oakleaf sprays.

War Commemorative Medal R

On 21 September 1928 a bronze medal was instituted for those who had served in the struggle for independence, during the period from 1 November 1918 to 18 March 1921. The *obv* shows the crowned Polish eagle with the *Virtuti Militari* on its breast; to lower left and right are the dates, 1918, 1921. The *rev* has the 3-line inscription, POLSKA/SWEMV/OBRONCY (Poland to her defender) in an oak wreath.

The ribbon is a rich deep blue with crimson-purple side stripes flanked by a narrow white stripe on each side, and with a narrow black stripe between the inner white and the blue; there is a very narrow blue edge. Foreign troops and civilians serving with the Polish army, were also awarded this medal.

Independence Cross and Medal R

These decorations were instituted on 29 October 1930, and were awarded for distinguished service in the struggle for independence.

The cross, 40 x 40mm, (although at least one is known, 38 x 38mm), is a rather narrow Greek cross, with the ends of the arms turned slightly outwards (rather like our Military Cross). The arms are enamelled black, with a central gold line; on the horizontal arms is the Polish inscription, BOJOWNIKOM NIEPODLEGLOSCI. The square gilt centre shows a stylised Polish eagle. The *rev* is similar, in black and gilt, but without the inscription. For special services the cross could be awarded 'with swords'.

The medal is in bronze, 35mm in diameter. The *obv* shows three hydras pierced by a sword; it has the same Polish inscription as the cross. The *rev* has the monogram, RP.

Both cross and medal have a 38mm black ribbon with 4mm red side stripes, inset about 1.5mm.

Photographic
Illustrations

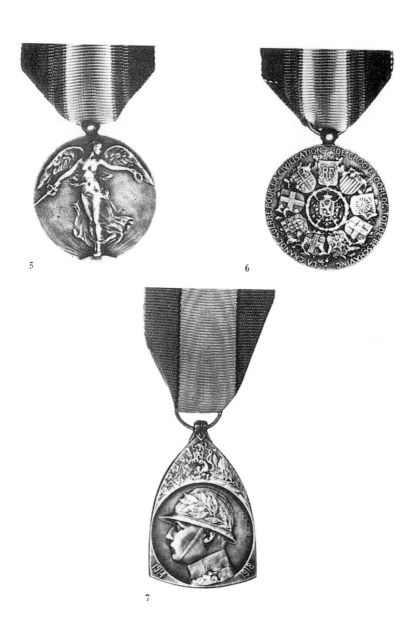

5 Belgium: Victory Medal (*obv*)

6 Belgium: Victory Medal (*rev*)

7 Belgium: War Medal, 1914–18

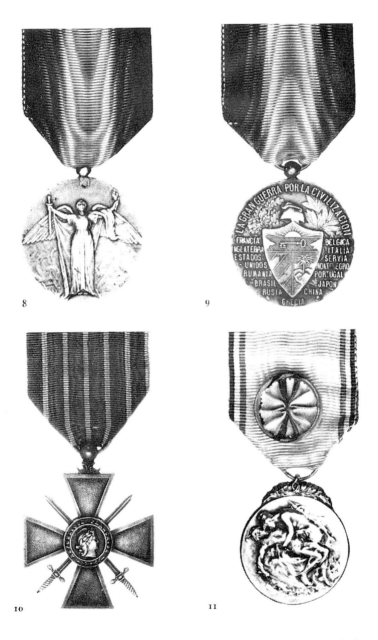

8 Cuba: Victory Medal (*obv*)
10 France: Croix de Guerre

9 Cuba: Victory Medal (*rev*)
11 France: Reconnaisance Medal

12 France: Victory Medal (obv)
14 France: Victory Medal, unofficial type (*obv*)

13 France: Victory Medal (*rev*)
15 France: Victory Medal, unofficial type (*rev*)

16 France: Médaille Commemorative Française, 1914–18   17 France: Croix du Combattant
18 France: Decoration for the Wounded

19 Great Britain: Order of the British Empire: badge of MBE (silver) and OBE (silver-gilt), Civil Division

21 Great Britain: Royal Red Cross with Bar for second award

20 Great Britain: Order of the Companions of Honour

22 Great Britain: Badge of an Associate, Royal Red Cross (ARRC)

23 Great Britain: Distinguished Service
Cross and Bar

24 Great Britain: Military Cross and Bar

25 Great Britain: Distinguished Flying
Cross and Bar

26 Great Britain: Air Force Cross and Bar

27

28

29

30

27 Great Britain: Distinguished Conduct
Medal with laurel spray Bar (replacing the
dated bars)

29 Great Britain: Military Medal (*rev*) and
Bar

28 Great Britain: Distinguished Service
Medal (*rev*) and Bar

30 Great Britain: Distinguished Flying
Medal (*rev*) and Bar

31 Great Britain: Air Force Medal (rev) and Bar

32 Great Britain: 1914 Star and Bar

33 Great Britain: 1914–15 Star

34 Great Britain: British War Medal, 1914–18 (*rev*)

35

36

37

38

35 Great Britain: Mercantile Marine War Medal (*rev*)

37 Great Britain: Victory Medal (*rev*)

36 Great Britain: Victory Medal (*obv*) with oakleaf spray for Mentions in Despatches

38 Great Britain: Victory Medal, South Africa (*rev*)

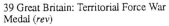

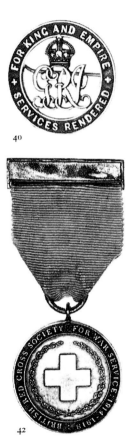

39 Great Britain: Territorial Force War
Medal (*rev*)

41 Great Britain: Special Constabulary
LSM (*rev*) with GREAT WAR Bar

40 Great Britain: Silver badge for those
discharged through wounds, etc

42 Great Britain: British Red Cross
Society's Medal for War Service

43

44

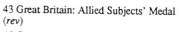

45

46

43 Great Britain: Allied Subjects' Medal (*rev*)

45 Greece: Victory Medal (*rev*) (later striking)

44 Greece: Victory Medal (*obv*) (later striking)

46 Italy: War Cross, 1918

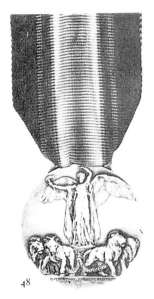

47 Italy: War Medal, 1915–18

48 Italy: Victory Medal (*obv*)

49 Italy: Victory Medal (*rev*)

50 Japan: Victory Medal (*obv*)
(French copy)
52 Portugal: Victory Medal (*obv*)

51 Japan: Victory Medal (*rev*)
(French copy)
53 Portugal: Victory Medal (*rev*)

54 Rumania: Medal for Bravery &
Loyalty, with swords

56 Rumania: Victory Medal (*obv*)

55 Rumania: Commemorative Cross,
1916–18

57 Rumania: Victory Medal (*rev*)

58 Serbia: Order of the Karageorge Star:
Cross for NCO's, etc., for bravery
60 USA: Distinguished Service Cross

59 Serbia (Jugoslavia): War
Commemorative Medal
61 USA: Distinguished Flying Cross

62 USA: Victory Medal (*obv*)

63 USA: Victory Medal (*rev*)

64 Austria: Medal for Bravery (1917, Emperor Karl type)

65 Austria: Iron Cross of Merit, 1916, with Crown, on ribbon of the Medal of Bravery

66 Austria: Karl Truppenkreuz, 1916

67 Austria: War Commemorative Medal

68 Austria: Tyrol Commemorative Medal, 1914–18

69 Bulgaria: Soldiers' Cross for Bravery, 1915 type

70 Bulgaria: War Medal, 1915–18, with ribbon for front-line combatants

71 Germany: Cross of Honour for the
Great War, for front-line fighters

73 Germany: Badge for Wounded Army
personnel, 1914–18

72 Germany: Cross of Honour for other
troops

74 Germany: Anhalt: Friedrich Cross

75

76

77

78

75 Germany: Bavaria: King Ludwig Cross

77 Germany: Free Hanse Towns:
Hanseatic Cross, Bremen

76 Germany: Brunswick: Cross for War
Merit, 1st Class

78 Germany: Free Hanse Towns:
Hanseatic Cross, Hamburg

79

80

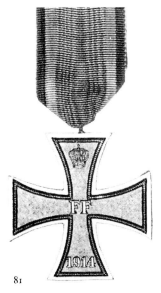

81

82

79 Germany: Free Hanse Towns:
Hanseatic Cross, Lübeck

81 Germany: Mecklenburg-Schwerin:
Cross for Military Merit, 2nd Class

80 Germany: Schaumburg-Lippe: Cross
for Faithful Service (*Steckkreuz*)

82 Germany: Prussia: Iron Cross, 1st
Class (1914–18 type)

83

84

85

86

83 Germany: Prussia: Iron Cross, 2nd Class (1914–18 type), with ribbon for combatants

85 Germany: Saxony: War Merit Cross, 1915 (*rev*)

84 Germany: Prussia: Cross of merit for War Aid, 1916

86 Germany: Saxe-Meiningen: Cross of Merit in War, with combatant's ribbon

87 Turkey: War Medal, 1915–18
(Decoration for distinguished service)

88 Turkey: War Medal, 1915–18 (unofficial
'improved' type)

89 Netherlands: Mobilisation Cross, 1914–18

90 Czechoslovakia: Victory Medal (*obv*)

91 Czechoslovakia: Victory Medal (*rev*)

92

93

94

92 Finland: War of Liberty
Commemoration Medal (*rev*)

93 Hungary: War Commemorative Medal
for Combatants

94 Poland: Cross of Valour

APPENDIX 1

Inscriptions on Orders, Decorations and Medals

The inscriptions listed here do not pretend to be comprehensive, but will, perhaps, be useful for identification purposes. It should be realised that in many cases the same, or similar, initials, monograms, or words are common not only to several different awards of a particular country, but to different states or countries, particularly those such as FÜR VERDIENSTE (For merit) or FÜR TAPFERKEIT (For bravery).

Not all initials or monograms have been included, as in many cases other inscriptions are sufficient to identify the piece; most *obv* inscriptions which merely give the ruler's name and titles are omitted where the country of origin is obvious.

●●●●●●●●●

A– Belgium: Croix de Guerre; Civic Decoration, 1914–18.
A.F. – Mecklenburg-Strelitz: Adolf Friedrich Cross.
A.R. – Saxony: Cross of Honour.
ADORATIO – IMITATIO etc. – Austria: Medal for Catholic Sisters.
AL MERITO MILITARE – Italy: Military Order of Savoy.
AL VALORE MARINA – Italy: Medal for Maritime Valour.
AL VALORE MILITARE – Italy: Medal for Military Valour.
ALBERTUS ANIMOSUS – Saxony: Order of Albrecht.
ALS BLIJK VAN'S LANDS ERKENTELIJKHEID – Belgium: Political Prisoners Medal (Flemish type).
AUGUSTUS, 1914, NOVEMBER, 1918 – Netherlands: Mobilisation Cross.
AUX VICTIMES DE L'INVASION, LA FRANCE RECONNAISSANTE – France: Medal for Victims of the Invasion.

BARBATIE SI CREDINTA – Rumania: Medal for Bravery and Loyalty.

C.E., 1914 – Saxe-Coburg-Gotha: War Commemorative Cross, 1914–18.
ČS – Czechoslovakia: War Cross.
ČS, 1918 – Czechoslovakia: Order of the Sokol (or Falcon).
C.W. – Württemberg: Charlotte Cross.
CAMPAÑA POR LA HUMANIDAD, LA JUSTICIA Y EL DERECHO – Cuba: War Medal, 1917–19.
CAMPANHAS DO EXERCITO PORTUGUES, 1916 – Portugal: Campaign Medal.
CAROLA KOENIGIN VON SACHSEN – Saxony: Carola Medal.
CAROLVS – Austria: Medal for Wounded.
ČESKOSLOVENSKÉ VOJSKO. ZA SVOBODU – Czechoslovakia: Jan Žižka Medal.
CONIATA NEL BRONZE NEMICO – Italy: War Medal.

DANSK KRIGSFANGERHJAELP, 1914, 1919 – Denmark: Red Cross Medal for Aid to Prisoners of War.
DAS DANKBARE DEUTSCHLAND ZUR ERINNERUNG AN DEN WELTKRIEG – Germany: Helvetia Benigna Medal.

DAS LAND TIROL DEN VERTEIDIGERN DES VATERLANDES, 1914–18 – Austria: Tyrol Commemorative Medal.

DE GROOTE OORLOG TOT DE BESCHAVING - LA GRANDE GUERRE POUR LA CIVILISATION – Belgium: Victory Medal.

DEM MILITAIR-VERDIENSTE – Lippe: Medal for Military Merit.

DEM TAPFERN – Baden: Karl-Friedrich Medal for Military Merit.

DEM VERDIENSTE – Saxony: Order of Civil Merit; Saxe-Weimar-Eisenach: Cross of Merit, General Decn. of Honour; Württemberg: Medal of the Order of the Crown, Order of Friedrich.

DEM VERDIENSTE, 1914 – Saxe-Weimar-Eisenach: General Decoration of Honour.

DEN 25sten AUGUST 1870 – Hesse: Military Medical Cross.

DER TAPFERKEIT – Austria: Medal for Bravery; Bavaria: Medal for Bravery.

E – Estonia: Order of the Cross of Liberty.

EA, VL (each twice), 1914 – Brunswick: Cross of War Merit for Women.

EA, 1914 – Brunswick: Cross of War Merit.

EL (monogram) – Hesse: Troops Decoration of Honour.

ELE (looks like ECE) – Hesse: Decn. of Honour for War Welfare Work.

E II – Saxe-Altenburg: Duke Ernst Medal, Medal for Bravery.

EN SOUVENIR DE SA COLLABORATION - TER HERINNERING AAN ZIJN MEDEWERKING – Belgium: Medal of the Natl. Committee for Assistance and Food Supply.

EN TÉMOINAGE DE RECONNAISSANCE NATIONALE – Belgium: King Albert Medal, Political Prisoner's Medal, 1914–18.

F – Anhalt: Friedrich Cross; Baden: War Merit Cross.

FA, 1914 – Oldenburg: Friedrich August Cross.

F.A.R. – Saxony: Friedrich August Medal, Commemorative Cross for Voluntary Sick Nursing.

FF (back to back) – Mecklenburg-Schwerin: Friedrich Franz Cross; Rumania: Order of Michael the Brave, Commemorative Cross.

FF, 1914 – Mecklenburg-Schwerin: Cross for Military Merit.

FW III R – Various Prussian awards.

FEODORA-MCMXV-MARIA PAVLOWNA-MDCCCXV – Saxe-Weimar-Eisenach: Decoration of Merit for Women.

FIDELITER ET (or &) CONSTANTER – Saxony Duchies: Ducal Saxe-Ernestine House Order (with gothic F, E, or B on the upper arm for Saxe-Altenburg, Saxe-Coburg-Gotha, or Saxe-Meiningen, respectively), Crosses and Medals of the Order; Saxe-Coburg-Gotha: Carl Eduard War Cross.

FRAUEN-VERDIENST-IM-KRIEGE – Saxe-Weimar-Eisenach: Decn. of Merit for Women.

FRIEDRICH. BATHALDIS. F.u.F.z.W.u.P. – Waldeck: Friedrich-Bathaldis Medal.

FUER VERDIENST – Saxe-Coburg-Gotha: Oval Carl Eduard Medal, Decoration for Merit in the Homeland.

FUER VERDIENSTE UM DAS ROTHE KREUZ – Prussia: Red Cross Medal.

FÜR AUFOPFERNDE DIENSTE IM KRIEGE (in gothic) – Brunswick:Cross of War Merit for Women.

FÜR AUSZEICHNUNG IM KRIEGE – Lippe: Cross for War Merit.

FÜR BADENS EHRE – Baden: Military Order of Karl-Friedrich, Karl-Friedrich Medal for Military Merit.

FÜR HEIMAT VERDIENST – Saxe-Weimar-Eisenach: Cross for Merit in the Homeland, 1914–18.

FÜR HELDEN MÜTIGE TAT, 1914 – Lippe: War Cross of Honour for Heroic Deeds.
FÜR KRIEGSFÜRSORGE – Hesse: Decn. of Honour for Welfare Work.
FÜR KRIEGS-HILFSDIENST – Prussia: Cross of Merit for War Aid.
FÜR MILITAIR-VERDIENST – Schaumburg-Lippe: Medal for Military Merit.
FÜR ÖSTERREICH – Austria: War Commemorative Medal.
FÜR PFLEGE DER SOLDATEN 1914 (in gothic) – Hesse: Military Medical Cross.
FÜR TAPFERKEIT – Mecklenburg-Strelitz: Cross for Distinction in War.
FÜR TAPFERKEIT UND TREUE – Saxe-Weimar-Eisenach: General Decn. of Honour.
FÜR TREUE DIENSTE – Reuss: Cross of Merit, *inter alia.*
FÜR TREUE DIENSTE IM WELTKRIEGE – Oldenburg: Medal for War Merit.
FÜR TREUE DIENSTE, 1914 – Schaumburg-Lippe: Cross for Faithful Service.
FÜR TREUE UND VERDIENST – Various (see Hohenzollern, Lippe, Schaumburg-Lippe, etc.).
FÜR TREUES WIRKEN IN EISERNER ZEIT, 1914 – Reuss: Medal for Devoted Service in Wartime. With 1915 – Waldeck: Friedrich-Bathaldis Medal.
FÜR VERDIENST or FÜR VERDIENST IM KRIEGE – Various German States.
FÜR VERDIENSTE UM DAS ROTE KREUZ, & c. – Württemberg: Karl-Olga Medal.
FÜR WERKE DER KRIEGSHILFE, 1917 – Mecklenburg-Strelitz: Adolf-Friedrich Cross.

GFC – Schwarzburg-Sondershausen: Cross of Honour and other awards.
GG (in ornate script, one reversed) – Schwarzburg: Anerkennungs Medal. Ditto, with 1914 below – Schwarzburg: Silver Medal for War Merit.
GW – Schaumburg-Lippe: Medal for War Merit.
GESTIFTER FÜR HILFREICHE NÄCHSTENLIEBE – Saxony: Carola Medal.
GRANDE GUERRA PELA CIVILIZACÃO – Brazil: Victory Medal.
GRANDE GUERRA PER LA CIVILITA - AI COMBATIENTI DELLE NAZIONI ALLEATE ED ASSOCIATE – Italy: Victory Medal.
GRATI PRINCIPS ET PATRIA CAROLVS IMP. ET REX – Karl Truppenkreuz.
GUILELMUS PRINCEPS DE HOHENZOLLERN – Hohenzollern: Bene Merenti Medal.
GVERRA PER L'UNITÀ D'ITALIA – Italy: War Medal.

H. XXVII – Reusz: Medal for Devoted Service in Wartime.
H. XXVII, 19–14 – Reusz: Cross for War Merit.
HR – Hungary: War Invalids' Badge.
HELVETIA BENIGNA – Germany: Helvetia Benigna Medal.
HIC BIMUS MANE OPTIME – Italy: Medal for Occupation of Fiume.
HONNEUR ET PATRIE – France: Legion of Honour.

IL FIGLIO CHE TI NACQUE DAL DOLORE TI RINASCE, &c. – Italy: Medal for Mothers of the Fallen.
IN ACTION FAITHFUL AND IN HONOUR CLEAR – Gt. Britain: Order of the Companions of Honour.
INTER ARMA CARITAS – Gt. Britain: British Red Cross Society War Medal, BRCS Special Service Cross.
ISÄNMAAM HYVÄKSI – Finland: Finlands White Rose Medals.

KRIEGER VERDIENST – Prussia: Soldiers' Medal of Merit.
KRIEGS VERDIENST – Württemberg: Wilhelm Cross.

KRIEGS-VERDIENST – Brunswick: Cross for Military Merit; Prussia: Military Cross of Merit, Military Decoration of Honour.

LA GRAN GUERRA POR LA CIVILIZACION – Cuba: Victory Medal.
LA GRANDE GVERRE POUR LA CIVILISATION – France: Victory Medal.
LAESO MILITI - MCMXVIII – Austria: Medal for Wounded.
LA VILLE DE LIÈGE À SES VAILLANTS DEFENSEURS – Belgium: Liège Medal.
LIBERTÉ, EGALITÉ, FRATERNITÉ – France: Médaille de la Fidélité Française.
LUCEMBURGEM VIRTUTI - CRÉCY, 1346 – Luxemburg: Medal for Volunteers.

MF (entwined) – Anhalt: Marie Cross, 1918.
MARELE RAZBOI PENTRU CIVILIZATIE – Rumania: Victory Medal.
MARNE-MEUSE/SOMME/AISNE.YSER-VARDAL – Luxemburg: Medal for Volunteers.
MÉDAILLE COMMÉMORATIVE DE LA CAMPAGNE - HERINNERINGS MEDAILLE VAN DE VELDTOCHT – Belgium: War Commemorative Medal.
MEDALIA DA VITORIA – Portugal: Victory Medal.
MERENTI – Bavaria: Order and Cross of Military Merit.
MERITO CIVILI TEMPORE BELLI - MCMXV – Austria: War Cross for Civil Merit.
MERITO DI GVERRA – Italy: War Cross.
MERITUL SANITAR – Rumania: Cross for Medical Merit.
MOBILISATIE - VREDE - EER – Netherlands: Mobilisation Cross.
MOBILISATIE - WAARDEERING – Netherlands: White Mobilisation Cross.

NA POLU CHWALY 1920 – Poland: Cross of Valour.

ORDO. TEUT. HUMANITATI – (Austria) Marianer Cross of the Teutonic Order.

PAR TEVZEMI 1918, 1920 – Latvia: Medal for War of Independence.
PATRIA - LA GUERRA DI DERECHO (or A LA FUERZE DEL DERECHO) – Panama: Medal of Solidarity.
PATRIAE AC HUMANITATI – Austria: Decoration of Honour for Merit to the Red Cross.
PELA JUSTICA E PELA CIVILIZACÃO – Brazil: Campaign Cross, 1917–18.
PER ASPERA AD ASTRA - PER CRUCE AD LUCEM – Italy: Medal for Army Chaplains.
PIIS MERITAS – Austria: Chaplains' Cross of Merit.
POLSKA SWEMV OB RONCY – Poland: War Commemorative Cross.
Pour/le Mé/rite – Prussia: Order 'Pour le Mérite' (For Merit).
PRAVDA VITEZI – Czechoslovakia: Order of the White Lion.
PRISONNIERS CIVILS DÉPORTÉS ET OTAGES DE LA GRANDE GUERRE – France: Medal for Civilian Prisoners, Deported and Hostages.
PRO DEO ET PATRIA – Hungary: War Commemorative Medal.
PRO PATRIA, HONORE ET CARITATE – Belgium: Queen Elisabeth Medal.

RECONNAISSANCE FRANÇAISE – France: Medal of Gratitude.

SALUS PATRIAE SUPREME LEX – Belgium: Croix du Feu.
SIGNUM LAUDIS – Austria: Medal for Military Merit.

SLESVIG 1920 – Denmark: Slesvig Medal.
SOUVENIR DE LA RESTAURATION – Belgium: Medal of the National Restoration.
SUOMEN KANSALTA 1918 – Finland: Medal of Liberty.
SVĚTOVA VALKA ZA CIVILISACI – Czechoslovakia: Victory Medal.

TAPFER UND TREU – Mecklenburg-Strelitz: Cross for Distinction in War.
TER VERDEDIGING DER VOLKSVRIJHEID – Netherlands: Amsterdam Burgerwacht Cross and Medal.
THE GREAT WAR FOR CIVILISATION - DE GROTE OORLOG VOOR DE BESCHAVING 1914–1919 – South Africa: Victory Medal.
TREU BEWÄHRT IN SCHWERER ZEIT 1915 – Lippe: War Medal of Honour.
TREUE UND VERDIENST – Hohenzollern: Princely House Order.

UNITÀ D'ITALIA 1848–1918 – Italy: United Italy Medal.
URHEUDESTA - FÖR TAPPERHET – Finland: Medal of Liberty.
UZ NARSUMA – Lithuania: Order of the Cross of Vytis.

V TĚŽKYCH DOBACH, 1918, 1919 – Czechoslovakia. Commem. Cross for Volunteers.
VALEUR ET DISCIPLINE – France: Médaille Militaire.
VER/DIENST – Austria: Cross for Military Merit.
VERDIENST IM KRIEGE – Schwarzburg: Silver Medal for War Merit.
VERDIENST UM DEN STAAT – Prussia: General Decoration of Honour.
VERDIENST UMS VATERLAND – Schwarzburg: Anna Louisa Award of Merit.
VIRIBUS UNITIS – Austria: Order of Franz Joseph, Gold, Silver and Iron Crosses for Merit.
VIRTUTE MILITARIA – Rumania: Cross and Medal for Military Merit.
VIRTUTI MILITARI – Poland: Order 'Virtuti Militari'.
VOLONTARIIS (or VOLUNTARIIS) 1914–1918 - PATRIA MEMOR – Belgium: Medal for Combatant Volunteers.
VOLONTARI DI GVERRA, MCMXV-MCMXVIII – Italy: Medal of Merit for Volunteers.
VOM FELS ZUM MEER – Prussia: Royal Hohenzollern House Order.
VOR DEM FEINDE (on bar) – Oldenburg: Friedrich August Cross.
VRIJWILLIGE BURGERWACHT 1918 – Netherlands: Amsterdam Burgerwacht Medal.

W. 1914 (FW 1813 on *rev*) – Prussia: Iron Cross (Grand Cross and 2nd Class).
W. 1914 (plain *rev*, pin fastener) – Prussia: Iron Cross, 1st Class).
WE 1915 – Saxe-Weimar-Eisenach: Wilhelm Ernst War Cross.
WR – Prussia: Order of the Red Eagle and other Prussian awards.
WALE/CZNYM – Poland: Cross of Valour 1920.
WELTKRIEG, FA – Saxony: War Merit Cross.
WELTKRIEG 1914–16 (on oakleaf bar) – Saxony: Friedrich August Medal, Carola Medal (both when awarded to women).

Y.C.C. 1914 – Ukraine: Cross of Legion of Ukrainian Sich Riflemen.
YSER – Belgium: Yser Medal and Cross.

27 – Finland: Sharpshooters' Decoration.
2 DECEMBER 1873 – Austria: War Medal, 1873–1916 (*rev*).

INSCRIPTIONS IN CYRILLIC LETTERS

Η ΤΑΝ Η ΕΠΙΤΑΣ	—	Greece: War Cross, 1916
МИЛОШ ОБИЛИЋ	—	Serbia: Medal for Bravery (Obilitch Medal).
ПЕТАР I 1904	—	Serbia: Order of the Karageorge Star.
ЗА ПРАВО ЧАСТ И СЛОБОДУ ЦРНЕ/ГОРЕ	—	Montenegro: Order of Freedom.
ЗА ТРУДЫ ПО ОТЛИЧНОМУ &c.	—	Russia: Mobilisation Medal.
ЗА ХРАБРОСТ	—	Serbia: Medal for Bravery.
ЗА УСЕРДИЄ	—	Russia: Medal for Zeal.
ЗА ХРАБРОСТЬ	—	Russia: St. George Medal, Medal for Bravery.
ЗА ХРАБРОСТЬ	—	Bulgaria: Soldiers' Cross for Bravery.

APPENDIX 2

Some firms who may be able to supply medal ribbons

GREAT BRITAIN –   A. H. Baldwin & Sons Ltd., 11 Adelphi Terrace,
London. WC2N 6BJ.
A. D. Hamilton & Co. Ltd., 7 St., Vincent Place,
Glasgow. G1 2DW
Spink & Son Ltd., 5–7 King Street,
St. James, London. SW1Y 6QS

BELGIUM –   Fibru-Fisch, Edmond Rostandstraat, 59,
B–1070 Brussels.

CANADA –   Eugene G. Ursual. P.O. Box 8096, Ottawa,
Ont., K1G 3H6.
The Military Exchange Ltd., 95 Yonge St.,
Toronto, Ont., M5C 1S8.

DENMARK –   M. W. Mørch & Sons, Eftf., Pederskramsgade 3,
Copenhagen.

FRANCE –   Arthus Bertrand, 46 Rue de Rennes,
F-75006 Paris.

GERMANY –   Die Orders-Sammlung, Wielandstr., 16,
1000, Berlin 12.
A. Thies, Bismarkstr. 28, 744 Nurtingen.
Henning Volle, Postfach 1613, Rehlingstr. 14,
78 Freiburg.

ITALY –   Ditta Alberti, Via Nino Bixio 6, Milan.
Ditta Cravanzola, Via del Corse 340, Rome
Stefano Johnson S.p.A., Piazza S. Angelo 1,
Milan.

NETHERLANDS –   Jacques Schulman BV, Keizersgracht 448,
Amsterdam C.
J. M. J. van Wielik, Noordeinde 9, The Hague.

APPENDIX 3

A Select Bibliography

It is difficult to provide a comprehensive bibliography, since nearly every modern book on orders and medals includes something, however limited its interest, on awards connected with the Great War. The selected works listed below include most of the more important items, although in nearly every case they cover a far wider field than 1914–1918.

· · · · · · · · · ·

General
Dorling. Capt. H. Taprell, DSO, RN. RIBBONS AND MEDALS. *London*, 1916 onwards Larger revised edition 1983; 320pp, and 24pp of coloured illus. of ribbons. Numerous illus. in the text.

Mathis, René. LES CROIX DE GUERRE. *Nancy*, 1924. 135pp, 11pl.

Purves, Alec A. COLLECTING MEDAL AND DECORATIONS. *London*, 1968. 3rd, revised, edition. 1978, 238pp, 15pl, line drawings.

Allies and Associated Countries
Belgium
Quinot, Henri. RECUEIL DES DÉCORATIONS BELGES ET CONGO- *Auderghem*, 1934. 5th edition. *Brussels*, 1963, with title, RECUEIL ILLUSTRÉ DES ORDRES DE CHEVALERIE ET DÉCORATIONS BELGES DE 1830 À 1963. 328pp, 39pl (12 in colour).

Central America
Guille, Lionel. THE DÉCORATIONS AND MEDALS OF THE CENTRAL AMERICAN COUNTRIES. *Stevenage*, 1952. 23pp (Publication No. 2 of the Orders & Medals Research Society).

France
Delande. M, DÉCORATIONS – FRANCE ET COLONIES. *Paris*, 1934. 104 pp, including 54pl (4 in colour, of ribbons). Large 4to.

Malécot, Yves (Ed) DÉCORATIONS OFFICIELLES FRANÇAISES. *Paris*, 1956. 291pp including 54pl (25 in colour); 2 facsimile documents, and numerous illustrations in the text. Large 4to.

Great Britain and the British Empire
Abbott, Peter E. & Tamplin, John. M. A. BRITISH GALLANTRY AWARDS. *London*, 1981 316pp, including 4 coloured pl, numerous illus in the text.

Bell, Ernest W. SOLDIERS KILLED ON THE FIRST DAY OF THE SOMME. *Bolton*, 1977. vi + 212pp. Lists some 18,000 officers and men, by regiments (with their regimental numbers).

BURKE'S HANDBOOK TO THE ORDER OF THE BRITISH EMPIRE. *London*, 1921. 704pp, 5pl in colour, of insignia.

Gordon, Major Lawrence L. BRITISH BATTLES AND MEDALS. *Aldershot*, 1947. 5th edition (revised by E. C. Joslin), *London*, 1979. 437pp, 43pl. coloured frontispiece, and ribbon chart.

Gould, Robert W. LOCATIONS OF BRITISH CAVALRY, INFANTRY AND MACHINE GUN UNITS, 1914–1924. *London*, 1977. 48pp.

Hayward, J. B. & Son (Pubr.). ARMY HONOURS AND AWARDS. *London*, 1974. 653pp. Originally published as part of the Supplement to the *Official Army List*, 1920.

Hayward, J. B. & Son (Pubr.). NAVAL AND AIR FORCE HONOURS AND AWARDS. *London*, 1975. 8 + 227 + 2 + 68pp. Originally published in the *Official Navy List*, April 1919 and in the *Royal Air Force List*, April 1920, respectively.

Hayward, J. B. & Son (Pubr.). HONOURS AND AWARDS, INDIAN ARMY, 1914–1921. *London*, n.d. (1978). (iv) + 302pp. A reprint of *Roll of Honour, Indian Army, Great War, 1914–1921, (Delhi*, 1931).

HONOURS AND AWARDS OF THE OLD CONTEMPTIBLES. *London*, 1915. Reprinted 1971. v + 58pp.

OFFICERS DIED IN THE GREAT WAR, 1914–1919. *London (HMSO)*, 1919. 262pp. Lists alphabetically, in order of precedence of regiments. Reprinted 1975.

NOTE: The 80 parts of *Soldiers died in the Great War* are rarely obtainable, but can be consulted in some public libraries.

Parfitt, G. Archer. THE AWARDS OF THE CROIX DE GUERRE (1914–18) TO UNITS OF THE BRITISH ARMY. *London*, 1973, 32pp. Illus. in the text. (Reprinted from the Bulletin of the Military Historical Society, November 1973).

Ruvigny, The Marquis de. THE ROLL OF HONOUR. *London*, 1916–19. 5 vols. 1435pp in all. Illus.

Regimental Histories

There are hundreds of books on regimental history, many of them dealing solely with the Great War period, sometimes limited to just one battalion. Those with lists of casualties, honours and awards are the most useful.

Greece

Dimacopoulos, George. GREEK ORDER AND MEDALS. *Athens*, 1961. Vol. 1. 78pp. 20pl.

Romanoff, Prince Dimitri. THE ORDERS, MEDALS AND HISTORY OF GREECE. *Rungsted Kyst, Denmark*, 1987. 223pp. Profusely illustrated, including 25 coloured plates.

Italy

Scandaluzzi, Franco. ORDINI EQUESTRI, MEDAGLIE E DECORAZIONE ITALIANE. np. (*Milan*), 1962. 9pp of text index, 131pl of line drawings; 3 hand-coloured pl of ribbons.

Japan

Peterson, James W. ORDERS AND MEDALS OF JAPAN AND ASSOCIATED STATES. *Chicago*, 1967. 110pp, 214 illustrations. (Publication No. 1 of the Orders & Medals Society of America).

Luxembourg

Schleich de Bossé, Jean R. LES DISTINCTIONS HONORIFIQUES AU PAYS DE LUXEMBOURG, 1430–1961. *Luxembourg*, nd (1962). 48pp, 36pl.

U.S.A.

Grosvenor, Gilbert (and others). INSIGNIA AND DECORATIONS OF THE U.S. ARMED FORCES. *Washington*, D.C., 1944. 208pp (with 2,476 reproductions in colour of medals, ribbons, etc.). A reprint, as a separate volume, of the *National Geographic Magazine*.

Kerrigan, Evans E. AMERICAN WAR MEDALS AND DECORATIONS. *New York*, 1964. New edition, *London*, 1973. xvi + 173pp, 4 col pl, illus, in text.

Robles, Philip K. UNITED STATES MILITARY MEDALS AND RIBBONS. *Rutland, Vermont/Tokyo*, 1971. 187pp (including 44 coloured plates illustrating 139 items), and a map.

The Central Powers
Austria

Falkenstein, Joseph von. IMPERIAL AUSTRIAN MEDALS AND DECORATIONS. *Sausalito, Calif./Plantation, Fla.*, 1972. xvii + 178pp, 1pl of ribbons in colour. Numerous illus. in text.

Měřička, Vaclav. ORDEN UND EHRENZEICHEN DER ÖSTERREICHISCH-UNGARISCHEN MONARCHIE. *Vienna/Munich*, 1974. 304pp, 60 col. pl, 255 illus.

Michetschläger, Heinrich F. DAS ORDENSBUCH DER GEWESENEN OESTERREICHISCH-UNGARISCHEN MONARCHIE. *Vienna*, 1918–19. 40pp, 26 col. pl, some 500 items illus, in text.

Prochazka, Roman, Freiherr von. ÖSTERREICHISCHES ORDENSHANDBUCH. *Munich*, 1974. 161 (+ 1) pp, 101pl, illustrating over 600 items. 2nd edition, 1979, in 4 volumes, 313pp. 146 plates.

Germany

Bowen, V. E. THE PRUSSIAN AND GERMAN IRON CROSS. *Stroud*, 1986. 336 (+ 6) pp, 1 coloured plate, Profusely illustrated.

Hessenthal, Dr W. H. E. von, and Schreiber, Georg. DIE TRAGBAREN EHRENZEICHEN DES DEUTSCHEN REICHES. *Berlin*, 1940. xxii + 563 + 32pp, 32pl. Supplement of 5pp of additions and amendments.

Klenau, Arnhard, Graf. GROSSER DEUTSCHER ORDENSKATALOG, BIS 1918. *Munich*, 1974. 228pp, 350 illustrations.

Klietmann, Dr Kurt-G. 'POUR LE MÉRITE' UND TAPFERKEITS-MEDAILLE. *Berlin*, 1966. 104pp, 19pl. (Virtualy an enlarged edition of his earlier book FÜR TAPFERKEIT UND VERDIENST, *Munich*, 1954).

Klietmann, Dr Kurt-G. DEUTSCHE AUSZEICHNUNGEN. *Berlin*, Part 1, 1957, later edition 1971, 21pp, 18pl (1 in colour, of ribbons); Part 2, 1971 333pp. Part 3, 1972. ANHALT, 63pp, 5pl.

Neville, Donald G. MEDAL RIBBONS AND ORDERS OF IMPERIAL GERMANY AND AUSTRIA. *St. Ives, Cambs.*, 1974. 94pp, incl. 52 col. pl.

Waldorf-Astoria (Pubr.). ORDEN - EINE SAMMLUNG DER BEKANNTESTEN DEUTSCHEN ORDEN UND AUSZEICHNUNGEN. *Munich*, nd (not before 1928, possibly c 1932), Large 4to. 56 unnumbered pp with 287 coloured cigarette cards.

Schreiber, Georg. DIE BAYERISCHEN ORDEN UND EHRENZEICHEN. *Munich*, 1964. 6 col. pl, 138 illus. in 7 folding pl.

Prowse, A. E. THE IRON CROSS OF PRUSSIA AND GERMANY, 1813–1945. *Wellington*, N.Z., 1970. 62pp (incl, 10 pl). Reprinted from the *New Zealand Numismatic Journal*.

Volle, Henning. BADENSORDEN, EHRENZEICHEN, PRÄMIEN MEDAILLEN. *Freiburg*, 1976. vi + 188pp, 24pl (including coloured pl of ribbons).

The Neutral Countries
Netherlands

Meijer, H. G., Mulder, C. P., Wagenaar, B. W. ORDERS AND DECORATIONS OF THE NETHERLANDS. *Venray*, 1984. 214pp, incl. 14 coloured plates. Profusely illustrated.

The Emergent Nations

Czechoslovakia

Měřička, V. ČESKOSLOVENSKA VYZNAMENANI. *Hradec kralove*, 1973. Part 1 –
1918–1938. 76pp, incl. 22 plates (2 coloured). Illus. in the text. (Text in Czech,
Russian, English, German and French).

General

Mathis, René. LES NOUVEAUX ÉTATS EUROPÉENS ET LEURS DÉCORATIONS. *Nancy*, 1929.
xvi + 327pp,illus.

INDEX

NOTE:

The key to the abbreviation indicating the countries concerned will be found in the
list of contents on pages 6 and 7.